SUFISM, MUSIC AND SOCIETY
IN TURKEY AND THE MIDDLE EAST

SUFISM, MUSIC AND SOCIETY
IN TURKEY AND THE MIDDLE EAST

Papers Read at a Conference Held
at the Swedish Research Institute
in Istanbul, November 27-29, 1997

Edited by Anders Hammarlund, Tord Olsson, Elisabeth Özdalga

SWEDISH RESEARCH INSTITUTE IN ISTANBUL
TRANSACTIONS VOL. 10

Front cover: A Mevlevi *sema* performance in Darphane, Istanbul.

Back cover: Calligraphy from the beginning of the nineteenth century saying: "Ya Hazreti Mevlana" (İstanbul Ansiklopedisi, vol. 5 p. 426, İstanbul, 1994).

© Swedish Research Institute in Istanbul and the authors.
Logotype: Bo Berndal

Prepared by The Economic and Social
History Foundation of Turkey
Printed in Turkey by Numune Matbaası,
Istanbul 2001
Distributor: Curzon Press, Richmond, England

ISBN 0-7007-1148-1

ISSN 1100-0333

Preface

One of the most powerful memories from my first visit to Istanbul in the legendary student movement year of 1968 is the sound of the *ezan*, the call to prayer. Especially the *ezan* of early dawn, called out before the noise of the swarming streets deadens the distinctness of any single sound, has ever since then been coupled with undefined, but excited expectations on my part of a different, at that time undiscovered world - life itself, as a matter of fact.

One summer night a few years after my first visit, I was sitting in a coffee-house in Eskişehir, a middle-sized town in Anatolia, when the *müezzin* called out the evening prayer. Wishing to share my appreciative feelings for the *ezan*, I said in halting Turkish: "How beautiful he sings!" Since people at the table smiled, almost with a kind of embarrassment, I understood that I had said something wrong. The *ezan* is not sung, but read! The proper expression would have been: "Ne güzel ezan okuyor!" (lit. How beautifully he reads the ezan!) Having corrected the sentence, however, I had second thoughts. What if, by insisting in evaluating the *ezan* from an aesthetic point of view, I had made another, yet more subtle mistake. Perhaps my first expression had been wrong in a double sense, not only grammatically, but also ethically.

This question touches on the complex and sometimes controversial issue concerning the role of music in different religious rituals. As for Islam, the opinions widely diverge on this question. The traditionally most common and most orthodox view is that liturgy (especially the reading of the Koran) admittedly may be supported by different forms of chanting, but the musical element in a religious ceremony should be kept under strict control, and not entice the listener or performer to neglect sacred meaning for musical enjoyment. This puritanism is not all-embracing, however. Within Sufism, the tradition of Islamic mysticism, music has developed more freely. The Sufi order (*tarikat*) which is especially connected with the development of sophisticated forms of ritual music, vocal and instrumental, has been the Mevlevi order, inspired by Mevlânâ Jalâl ad-Dîn Rûmî (d. 1273).

One of the most remembered Psalms (Nr. 42) in the Bible reads: "As the hart longs for flowing streams, so longs my soul for thee, O God." The same mystical longing is expressed by Mevlânâ in the very first part of his massive Sufi poetical work, *Mesnevi*, but through another metaphor, the *ney*, the reed flute. In the hands of the *neyzen*, the *ney* expresses its longing for the root, from which it once was cut off. The fact that the *ney*, a musical instrument, is chosen as an essential symbol for the mystical longing of the Mevlevi dervishes, is a telling evidence of the importance of music in this order.

The Mevlevi order has been especially important for the development of music in Ottoman society, both as sacral, mystical music and as secular, art music. It is characteristic of the development of Ottoman art music, mainly played at the court, but also in homes of people of high station, that many of the performers were

Minarets carrying the sound of the *ezan* into the busy city life of Istanbul.

Mevlevi dervishes. Close co-operation between performers of sacred and secular music developed, especially during the seventeenth and eighteenth centuries, and was part of an early process of secularization of Ottoman society. In spite of the fact that many dervishes took part in performances of secular art music, and that the musical performances of the dervish lodges made use of the same instruments and structural forms as art music, the genres of sacred and secular music were strictly separated; the *ayin* played in the dervish lodge was clearly distinguished from the *fasıl*, played at the court. Still, the firm distinction between art music, on the one hand, and the chanting of the Koran, on the other, that had been most common in Islamic religious thought, was blurred, and the religious *ayin*, and the secular *fasıl* could both be categorized as music - *mûsîkî*. This also means that, in such a context, evaluating the *ezan* on aesthetic grounds would most probably not have been blamed, even though posing such a question was culturally like singing out of tune.

During the last two or three decades, the Mevlevi ceremony, *sema*, with the "whirling dervishes" has become very popular inside, as well as outside, Turkey. The first time I visited a Mevlevi *sema* was in Konya in 1972. The performances were held in the sports center of the city, and in spite of the somewhat profane atmosphere in the hall, I was truly enchanted. About twenty years later I attended the same ceremony together with students from my Sociology of Religion class at the Middle East Technical University in Ankara. Since we had to travel almost 300 kilometers to get there and did not have the financial means to stay overnight, we had to visit one of the afternoon performances. This turned out, however, to be a very different experience. Above all, the audience was different. In fact, the matinees were especially organized for women, who could not stay over night when they traveled without their husbands. They came in busloads from far and near, together with their young children, and filled the hall with chattering, soft drink bottles, and sunflower seeds. On top of all this muddle, the performance itself was cut almost half-way, a kind of short-cut *sema*, specially arranged for touristic purposes.

I was filled with disappointment and confusion. The *sema* had become a mass attraction and had totally lost its enchantment. Apart from contempt for the womanish audience, this slipshod piece of work also reflected the profanation that occurs when sacred rituals are brought out on the market. The inevitable question posing itself as a result of this is: "What happens to the inner structure of the musical form itself under such dramatically changed conditions?"

Today there is a renewed interest in classical Ottoman sacral and art music in Turkey. This trend runs parallel to an increased concern for cultural, ethnic and religious identities, and the rising tide of religious revivalism sets the tone. However, the social and cultural conditions where these renewed trends develop are very different from the ones that prevailed several centuries ago. What, now, has happened to different forms of Sufi music as society, with its political institutions, social structures, and cultural traditions, have undergone profound changes? These intriguing issues are addressed in this book, which is a collection of papers read at a conference entitled "Tasavvuf, Music and Social Change in Turkey and the Middle East" held at the Swedish Research Institute in Istanbul from 27th to 29th November, 1997. The conference was part of a wider concentration of programs focusing on "Islamic culture".

The book is divided into five parts. The first part on "Tasavvuf and Music" contains a single chapter written by Annemarie Schimmel, and is a general introduction to the role of music within Islamic mysticism. The second part, "Method and Aesthetics", consists of three chapters, where various methodological problems involved in the study of music and social change are addressed. Dag Österberg presents a three-fold framework for the socio-musicological analysis: music as expression, music as structure and music contained in a context. These three notions help in classifying different musicological analyses and relating them to each other. Amnon Shiloah problematizes the concept of change by asking: "Change for whom? Is it for the objective outsider, or for the people who practice the music being evaluated?" Professor Shiloah brings up the emic/etic dichotomy and other methodological issues in relation to a rich material on Near Eastern Muslim and Jewish liturgical and ritual music. Anders Hammarlund builds his discussion on an analysis of the development of art music in the West, and relates that to patterns of musical change among different performing communities among Turkish, Iranian and Syrian-Orthodox immigrants in Sweden. Hammarlund introduces a number of theoretical pairs of concepts, where he specially emphasizes the form/spirit (eidos/ethos) dichotomy and its relevance in the analysis of musical change among present-day performers.

The third part, "Structure and Evolution" contains three chapters on Ottoman classical music. Evrim Binbaş's chapter deals exclusively with Mevlevi music and *sema* in the fifteenth and sixteenth centuries. Walter Feldman and Edwin Seroussi discuss the relationship between ritual and art music in Ottoman society. Both authors point out the fact that the Mevlevi dervishes constituted an important part of the performers of art music at the court. There was a markedly mutual influence between ritual and art music in the Ottoman Empire, all the way up to the end of the nineteenth century. While Walter Feldman discusses the development of one section of the Mevlevi *ayin*, the "third selam", and its relation to developments within classical art music, Edwin Seroussi's analysis concerns the influence on

Ottoman art music from yet another source, namely Jewish ritual music. Seroussi's chapter, therefore, elaborates on the mutual relationship between the synagogue, certain Sufi orders, and the Ottoman court.

The fourth section, "Change and Continuity in the Modern Era", begins with a chapter by Cem Behar, which contains an analysis of how modernizers of the early Turkish Republic encroached upon and distorted old musical traditions, so that they would fit the official image of the social and cultural backwardness of late Ottoman music. The author discusses how zealous reformers like Hüseyin Sadettin Arel (1880-1955) and Dr. Suphi Ezgi (1869-1962), in the name of rationalization and secularization, even went as far as to invent a metric form (*usul*) that had never existed before. Orhan Tekelioğlu continues the analysis of the effects of the musical reforms imposed from above by the leaders of the young Turkish Republic. He concentrates on a magazine, *Nota*, which, due to the fact that it did not follow the official, allegedly progressive and enlightened line, ended in closure.

Nedim Karakayalı, questions the East/West dichotomy and denies its usefulness for the analysis of contemporary musical forms. He extends his criticism also to ideas of border cases and "in-betweenness", claiming that such models are still dependent on the same dichotomous concepts. Karakayalı argues that musicologists should try to be as imaginative in their search for new concepts as many composers and performers of contemporary music are in finding new artistic expressions.

The following author takes us to a different area: the Balkans. Nathalie Clayer describes musical developments in Albania after the collapse of the Ottoman Empire. She draws attention to a tendency of the twentieth century towards Albanization/nationalization of Sufi music, especially among the Bektashis.

The last section, "Sufi Music and the Media", contains a single chapter by Jean During. He addresses the question of the influence of modern mass media and new techniques in the transmission of music on the old Sufi traditions. Some Sufi groups totally reject any interference from mass-media, while others try to use them in order to present an attractive picture to the public. With special reference to the Ahl-e Haqq in the Kurdish areas of Iran, Jean During addresses the question of secularization and what happens to the sacred, inner message as the order is drawn into the public arena.

This work is intended for anyone interested in music and musicology, but, since the discussions sometimes require special knowledge, the book opens with an introduction by the co-editor Anders Hammarlund, where certain technical terms and concepts belonging to the Islamic musical tradition are explained. Through this "annotated glossary" we hope that some of the select discussions on Islam and music contained in this volume will be accessible to a wider public.

As organizer of the conference, I want to convey my hearty gratitude to all participants in the conference, and especially to Professor Cem Behar of Boğaziçi University in Istanbul, and Dr. Orhan Tekelioğlu of Bilkent University in Ankara, both of whom were also particularly helpful during the preparations for the conference. I also owe special gratitude to Sigrid Kahle, who summarized and mediated her impressions of the conference to the Swedish press, and to the warmhearted support of the hosts at the Swedish Research Institute in Istanbul, especially the then secretary, Kari Çağatay, and the director of the Institute, Bengt Knutsson. Without their steady encouragement it would hardly have been possible to realize the conference. I also want to express my thanks to the Board of Trustees of the Swedish Research Institute in Istanbul for their generous financial and moral support and to Gunvor and Josef Anér's Foundation in Stockholm, which made this publication possible. The copy-editors at The History Foundation in Istanbul, especially Gülay Dinçel and Saliha Bilginer are also cordially remembered for their patient work.

Istanbul, January 2001
Elisabeth Özdalga

Contents

Introduction: An Annotated Glossary

ANDERS HAMMARLUND

"Remember God as often as possible!" This Koranic injunction is a main point of reference for Sufism, the esoteric and mystic expression of Islam. This publication deals with one of the media of this expression, namely music, its forms, functions, uses, and development. It should be stressed, however, that Sufi music never was a marginal, sectarian phenomenon in the musical culture of the Muslim world. On the contrary, it constituted the main outlet for musical creativity in a religious context - and the religious context in traditional Islamic societies was almost all-embracing. The study of Sufi music, therefore, is a study of the highroad of music in Islam. However, Sufi music was not practised in the mosque; it did not belong to the formal and legalistic sphere of official religion. It was created and performed in a multitude of other settings, by learned men in palaces as well as by illiterate peasants.

Zikr (*dhikr*) means remembrance, or, recollection, and this term also denotes the ritual event, the act of fulfilling the above-mentioned injunction. There were always many different ways of organising such events, but common to all of them is the aim to reach a heightened mental state, an experience of total presence and mystical union, not necessarily ecstasy - often the experience has more of an inward, intellectual quality, and it is not always given a vivid physical expression.

During the *zikr* events many different methods and media are used in order to reach the experience of sacrum: recitation, meditation, dancing, breathing techniques etc. Music is among the most common vehicles used and this aspect of the *zikr* is called *sema* (*samā'*) listening, or audition. *Sema* became a general term for Sufi music (in some traditions including dancing). But there is no unified and standardised *sema*. It can be performed on a synthesiser as well as on a traditional reed flute. *Sema* simply denotes the use of musical structures in a *zikr* context. It is not bound to any specific style of music.

In the many different Sufi orders of confraternities, *tarikatlar* (pl. of *tarikat*, *ṭarīqa*), a great variety of musical traditions and repertoires evolved. In Turkey and the Middle East, the area focused on in this book, the most elaborated and well-known of these is the *ayin* of the Mevlevi order, linked to the famous dance of the so-called whirling dervishes. *Ayin* is the term for the formalised ritual sequence, but it also denotes the specific set of musical pieces linked to the ritual, a suite-like arrangement of instrumental and vocal compositions.

In Ottoman society the Mevlevi order gradually took the role of an intellectual and artistic elite. Its *ayin* consequently shared many features with the "secular" court music, the *fasıl*, e.g. compositional forms like the *peşrev* and the *saz semai*. The cultivation of *musiki* (*mūsīqā*), the traditional art music in Turkey and the Middle East, was in fact largely dependent on the Mevlevi *sema* practice.

The Musical Material

Let me now say a few words about the musical structures and means of expression used in Sufi contexts. It is important once again to realise that theoretically any musical language capable of conveying the sacrum could be used as *sema*, including music in the "Western" tradition. Any simple equation of Sufi music with "oriental, Middle Eastern" music, therefore, is incorrect. But since this book mainly deals with Sufi traditions in Turkey and the Middle East I think it might be helpful for the reader to be updated concerning the basics of the music of this region. The musical material (scales, melodic formulae, rhythms) used by the Sufi confraternities is specific to the culture of western Asia generally, not only to Sufism and not even to Islam. The local Christian and Jewish communities share these musical resources with the Muslim majority. In *musiki*, the intellectually underpinned music, the concept *makam* is central (*maqām*; *dastgâh* is the analogous Persian equivalent). A *makam* can be described as a kind of family of melodic formulae, sharing a common set of pitches ("scale") and certain patterns of melodic movement. Each *makam* has a specific expressive character. Dozens of *makam*s are frequently used in musical practice, but about 200 have been registered by the musicologists, and the number is not yet finite - new *makam*s are still being created. A *makam* is most distinctly rendered in the *taksim* (*taqsīm*), which is a non-metric improvisation, often used as an introduction to a set of pre-composed pieces in the same *makam*. Most pre-composed pieces (though not all of them) have a regular beat and are based on metrical cycles, *usul*s, which, in ensemble playing, are rendered as rhythmic patterns played on percussion instruments.

Some Musical Instruments

Of the musical instruments used in traditional Sufi contexts, the *ney* has to be mentioned in pride of place. This simple, rim-blown flute has been a symbol of Sufism since the days of Rumi, and in the Mevlevi *ayin* it is still the lead instrument. The *ney*

A Mevlevi playing the *ney*.

Ney and *kanun*.

Kanun

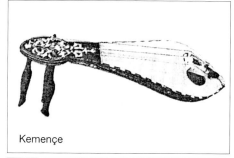

Kemençe

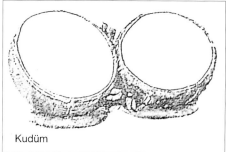

Kudüm

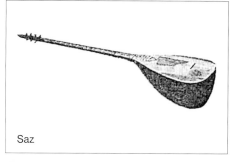

Saz

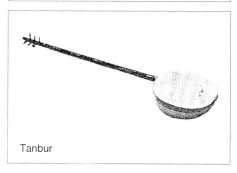

Tanbur

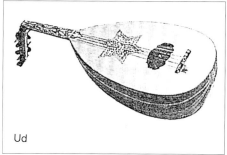

Ud

is made from a piece of hard bamboo-like reed, and is ca 40-80 cm. long. The Ottoman/ Turkish *ney*, which has six finger-holes, with one thumb-hole on the reverse, is equipped with a conical lip-rest. Persian instruments (*nay*) have five finger-holes and lack the lip-rest, but are furnished with a metal tube at the upper end, facilitating a very peculiar playing technique with the instrument inserted into the mouth cavity and fix-ated against the upper teeth; the airstream is then directed against the rim with the help of the tongue. The Turkish and Arabic playing technique is less complex, but the sound ideal everywhere is very different from the classical western flute timbre. The low reg-ister with its somewhat hoarse and fiery, very sensual sound is especially associated with spirituality. Variants of this instrument can be found all over western and central Asia, and its use in ritual contexts hark back to shaman traditions existing long before the advent of Islam.

Another type of instrument we often come across in Sufi contexts is the long-necked lute. In Mevlevi and traditional art music in Turkey the *tanbur* is the preferred variant, whereas the *bağlama* (also called *saz*) dominates in rural Sufi and Alevi milieus. The *setâr* is a Persian variant.

The *ud* (*'ūd*) is a lute of another type, with a short neck, a pear-shaped resonance body and six courses of strings. The variants used in Turkey and the Middle East are close relatives to the European Renaissance and Baroque lute, which actually evolved from instrument types taken over in mediaeval Europe from early Islamic culture.

In Turkey the *kemençe* is a bowed instrument of lira type with three strings. In other parts of the Islamic world similar names are given to different forms of spike-

Mehter takımı - the Ottoman military band.

fiddles. In many Sufi contexts the *kemençe* was replaced by the western violin during the nineteenth century.

Then there is the *kanun* (*qānūn*), a plucked zither, which is a common instrument in many forms of traditional music in Turkey and the Middle East. In Iran, however, the *santûr*, a dulcimer, has a stronger position.

As for percussion instruments, the *kudüm*, a pair of small kettledrums, used in Mevlevi and other Sufi music in Turkey should be mentioned. Generally, big frame drums called *def*, *bendir*, *daire* etc. seem to be associated with Sufi *zikr* music in western and central Asia.

It is important to point out that the tasks of these instruments in ensemble interaction are different from the roles of the instruments in the classical Western orchestra. The traditional musical culture of Turkey and the Middle East is basically monophonic, i.e. in any piece of music there is just one single melodic line which is played in unison or in parallel octaves by all the melodic instruments of the ensemble. (Due to the specific properties of the different instrument types, the actual rendering of the melody is always slightly divergent, which gives a certain heterophonic richness or thickness to the ensemble sound). Multi-part music, polyphony and harmonisation are alien to this system, which focuses on the subtle modal development of the melodic material.

Traditional ensembles (except for the Ottoman military band, the *Mehter*) were small and did not reach orchestral dimensions, even if the Mevlevi *sema* sometimes was accompanied by rather large groups of players.

Music and Society

Until the twentieth century, music was not an independent social field in the societies of western Asia; there were no civic music institutions such as concert halls or conservatoires. *Musiki* was cultivated by dilettante literati belonging to the Ottoman elite and by non-Muslim professional musicians socially dependent on this dominating stratum, mainly in big cosmopolitan urban centres such as Constantinople, Saloniki, Damascus and Alexandria. In this environment there had been a certain influx of European musical concepts and elements already since the eighteenth century (e.g. the introduction of Western notation), which contributed to the development of a fairly homogenous urban style. In the countryside, however, the concept *musiki* was unknown; music-making was integrated into other social activities and was not conceptually separated from them.

The conditions for the emergence of an institutionalised musical life were created only by the modernising, nationalist regimes of the early twentieth century. Western music was introduced and encouraged by the reformers, but the traditional forms of music were also deeply affected by the political and social changes. Gradually both *musiki* and the many different forms of rural, musical folklore were theoretically redefined according to western musical concepts. Formalised training was substituted for the traditional, predominantly oral, methods of transmission and artisticsocialisation.

These modernising efforts - greatly enhanced since the 1950s by increasing medialisation and urbanisation - created a new, vast and diverse societal area of music in which traditional art and folk genres became only musical subfields. All kinds of Western, international art and popular music (like opera, jazz, rock etc) soon obtained their own local niches. A domestic commercial music industry emerged and thrived on diverse synchretic fusions, of which the best known, perhaps, is the Turkish *arabesk*. In this sometimes kitschy but immensely popular blend of traditional Middle Eastern and European music material, fashioned with the help of electronic, multitrack studio equipment, the politically strictly upheld division between Western secularistic modernity and eastern Islamic traditionalism was challenged. In *arabesk* and other medialised genres elements from different forms of Sufi *sema* are important components. This should not be surprising, since the *sema* had been a main outlet for musical creativity in traditional society. However, the use of stylistic traits from the *sema* does not automatically imply a religious commitment. In a world of globalised media and collage aesthetics the music material is becoming increasingly free-floating and secularised.

PART I
TASAVVUF AND MUSIC

The Role of Music in Islamic Mysticism

ANNEMARIE SCHIMMEL

Ladies and gentlemen,[1] I cannot claim to be either a specialist in music or a musician; rather, I am simply a lover of Sufi music. Let me therefore begin with a little story about an event that happened long long ago in connection with the Mevlevi *sema*. I had joined the *İlâhiyat Fakültesi* in Ankara in the fall of 1954. In early December I received an invitation from Mehmet Önder, the director of the Mevlâna Müzesi [museum] in Konya, to participate in the celebration of Ḥaẓret-i Mevlâna's anniversary that was to be held there on December 17 and was asked to give a speech on 'Mevlâna's influence in East and West'. A few days before travelling to Konya I had a dream: the Mevlevis were turning like white butterflies as heavenly music filled the air. Apparently, there was no possibility that this dream might foretell a real event, as the dervish lodges had been closed since 1925, and no trace of the ritual remained. Nevertheless, I told my lovely dream to one of my colleagues in the Faculty, a *hafız* with a wonderful voice who - as I learned - was also to attend the celebration, and with a smile he said: "Perhaps it was a true dream!"

Ḥaẓret-i Mevlâna.
Drawing based on a miniature.

---

1 Professor Schimmel as usual gave her lecture without using manuscript. The following text is a transcription made by Tord Olsson from a tape-recording, edited and corrected by Annemarie Schimmel herself.

A calligraphy from 1843 saying: Yâ Hazret-i
Mevlânâ Muhammad Jalâl ad-Dîn Rûmî.
From: C. Kerametli, *Galata Mevlevihanesi*, Istanbul 1977.

My mother and I reached Konya on a cold, rainy afternoon, and after a sumptu-
ous dinner at the home of our generous hosts, the two of us were taken to an old
house in the heart of the town, where we encountered a number of elderly men with
strange looking parcels. These were opened - and what should appear but dervish
hats, reed flutes, tennure and whatever was required for the *sema*! My mother and I
were placed in the two armchairs in the otherwise empty hall, and the music and the
whirling began: it was the first time in twenty-nine years that the old dervishes performed the ritual together. They had come from Afyon Karahisar, Trabzon, Ankara,
and İstanbul to celebrate Hazret-i Mevlâna. Halil Can was playing the flute while my
colleague, Hafız Sabri, recited the *na't-i şerif*. We were slowly drawn into the sea of
music and of whirling and lost ourselves in the rhythm, the sound, and the spirit.

I had loved Hazret-i Mevlâna even as a teenager, and had translated some of his
lyrical poems into German verse as soon as I had learned enough Persian. Not only
that, I came to study the form and content of his work as well as his influence in the
world of Islam and in the West. Whenever I lecture about him, I like to start with a
little anecdote found in Persian hagiography (such as Jami's *Nafahât al-uns*) and rendered into German verse by our great orientalist-poet Friedrich Rückert (1788-1866).
It reads as follows:

> Once our master Jelaladdin said this:
> "Music is the creaking of the gates of Paradise!"
> Whereupon one of the stupid idiots remarked:
> "I do not like the sound of creaking gates!"
> And Mevlâna answered:
> "You hear the doors when they are being closed,
> but I, I hear them when they are opening!"

This anecdote shows us very clearly the importance of music in the Sufi tradition
and, in particular, in the life and thought of Mevlâna.

After the dervish lodges had been closed since 1925, the first celebration of Hazret-i Mevlâna's anniversary was held in 1954. Halil Can (on right, see text) was playing the *ney* in the celebration.

Music is a means to draw the soul closer to God, and for this reason, it played an important role in Sufi life. However, it was also objected to by many of the stern, sharia-bound Muslims. We know that as early as 867 a *samakhana* was opened in Baghdad where the Sufis - at that time a small group of pious men - used to meet once in a while. It was their recreation after days and nights of intense religious exercises, a relaxation that allowed them to give themselves to the attraction of love, to forget their intellectual striving. The orthodox objected to this practice mainly because worldly love songs were recited which spoke of human love relations instead of concentrating upon the Divine Grandeur and Majesty as taught through the words of the Koran. Furthermore, it could well happen that some listeners might get up and whirl around their own axis, in a state of rapture. This again seemed to be incompatible with the rules of proper religious behaviour. An early story from the Sufi tradition points to this danger: a master who died shortly before 900, appeared after his death to someone in a dream. As usual in such stories, the dreamer asked him: "What did God do to you?" And the Sufi answered: "God scolded me and said: You have always described Me under the names of Salma and Leyla. Had I not known that at one moment you really thought of Me, I would have cast you into Hell!" That means, the mixing of worldly love as expressed in beautiful songs with Divine Love seemed to the early orthodox believers extremely dangerous, as much as it was to permeate later Sufism.

The early sources describe how often music was practiced among the Sufis of Baghdad and elsewhere, and how most of the participants would get up to whirl. Only Junayd, the master of the sober "Baghdadian" tradition (d. 910) would never move during such a concert. When one of his friends asked him the reason for his behaviour he answered with the Koranic quotation: "You see the mountains and consider them to be firm, yet they move like clouds" (Sure 27, 90). That is, the real movement happens in the heart, not in the limbs. Yet, many of Junayd's contemporaries loved to participate in the *sema*-meetings and abandon themselves to an ecstatic or pseudo-ecstatic state. And even though many great masters objected to music and whirling, such meetings became popular everywhere. In the famous handbook of Sufism by Abu Hafs Omar as-Suhrawardi (d. 1234) we find the following remark:

> Music does not give rise, in the heart, to anything which is not already there.
> So he, whose inner self is attached to anything else than God is stirred by music to sensual desire, but the one who is inwardly attached to the love of God is moved, by hearing music, to do His will.... The common folk listen to music according to nature, and the novices listen with desire and awe, while the listening of the saints brings them a vision of the Divine gifts and graces, and these are the gnostics to whom listening means contemplation. But finally, there is the listening of the spiritually perfect to whom, through music, God reveals Himself unveiled.

For this reason some Sufis thought that the *murid* on the first stages of the path should not be allowed to participate in the *sema*. Only those who were already mature and could not be tempted into dangerous sensual desires by listening to love songs might attend such concerts. And while some *tariqa*s allow the practice of music, others - the so-called sober orders - prohibit it.

Literature about music, and whether or not it is permissible to use songs in a religious context, fills hundreds of books and treatises, and *fatwa*s have been issued concerning this problem, since scholars have not been able to agree on this issue. That holds true for the entire Islamic world, be it ancient Baghdad or medieval Delhi, Cairo or Bukhara. Even in Ottoman Turkey the opinions of scholars and Sufis concerning *sema* differed widely. We can understand that austere theologians objected to *sema* when they saw Auhadaddin Kirmani tearing off the frocks of young, unbearded *murid*s to dance breast to breast with them; even a great mystical leader like Mevlâna's friend Shams-i Tabrizi disliked such performances. On the other hand, many lay people loved to watch the Sufis whirling about; and when they, in a state of ecstasy, tore up their frocks the spectators would collect the shreds, *tabarrukan*, "for the sake of blessing". They believed in the religious power of music which, so to speak, oozed not only into the bodies of the whirling dervishes but also into their garments. Thus, in the Persian work of Hujwiri, the saint buried in Lahore about 1072, we learn that as early as the eleventh century "people thought that Sufism consists mainly of dancing". This remark reminds us of modern trends in the West where courses in Sufi dance are being taught to people who know nothing about the spiritual roots of Sufism. Almost everyone in the medieval Muslim world was well aware of the healing powers of music. This becomes particularly evident in Turkey: Divriği and Edirne are just two places where we still find buildings in which music therapy was used - as it is still today in Turkey, as well as in Central Europe. Many centuries ago, the Şifaiya in Divriği (built 1228), the most impressive building in Anatolia, was a centre of this kind of therapy. In the central hall of the huge building you can see a large basin into which water flows, and from this basin a complicated spiral carving leads the water into a small basin, producing a sweet sound when the drops fall into the lower basin. Listening to the soft, silvery sound of the falling drops, the soul is carried step-by-step into a different world; mentally disturbed people were able to find peace, perhaps even healing, by listening quietly to the water music. The effects of the healing power of music are well known in India as well, and numerous are the stories told about the magic quality of music.

Such stories abound in Sufism, and it might well happen that some austere jurist who disliked music and disapproved of it was converted - often by means of a dream.

Among the great lovers of music and *samâ* was Abû Said-i Abû'l-Khayr (d. 1049) in Mihana, a place close to the southern border of today's Turkmenistan. One of his neighbours, who disliked his behaviour, dreamt one night that Abû Said was calling him: "Get up and dance for the sake of God!" Horrified he awoke and recited *A'udhu billâhi min ash-shaytân ar-rajîm!* for he thought he had been tempted by satanic powers. He went to sleep again, and lo, the same dream repeated itself, and he, as a good Muslim, reacted again by reciting the formula of refuge. But when the dream occured for the third time he was disturbed (as the threefold repetition of a dream is a sign of its veracity) and got up to visit Abû Sa'id. When he reached the master's house he heard him call: "Get up and dance for the sake of God!" And he participated in the *samâ* and became a disciple of Abû Sa'îd and a lover of music.

This is only one of the numerous stories told in Sufi sources about the influence of music and whirling dance on the human heart.

The greatest representative of the musical tradition is, without doubt, Mevlâna Rumi who - as we mentioned - understood that music means the opening of the gates of Paradise. When his spiritual beloved Shams-i Tabrizi disappeared, Mevlâna forgot all about his scholarly pursuits - at least for some time - and instead began to listen to music and whirl around himself while dictating poetry in a state of near unconsciousness. He probably began by saying some *rubâ'iyât*, quatrains, a genre that has been associated with the *sema* since its early days. He may also have recited not only Persian but also Arabic poetry, as he was well versed in classical Arabic poetry, especially in the work of al-Mutanabbi (d. 965); and in addition to delightful Arabic songs, we find Arabic and Persian lines intrinsically interwoven in some of his ecstatic poems. Anyone who has read his lyrical poetry, which came to him like a gift from the Unseen, will have realized that in many of those poems, the rhythm can be followed by handclapping, although all of them are written in classical *'arûz*, the Arabo-Persian quantitative meter. Many of them indeed impel the reader or listener to get up and turn around. In some of his early poems Mevlâna indeed refers to the mysterious change he experienced in his life: he, the learned theologian, was transformed into a lover who found his inspiration through music.

None who has read Mevlâna's poetry - be it only the first eighteen verses of the *Mathnavi* - can deny that music was a divine force for him. One aspect of his poetry is his clever use of musical imagery. That may sound more or less like a literary problem, but I think that this imagery shows how strong the impact of music as a life - giving force was on him. Did he not feel after the first disappearance of Shams that the breath of the Beloved made him sing as though he were a flute? Every moment, he feels that he is moved, so to speak, by the breath, by the finger of the Beloved, and is nothing but the instrument of a higher power. The story of the *ney*, the reed-flute, at the beginning of the *Mathnavi* expresses this feeling in perfect form, because the *ney* is, as all of us know, the instrument closest to the human voice. But the flute can only sing when someone breathes into it. Without the breath of the Beloved - so says Rumi - without the influx of the *nafas ar-rahmân*, the "Breath of the Merciful" human beings cannot act, speak, or think, just as the flute cannot reveal its secrets unless the musician breathes into it. This is a recurrent theme in the *Divân-i Shams* and, to a certain extent, in the *Mathnavi* as well. The *ney* is the symbol of man who is separated from his primordial roots, just as the flute is cut off from the reedbed. But - and this has to be kept in mind - only by being cut off is it able to tell the story of eternal longing; for the soul longs for home, longs for the time "when it was as it was before it was" (as Junayd put it) - that is, before the act of creation, in which the Absolute Divine Unity manifested itself through creation, and multiplicity appeared.

The story of the *ney* divulging the secret of the Beloved is, however, not Rumi's invention. In an article published in 1932, Helmut Ritter discusses the introductory poem of the *Mathnavi* and shows that the story comes from the ancient Near East: it is the story of King Midas of Gordion (incidentally, a place close to Konya). King Midas had donkey's ears, a secret which he one day told to his minister under the condition never to reveal it. But the minister, smarting under the burden of this terrible secret went to a lake to tell it to the the lonely water. However, the reeds that grew in the lake listened as well, and when someone cut a reed to made it into a flute, the flute revealed the whole story... There is also an Islamic version of the tale which we find in Sana'i 's *Hadiqat al-haqiqat*. It is said that Hazret Ali could not bear all the spiritual wisdom entrusted to him by the Prophet and told it to a lake in the wilderness, and again it was the flute that revealed to mankind some of the Prophet's deepest secrets. Thus, Rumi stands in an old tradition of flute stories; but it is his version of the reedflute that has become the unsurpassable expression of the soul's constant longing for its homeland in God's infinity.

Rumi's story of the reedflute has been taken over into all the areas where Persian is used, and allusions to it permeated Persian, Urdu, and even Bengali poetry. An interesting case is that of Shah Abdul Latif Bhitai, the great mystical poet of Sind (d. 1752). He used the motif of the *ney* in the story of Marui. Marui, a village girl kidnapped by the ruler of Amarkot, refused to have anything to do with him, regardless of the presents he showered upon her, for she constantly longed for her village, for her friends. She is the symbol of the soul that longs for home, for the First Beloved, and cannot be seduced by any worldly goods or gifts offered to her. When Shah Latif tells her story, he translates into Sindhi the beginning of Rumi's *Mathnavi,* for Marui is the human representative of the flute that is cut off from its roots.

Again, in the Indian subcontinent we find the towering figure of Muhammad Iqbal, the spiritual father of Pakistan, who used the motif of the complaining flute in his early Persian *mathnavi, Asrâr-i khudi* (1915). His emphasis, however, is on the necessity of separation, for separation is the secret of creativity - could the reedflute sing if it were not cut from the reed bed? Longing, that is longing in love, enables the human being to speak and thus to become creative.

Rumi's reedflute appears in various forms in the poetry of the countries between Turkey and India. In Bengal, this imagery is sometimes blended with the lovely flute played by Lord Krishna in the Hindu tradition - for his mysterious flute captivates the human heart and draws it to the Divine Beloved.

But it is not only the flute that serves as a fitting symbol of human beings in Rumi's work, the drum or the tambourin as well can represent the lover, for without the touch of the beloved's fingers the drum would be silent. Still, the poet may ask the beloved not to hit him too hard lest his body may be torn to pieces.... Or else, the human being resembles a *rabâb* which was, besides the *ney*, Mevlanâ's favorite instrument. Again, the *rabâb* can sing only when it is "caressed" by the fingers or the plectrum of the musician. Is not the lover like a *rabâb*, his nerves being the strings which react when the beloved's fingers touch them? I think we should understand an anecdote told about Mevlâna in this context. One day, he was watching his students studying Ibn Arabi's *Futûhât al-makkiyya* when Zaki the *rabâb*-player entered the room and began to play. And Mevlâna said - so it is told: "Don't you think that Zaki's *futuhât* are better than the *Futûhât al-makkiyya*?" For in music he found the movement of love, the divine attraction, without cerebral exertion.

Other instruments as well play a role in Rumi's poetical cosmos; each of them can serve as a symbol for the human heart that is moved only when the hand or the breath of the Divine Beloved moves them to express their love and longing.

Of course, musical imagery is not restricted to Mevlâna, although he is probably the most eloquent representative of this poetical device, as it was for him not merely an artistic image but the expression of his own experience. We may, in the course of Persian poetry, think of the poetry of Khaqani (d. 1119), whose musical imagery has been studied by a young Dutch orientalist, Anna Livia Beelaert. Is it not an amusing idea to compare the *barbat*, the great bulky string instrument, to a fat lazy person who will sing only when "you twist his ear", that is, tune it properly?

For Rumi, however, it is not only the song of the instruments that inspires him. Even more frequently does he allude to the *sema*, the dancing movement that permeates all of creation. And as often as Persian and Turkish poets may have used musical imagery, Rumi is probably the only one who has explained creation in terms of a musical image. That the voice of the Divine Creator is the reason for creation is an idea found in quite a few traditions, but Mevlâna goes further. Everyone knows the Divine address in Sura 7, verse 172, when God addressed the not-yet-created beings by the words: *Alastu bi-rabbikum* (Am I not your Lord?), and they answered, *balâ shahidnâ*, (Yes, surely we give witness to it), lest they can deny their pledge at the Day of Judgment. To Mevlâna, the words *alastu bi-rabbikum* are a musical sound, and listening to this primordial music, Not-Being suddenly begins to dance, to whirl around, so that out of this dance, stars and suns, atoms, animals, and flowers emerge, all of them moved by the creative Divine music.

> A call reached Not-Being, Not-Being said: "Yes (*balâ*),
> I shall put my foot on that side, fresh and green and joyful!"
> It heard the *alast,* it came forth running and intoxicated;
> It was Not-Being and became Being; [manifested in] tulips and willows and
> odoriferous herbs! (*Dîvân-i Shams Nr. 1832*)

This is probably the most beautiful and ingenious myth of creation one can imagine as it translates into poetry the empowering role of music. The Divine address is understood here as the first song to which the not-yet-created beings responded and thus were endowed with existence.

From this interpretation of creation, one understands why Rumi's whole work, and especially the *Dîvân-i Shams*, is permeated with musical imagery. He sees that everything, still under the spell of the Primordial Music, is dancing: the atoms spin around their centres, the planets turn around the sun; for in listening to music, the soul leaves its normal orbit and enters higher spheres. It whirls around a spiritual sun and receives strength from it. And this spiritual sun unites all the different atoms into a pattern through which the harmony of the cosmos is revealed. Dance permeates not only the living beings - the child dances in the mother's womb as the dead dance in the shrouds when they hear the name of the Beloved. Flowers and birds, dragons and djinns dance, and the garden is involved in constant dance; the nightingale - the imam of the birds - sings, and while all flowers listen to him, they grow as though they were dancing. Perhaps the loveliest expression of that everything created is dancing is found in a *rubâ'i* where Mevlâna praises the sun-like Beloved who comes in spring, while love resembles the spring breeze that quickens the trees and branches, which seem be to dead after winter's tyrannical rule, and every twig, touched by this breeze, dons a green dancing-gown and begins to move joyfully. Only those not touched by the breeze of love are dried up. They have to be cut off and thrown into the fire - as Sura 111 refers to the firewood carried by Abu Lahab's wife.

Whatever Mevlâna sings, whatever he feels, is in some way or the other connected with love, that is with the music of love. It is this presence of music and love that makes his poetry eternal.

Mevlâna's ideas have been taken up by later poets in the Mevlevi order, especially within the Turkish tradition. One has only to think of the poetry of Galib Dede, the sheikh of the Galata Mevlevihanesi (d. 1799). But it is little known that even Yahya Kemal composed a beautiful ghazel in honour of Hazret-i Mevlâna. The lovely poem by Asaf Halet Çelebi, *Sema-i semavi*, in which the poet has captured the secret of the whirling, of the movement that permeates everything created, once the music of love has touched it, should not be forgotten either:

> The trees, donning their dancing gowns
> supplicate in love
> Mevlâna

> The image in me:
> is a different image
> how many stars fall
> into my interior dance!
> I whirl and I whirl
> the skies whirl as well
> roses bloom out of my face

> The trees in the garden, in sunshine
> "He created Heaven and Earth"
> the serpents listen to the song of the reed
> in the trees donning their dancing gowns

> The meadow's children, intoxicated...
> Heart
> they call you

> I look, smiling, at suns
> which have lost their way...
> I fly, I fly
> the skies fly...

It would be easy to provide numberless examples from our wonderful collection of poetry from the Islamic tradition devoted to the secret of music and whirling dance. Such an anthology would prove that despite the aversion of many Muslims to these experiences, the lifegiving power of music has always been recognized in Islamic lands. Whether you listen to Sufi music in Morocco, where traditional Andalusian tunes are still alive, or hear the recitation of the *dalâ'il al-khayrât* at Jazûlî's tomb in Marrakesh, or attend the *dhikr* of the Sufis in Khartum or the song of the devotees at Bhit Shah in Sind - the tradition is very much alive. It is a power that permeates our lives. Yet, we should also understand the criticism voiced by the orthodox, because music, as we have seen, is something that takes the human being out of himself, brings him into another sphere, and thus may divert him from the responsibilities of daily life and the ritual duties of the believer. The tension between Sufism, with its love of music, and the sharia-minded people, with their aversion to, and perhaps fear of, music, can be explained in technical terms as the tension between the religion of *nomos,* the religious order, and reglementing law of orthodox circles (this also holds true to a certain extent in Christian history), and the religion of *eros*, Love. Goethe once spoke of the "Doppelglück der Töne und der Liebe", the twofold happiness growing out of the combination of music and love. This combination was something admired and longed for by many seekers, as it was regarded as dangerous and disturbing by others. These attitudes have continued among the pious throughout the centuries.

As we shall see in our conference, different aspects of music and the multiple aspects of Sufism have developed during the ages, sometimes increasing, sometimes dimishing. Moreover, it cannot be denied that in many modern manifestations of Sufism in the West, the emphasis lies much more on the ecstasy induced by music than on the religious, Islamic aspects of Sufism. This is a problem that produces much confusion.

But before I end my brief survey of music and the Sufis, let me read some lines from one of my favorite poems by Rumi, in which he calls his beloved to lead him to the *sema* and thus to the sphere of love:

> O come, o come! you are the soul
> of the soul of the soul of whirling!
> O come! You are the cypress tall
> in the blooming garden of whirling!
> O come! For there has never been
> and will never be one like you!
> O come! Such one has never seen
> the longing eye of whirling!
> O come! The fountain of the sun
> is hidden under your shadow!
> You own a thousand Venus stars
> in the circlying heavens of whirling!
> The whirling sings your praise and thanks
> with a hundred eloquent tongues:
> I'll try to say just one, two points
> translating the language of whirling.
> For when you enter in the dance
> you then leave both these worlds.
> For outside these two worlds there lies
> the universe, endless, of whirling.
> The roof is high, the lofty roof
> which is in the seventh sphere,
> but far beyond this roof has reached
> the ladder, the ladder of whirling!
> Whatever there appears but He,
> you tread on that in dancing:
> The whirling, see, belongs to you
> and you belong to the whirling.
> What can I do when Love appears
> and puts its claw round my neck?
> I grasp it, take it to my breast
> and drag it into the whirling.
> And when the bosom of the motes
> is filled with the glow of the sun:
> They enter all the dance, the dance
> and do not complain in the whirling!

PART II
METHOD AND AESTHETICS

General Socio-musicological Concepts: Expression, Structure, and Context

DAG ÖSTERBERG

The position of music in social life can be described from many perspectives, and their validity depends upon the kind of music in question. Here, I want to present three perspectives which seem to me highly important. I present them as distinct, even as competing perspectives; yet, in a concrete investigation, they may blend or merge.

The first perspective is based on the concept of *expression*: it makes us discover how music expresses social situations and social relationships.

The second perspective is based on the concept of *structure*: it opens up a field of interpretation where what is looked for is musical structure and similarity between musical and other social-cultural structures.

The third perspective - somehow at odds with the fore-mentioned - is based on the notion of a social setting or *context*: the question revolves around how the context has an impact on the music, how it contributes to the construction of music itself.

Music as Expression and Expressive Activity

The notions of expression and *expressivity* are fundamental or categorical, being on a par with the notions of cause and *causality*.[1] The human body is a field of expression and as such it is understood immediately, spontaneously, by all of us, from our earliest childhood. Joy and well-being, anger and fear express themselves through the human body, as sparkling eyes or a frightened gaze, as hilarious laughter or as "another shade of white", as liveliness or a depressed bodily poise - and so on. This primordial expressivity is part of our constitution, and one which we share with animals. It is there before any reflexive thought; we express ourselves before having any thought about it, and perceive the expressions of others in the same way, *pre*-reflectively. What is expressed is not the *cause* of the expression, nor is the expression an arbitrary *sign* of what is expressed; the expression somehow alters, unfolds or develops, enriches what is expressed. Expressivity is an *internal* relation between that which is expressed and the expression.

From at least 1750 - the end of Baroque, rhetorical music and the beginning of the dominance of a simplified, melodic-harmonic music - music in the West has mostly been understood as having to do with the *expression of feelings*. First, within the movement termed the Enlightenment, and within the so-called Rococo era, music was connected with the arousal of emotions; music within the Romantic movement

---

1 Cf. Ernest Cassirer, *Zur Logik der Kulturwissenschaften,* 1942, ch. II; or idem., *Philosophie der symbolischen Formen* (Philosophy of symbolic forms), vol. II, 1925.

in the strict sense, where music - instrumental music - was described as the opening up of a world of *infinite, sublime* emotion, above the sentiments and feelings of everyday life. From these cultural movements history has retained the moment of expressivity, up to the time when Stravinsky, in order to shock or provoke, stated that music did not express anything at all; or when the school of *neue Sachlichkeit* - "new objectivity" - tried to detach music from any kind of romanticism. But this anti-romantic attitude never became prevalent in Western culture, and, therefore, playing and listening to music still belong to the domaine of expressivity.

What kind of social relationships and structures does music express? With regard to Western music, the answer is simple - at least on a first level. Almost all Western music played today employs the major/minor scales or code, and is written on the basis of the theory of harmony founded by Rameau in the eighteenth century and refined to perfection by Riemann and others around the turn of the twentieth century. Within this musical code the minor connotes a more sad state of mind, whereas the major connotes a more joyful mood. Further, the consonant chord connotes harmony and concord, that is, unanimity and mutual affirmation within a social group; a dissonant chord connotes conflict, disagreement, hostility. A Western musical composition is constituted of the perpetual shift between the major and minor scales, between consonance and dissonance and modulations between the scales and the chords. Now, an obvious and established interpretation is that classical works of music from the last three centuries, as a rule, express the affirmation of *social solidarity,* and also express how social antagonism and struggle is lived through and overcome. In the end, social harmony is established or re-established. Consonant music has primacy over dissonant, social unity primacy over social conflict and deviance. It is along these lines that the classical, dominant music of the West has been interpreted for a very long time. This interpretation tends to make Beethoven the greatest of all composers, for in his compositions the momentum of conflict and tension is very strong; nevertheless unity and consensus get the upper hand at last. Analogy with the action of a film may be helpful; in the end, order is reestablished, what is positive and affirmative comes out victorious. Beethoven's music - and, to a certain extent, Beethoven as a person - is seen as expressive of a heroic, militant attitude towards life; this music is *edifying,* since it calls upon us to fight for what is just and true.

The next step in this line of reasoning is to consider the rôle of harmony and dissonance in music generally, relating this to social conditions. Classical music tended to become increasingly disharmonious and dissonant, and this was interpreted as expressive of increasing social unrest and conflict. Around 1910 the music of Stravinski and Schönberg was dissonant to the extreme. The latter, Schönberg, belonged to the general Expressionist movement in German art at the time. Dissonant music, such as that of the Schönberg school, claimed to be true music, since it expressed social conflicts and anxiety.

Consequently, very harmonious music may be deemed overly conflict-evading, trying to hide the conflicts in social life, and therefore, to express the wish to preserve the powers that be. Such music may be *ideological*, in the Marxist sense, being a not quite reluctant victim of social illusion. Of course, a huge bulk of music played in the West creates illusions in this sense, an extreme case being the so-called Muzak, which is devised in order to create nothing but harmonious feelings. But it must be noted that much music does not have this character; especially, rock music may express quite violent emotions, and thus show aggressive feelings in and towards society.

The accusations of immorality and indecency levelled against some forms of music - such as jazz music in the 1920s - also apply to the expressivist kind of music; the charge is that this sort of music expresses certain unwanted attitudes and feelings, and thus demoralises the listeners.

Structure and Structural Interpretation

Here, the word *structure* is taken in the sense of structural linguistics, a sense which was generalised and imported into the social and cultural sciences and the humanities with the *structuralist* movement in the 1960s. Structural interpretations offer themselves as an alternative to expressivist interpretations. For, just as the actual use of a language does not express its underlying structure, i.e. its grammar, nor the making of the various food dishes express the underlying structure codifying what we term a "cuisine" in a broad sense, i.e. the French cuisine, the Chinese cuisine and so on, in the same way the structure conditions the actual ways and modes, but is not expressed by them. (Foucault's "archeology of the sciences of man" is a model case.)

In the same way, a structural interpretation of music searches for the underlying condition of musical activity, its grammar, code or structure. Sociologically, this entails the search for parallells and homologies, or isomorphic relations between different fields.

Weber's essay on music is an early example of structural interpretation.[2] Concerned with the specificity of Western culture, its "spirit", he described various fields of culture as variations on a basic theme, that of means-towards-an-end-rationality. This rationality he claimed to be present within the economic sphere, within the field of law, the field of religion, the field of science, of architecture - and within the domain of music.

According to Weber, the specific rationality of Western music has to do with the tempered scale; which offers a solution to the "problem of the fifth's circle". By tempering the scale, the series of fifths "comes full circle", so to speak, making possible the progression of chords and the modulations which characterize the theory of harmony and Western music in general. Another specific trait is the system of musical notation; when music is written down, this permits large musical structures or texts to be composed, such as the huge polyphonic webs created in the Renaissance era, or the symphonies of the modern era. Weber endeavoured to show that the basic structure of Western music was similar to the structure of other fields, without claiming that the one was the "cause" or the "expression" of the other. The notion of structure - as that of expression - is also fundamental, or categorical. Therefore, structural interpretation can be undertaken for its own sake, as an end in itself.

Another great example is the socio-musicological interpretation of Thomas Mann - and his advisor, Adorno - in the novel *Dr. Faustus*. The book is about the catastrophic development in Germany, leading to the regime of National Socialism and the Second World War. This is seen by Mann as the decay of bourgeois humanist culture, the giving-in to another culture, that of "fascism", which praised ruthless force. On the level of music, Mann discerns a parallel structural process - the decay of harmonic music which had been the system of the bourgeois era since the renaissance, and its giving way to a new music of anti-humanism, celebrating the archaic, the primitive, barbaric force. The same basic theme is thus played on two different registers, so to speak.

---

2 Max Weber, *Die rationalen und sozialen Grundlagen der Musik*, 1921, posth.

Further examples could be shown as attempts to make music part and parcel of a political or national movement. The Norwegian composer, Grieg, wished to write Norwegian music even at a time when Norway did not exist as an independent state within the international system of states. Grieg wanted to contribute to the nation-building of Norway. Although trained in Germany in the Schumann school of Romanticism, he wanted to create specifically Norwegian music. He took up the study of the music of the peasants, transforming it into concert hall or salon music. At that time, the peasant movement was making great progress in Norwegian political life, and contributed much to the founding of the new Norwegian state in 1905. That is: the propagating of peasant music was thought of as structurally similar to the propagating of the peasants' political and economic interests. Others have tried to impose a way of listening to this music, stressing its naturalness, since Norwegian culture connotes a love of nature and the spending of leisure time in nature; peasant life, also, is - or was - nearer to nature than urban life. Thus, there are structural parallels to draw between Norwegian music and Norwegian social and cultural structure.

In this case, there is a *deliberate* intention to create a structural parallel or iso-morphic relationship. More often, perhaps, the structural relationship between music and its social setting, on the one hand, and music and other fields, on the other, exists unintentionally.

But there is also the possibility of a complementary relationship. The structure of music and of socio-musical relations may be very different from the main structures of society, and, for this very reason maybe, is what it is. The instrumental-expressive dichotomy according to Parsons[3] is famous: premodern society was more undifferentiated; modern society differentiates between the sphere of instrumental activity and thought, and the sphere of feelings and expressivity. Thus, very emotional, expressivist music may be complementary to the emotionally more neutral sphere of modern capitalist economy and work.

This notion of complementarity and differentiation, one should note, is essentially connected to the notion of social function; on this point, therefore, structural interpretation tends to merge with functional analysis.

Music and Context

Finally, I come to the contextual or situational interpretation of music. It springs from a very simple observation, i.e. that the social setting of music can have a considerable impact on what we hear. Thus, a pattern of sounds, acoustically the same, can be taken to mean or express interpersonal love, or a religious attitude of devotion and awe. To take a well-known example, the chorale which recurs again and again in Bach's *Passion of St. Matthew*, was originally a love song (Mein Kopf ist so verwirret, das macht ein Mädchen zart). The melody itself has been entirely re-contextualised; it has a new, religious text, it has become transformed from a solo song into a chorale, and it is sung in a different context, the protestant churches. For long now, we can all hear how this melody expresses Bach's pietist-sentimental Christianity. But since the melody at first intrinsically belonged to a text on love-sickness, it cannot be the music itself, but the context, which determines the meaning of this music.

Another example could be the second, slow movement of Chopin's second piano sonata, which is played at great, public funerals, such as the funeral of King George V.

---

3 See, for instance, Parsons and Shils, *Towards a General Theory of Action*, 1949.

of England. This movement expresses sorrow and sadness. However, we can readily conceive of a different interpretation - that the music is grave, but not necessarily sorrowful. But since it has served so often as funeral music, it has become virtually impossible to hear anything else than sorrow expressed even when it is played outside the funeral setting. (Chopin himself, as is well known, disapproved of "program music".)

From these and similar examples one can go on to suggest that these cases may not be exceptions, but exemplify the rule - i.e. that the context accounts for much of what is termed 'the meaning' of music.This is moderate contextualism (to which I subscribe). One may even go further, to the extreme, and maintain that *all* meaning in music is contextual. This is radical contextualism (to which I do not adhere).

The thought that music is contextual may be met with resistance, or even anger, especially in Western culture, where the notion of "pure or absolute music" is very important. The corpus of string quartets, symphonies and concertos which has been produced since the time of Haydn and Mozart constitutes, as it were, the basis of Western classical high culture music, with claims to universal intelligibility, appealing to the humanistic aspirations of all humankind. On the other hand, it can easily be conceded that social and cultural context is all-important for the perception and understanding of *other* branches of music, such as popular music or rock music. Here, it is said, the musical material is itself so poor that it cannot stand alone; it gets its meaning from the setting - one cannot listen to it in the same way one listens to chamber music. A rock concert is above all a social occasion, not a musical occasion.

The answer to this is that the proponents and lovers of classical music may be context-blind. They may over-look the contextual aspects of their own cherished music, in which they can not easily discern such aspects, as when it comes to types of music they care less about. Moreover, they forget or ignore that this notion of "absolute" music is no older than approximately 200 years; up till then, vocal music - and above all, opera - was considered the highest form of music, by far superior to instrumental music. At that time, around 1790, an important change took place, instigated by a circle of German writers and musicians. They claimed instrumental music to be the supreme art, not in spite of, but because of its non-verbal character. This enabled it to express and reveal insights of profound wisdom. This romantic claim was resisted by great thinkers such as Hegel, but somehow it won acceptance over the years. Few, if any, consider today that opera ranks above symphonic music.

This rise of instrumental music was itself connected to contextual changes, and social changes in a broader sense.

Opera was the musical art form of the nobility and the ruling classes. It was *rhetorical* and *representational;* its setting was that of the great opera houses, with their private boxes, rented by the nobility and the rich. People came to see and listen, but also in order to meet others, to be presented to new aquaintances and so on. The opera plot borrowed its themes from ancient mythology; the conflicts between goddesses and gods were regarded a proper subject matter - it somehow mirrored the situation of these noble and mighty spectators.

Instrumental music had other settings - the concert hall and the home - and a different public, the bourgeoisie and the middle classes, who now gained more access to public life than earlier, since the position in society of the nobility had by now weakened. The listening itself became more important: it became similar to the proper behaviour in the church i.e. silent, devotional. The concert hall was a more egalitarian setting than the opera house, and more centered upon the music. In the setting of the bourgeois home, music came to be associated with intimacy and privacy, as a contrast with public, social life. The public concert hall and the bourgeois home were complementary, both creating a setting for instrumental music favourable for its interpretation as the supreme art, expressive of the sublime. If we add to this the new musicological discourse brought into circulation, we can see how the meaning of instrumental music as profound, absolute music, is a social and cultural institution among other institutions. Today, this position has been shaken for many reasons, such as, for instance, the wide-spread use of extracts of classical music - famous themes, motifs, melodies - in advertising, or as an interlude in computer games, or as music played while we are waiting on the telephone. The *aura*, the sacred ring of classical music becomes worn away by this unceasing re-contextualization.

This process began with the gramophone record and the broadcasting of music. When music was played everywhere, and mostly through the medium of the phonograph, it became less and less connected with a definite setting. We should not say that is was decontextualised, since there is always a context. What happens then? The first possibility: music may become increasingly a matter of individual interpretation, any individual giving it a singular meaning, through a highly individualized context. If so, the meaning of music as a common cultural symbol with which to identify may wither or fade away. But there is a second possibility: public commentators - in the mass media - may interpret the music and impose their interpretation on the masses. The role of journalism in music - serious, light, classical, folk, regardless of what kind - is very great. Journalists and musicologists may somehow construct a cultural symbolism which, supplanting the original symbolism, becomes attached to a definite, lived-in social setting. There is a third possibility: the meaning of music may be defined by relating it to some broad category of social setting - such as church music, ball-room music, concert hall music; and when we listen to music through the medium of the compact disc or the radio, when listening to sacred music we may listen as if we were actually in the church; as if we were in the concert hall when listening to a symphony; as if we were in a dance hall or restaurant when listening to dance music, and so on - although we are, in fact, driving a car through the streets of a city. This kind of imaginary setting and imaginary listening blend with the highly individualised or privatized listening mentioned as the first possibility. The outcome is quite uncertain. It seems, therefore, safe to conclude that listening to music through the medium of the phonograph or otherwise makes the meaning of music more indeterminate than before.

To the extent that music is contextually determined, it is extremely susceptible to changes; for when the setting is altered, so is the music. What we are now confronted with is a socio-musical flow or process where every fixed meaning is provisional, bound to pass away.

Concluding Remarks

This discussion is intended as a conceptual clarification. Music has a position of paramount importance in the world today; at the same time, as an aspect of rapid globalization, there are all kinds to be heard and practised. This is perhaps the main reason for looking at music and musical change from more than one perspective; music today is a field where the hegemony of classical Western music is challenged more than ever - the trend is towards a musical field constituted of a vast number of subfields, each of them claiming its right to exist on an equal footing with the others. In this situation, I have found that the basic concepts or categories presented here shed light on the difficulties of understanding and interpreting music and musical change.

Patterns of Change and Continuity in Liturgical and Ritual Music

AMNON SHILOAH

My keen interest in the phenomenon of change has been an important catalyst in my research on past and present Jewish and Arab musical cultures. It also helped determine my basic approach when seeking a response to the fundamental question of the evolving relationships between their past and present. The impetus to deal with this question developed as a result of my growing acquaintance with the wealth of Arab and Hebrew sources related to exploring the various aspects of music. The study of those sources is extremely revealing and provides the seeker with a mine of invaluable information about the intellectual world of the thinkers and theorists of music in bygone days.[1] Their writings and reflections inform us of earlier concepts held about music, the conflicting attitudes toward which have been a matter of long-standing harsh and passionate debate between opponents and supporters, namely from a legal and theological point of view,[2] the role of music in the life of man and society, and the norms of its practice.

In light of the image obtained from analysis of the sources, one is naturally tempted to raise the pertinent and intricate questions as to whether and to what extent the musical theory and practice of present-day living musical styles descend from early classical musical traditions, or deviate from them. However, since the musical heritage was transmitted entirely by ear, and provides us with no musical documents earlier than the first recordings made at the beginning of this century, we cannot know with any certainty how the music sounded. This difficulty is exacerbated by changes that have affected music in the course of time, particularly during the last hundred years or so. Nevertheless, reasonable and helpful comparisons can be made on the level of ideas, of concepts held about music, musicianship and musicians, theoretical features, performance practices, and predominant forms and genres, as well as instruments - including their uses and functions.

In face of this complex situation, I have come to the conclusion that, with a view to understanding properly the nature of the eventual changes undergone in the current musical traditions, it is necessary to refer to the question of relationships between past and present, of tradition. In other words, in this case one should adopt an approach which appropriately combines the diachronic and synchronic aspects; this implies the ability to analyze actual living styles and their performing practices in the light of all that can be inferred from the sources. My experience in using this approach, as well as my acquaintance with various modern theories about change, has led me to suggest in a recent study that most extant ethnomusicological and anthropological theories on cultural change and musical change - particularly those

---

1 See, A. Shiloah, *The Theory of Music in Arabic Writings, c. 900-1900*, (RISM, Bx, Muenchen: Henle Verlag, 1979), 512+XXVIII pages.
2 A. Shiloah, "Music and Religion in Islam", *Acta Musicologica*, LXIX/2, (1997), pp. 143-155.

concerned with the historical dimension - would be neither sufficient nor exhaustive in that they are essentially founded on observations and analysis of living musical traditions belonging primarily to tribal cultures. Hence, too, they generally lack the type of living evidence mentioned above; this does not mean that I suggest rejecting or ignoring those theories, but I do suggest avoiding putting one's sole reliance on them.[3]

A great many publications dealing with theoretical or practical cases of musical change appear under the dichotomous label of continuity and change, implying that change can or should be assessed only against a given or assumed continuity. Yet the relationship between continuity and change, and the criteria by which the line separating them should be determined, let alone the definition of the nature of change as a whole, is unclear. In dealing with these and other related features, the late J. Blacking wrote in his analysis of different theories of change the following statement: "All evaluations of musical change tell us more about the class and interests of the evaluators than about the nature of musical change".[4]

Many scholars who rely on the available theories of change, consider the period coinciding with exposure to Western culture and techniques as a kind of a line of demarcation attesting to considerable or radical change, that is, the advent of something new as compared to traditional or classical music. Pursuant to the approach I have suggested, one must ask the following questions: Are those changes all the consequence of exposure to Western music and its influence? Do they represent a break with the period before there was contact? Were they indeed an instance of sudden innovation, or, perhaps the consequence of a different pattern of a culture-bound phenomenon? In referring to all these cases, it is essential to compare change in past and present periods. I did so in a recent study, using Erik von Grünebaum's dichotomy: orthogenesis vs. heterogenesis, by virtue of which he analyzed the basic differences in the process of change between past and present in the case of Muslim culture.[5]

Before delving further, it is important to keep in mind the following general clarifications, some of which will be mentioned or implied in the second part of this paper, while others will be left aside because they require special and extensive development.

A general examination of the relevant musical cultures throughout the ages reveals that change has affected mainly the category of sophisticated and recreational music, much less that of religious and folk music, as we shall see later. Music of the pre-contact period or the period preceding modernization should not be considered as some sort of "original" "authentic" static and unchanging tradition, nor should all the innovations introduced under the impact of Western music be viewed as unwelcome alterations devoid of authenticity. It should rather be affirmed that manifold permutations characterized music in the past, and a wide variety of stylistic types and changes emerged under the impact of new conditions such as those enumerated in many of Salwa al-Shawan's studies on music in modern Egypt,[6] or those defined in Shiloah-Cohen's "Dynamics of Change".[7]

---

3 *Idem.*, "Between Written and Oral Cultures - Past and Present as Incorporated into Muslim and Jewish Musical Traditions", *Musica e Storia*, vol. V, (Fondazione Ugo e Olga Levi, Societa editrice il Mulino,Venezia), 1997, pp. 153-164.

4 J. Blacking, "Some Problems of Theory and Method in the Study of Musical Change", *Yearbook of the IFMC*, 9 (1978), p. 4.

5 See, *supra*, note 3, 162-163.

6 S. el-Shawan Castelo-Branco, "The Traditional Arab Music Ensemble in Egypt since 1967: The Continuity of Tradition Within a Contemporary Framework", *Ethnomusicology, 28/2*, (1984), pp. 271-288; *Idem.*, "The Heritage of Arab Music in Twentieth Century Music", *Musica e Storia*, vol. V, (Fondazione Ugo e Olga Levi, Venezia), 1997, pp. 205-213.

7 A. Shiloah and E. Cohen, "Dynamics of Change in Jewish Oriental Ethnic Music in Israel", *Ethnomusicology, 27/2*, (1983), pp. 227-252.

In view of the predominance of change which occurs in different ways and varying degrees of intensity throughout the ages, I prefer to consider the different directions or various dynamics of change as a continuity-in-change, paraphrasing Nettl's subtle definition "The continuity of change". An eminent scholar who has contributed much to the study of change. Nettl used this label phrase as a title for a chapter of his book *The Study of Ethnomusicology*.[8] Such an approach attempts to extend the conceptual frame of reference in order to accommodate a wider scope of empirical variations.

Historically speaking, the "Great Musical Tradition"[9] established soon after the advent of Islam, and widely accepted by both conquerors and conquered, is in itself a product of change that came into being as a result of a well-controlled and deliberate process. This was a type of radical change which transformed the conqueror's pre-Islamic predominantly tribal music into sophisticated urbanized art music by way of willingly accepting the influence of the conquered, provided the latter accept certain conditions, namely full adherence to the process of "Arabization"[10] conceived as a means of unification. One witnesses here the creation of a skillful fusion in which the strong - the conqueror - did not seek to impose his culture on the conquered but rather sought a way to create "new arrangements" perceived by both conquerors and conquered as an outgrowth of the old. Moreover, it seems to me that the nature and pattern of change that brought about the successful fusion also presaged future change of the same type - other "adaptive strategies" that are corroborative of the principles and conditions that gave birth to the Great Tradition. The following is an interesting example from the first period which coincides with the crystallization of the Great Tradition. It is commonly admitted by the specialists that as part of the process of Arabization, the achievements and norms of pre-Islamic classical poetry became a model of creativity for all poets of the Islamic period. However, recent studies indicate that, due to Persian influences, post-Islamic poetry underwent subtle transformations, particularly in love-poetry, which corresponded better to the new conditions of urban life; those transformations were so well integrated as to give the general impression that the new is identical with the old. This type of orthogenetic change also had an impact on the music, because poetry was an essential component of the new sophisticated musical style. I believe that this readiness to absorb compatible foreign elements ensured what I have called continuity-in-change until the appearance in the nineteenth century of another type of change, heterogenetic in nature.

A similar openness in the case of Jewish music can be partly explained in view of the special circumstances that have surrounded Jewish life for two thousand years; during that time multiple traditions crystallized in many lands spread over the four corners of the earth. Here also, special restrictive conditions have determined the scope and types of change. In both cases the base line for reference is flexible and often movable.

Viewed against this general background, the definition of the phenomenon of change as applied here confronts three major difficulties:

1. Lack of a single accepted theory of the highly complex phenomenon of change, a theory which clearly defines its nature, endeavors to measure it, and to seek patterns and consistency.

---

8 B. Nettl, *The Study of Ethnomusicology*, (Urbana: University of Illinois Press, 1983), ch. 13.

9 This concept designates, in our context, the sophisticated musical art style elaborated in Near Eastern music after the advent of Islam and widely adopted by the cultures under Islamic influences.

10 The process of Arabization and its importance for the development of the Great Musical Tradition is described in A. Shiloah, *Music in the World of Islam*, (London: Scolar Press, and Detroit: Wayne State University Press), 1995, pp. 21-25.

2. Who is to determine change in a musical system? Should it be an objective outsider, or those who practice the music being evaluated? This brings to the fore the full significance of the emic/etic dichotomy. Most available studies seem one-sided and fall into the snare of subjectivity, as suggested by Blacking's statement cited above: "all evaluations of musical change tell us more about the class and interests of the evaluators than about the nature of musical change".[11]

3. The third problem pertains to the special instance of musical traditions for which we have a wealth of written sources and historical evidence that must be taken into consideration in the study of the types of change evinced by their modern counterparts. Because of the magnitude of this subject, I suggest focusing on one genre or category which corresponds to the major theme of religious or liturgical and ritual music.

In his monumental book, *The Anthropology of Music*, Alan Merriam contends that: "Within a musical system different kinds of music are more or less susceptible to change; thus it is assumed that less change can be expected in religious than in social or recreational music. The basis for the assumption is apparently that religious ritual depends upon music, while recreational music, for example, is used simply as accompaniment to other activities...the argument is that religious music is so much a part of general religious practice that it cannot be altered without altering other aspects of ritual."[12] Elsewhere in the book, Merriam clarifies the relationship between religious and other music saying that religious beliefs are expressed through musical prayer, myth and legend set to music, cult songs, songs of divination, and others, providing many examples in both cases, all of them referring to tribal cultures. There is nothing intrinsically wrong in this, but it makes the universal aspect of the statement hard to accept. Indeed, while the general statement that less change can be expected in religious music can be easily proven, many details of the theory confront us with a rather intricate situation for which different and contrasting responses should be taken into consideration. First and foremost, legal rabbinical and Muslim religious authorities from the start developed a reserved and sometimes hostile attitude regarding music *per se*, an attitude which varies between complete negation of the use of any musical component or instruments in ritual to various compromises or a tacit tolerance which willy nilly attempt to restrict the role of music in worship. This approach, which derives its essence from the concept about music that is common to authorities of both religions, was nevertheless somehow counteracted by the advent of other ideological interpretations and adaptive strategies.

Following the destruction of the Temple of Jerusalem by the Romans in 70 A.D. and the widespread dispersion of the people of Israel, the splendor of the Temple ritual gave way to an intimate synagogue worship. Prayer and praise replaced the sacrificial offerings and spectacular musical performance provided by professional choirs and instrumental ensembles. In accordance with the new rabbinical approach, cult became inextricably bound to the word and to the worshipper's individual devotion, described as "service of the heart". Hence, prime attention was given to cantillation and psalmody as fundamental musical forms. The term 'music' is altogether avoided when speaking of this type of chanting, even when it later embodied an ornate and melismatic form; one rather finds terms like 'to read' or 'to recite' which aim to emphasize the pre-eminence of the text in this combination of words and musical sounds. Accordingly, biblical and Koranic cantillation does not envelop the text with a musical ambience but seeks to identify itself, by virtue of the musical

---

11 See, *supra*, note 4.
12 A. Merriam, *The Anthropology of Music*, (Evanston: Northwestern University Press), 1964, pp. 217-218.

component, with the divine essence embraced by the text. In the protracted debate over the permissibility of music, this sacred aspect expressed in sound has led to the exclusive ideological application of the concept music to all types of composed music based on esthetic and compositional norms, that is to say, secular art music whose chief purpose is to please the ear and delight the senses, entertaining the soul. Thus art music came to symbolize the profane, implying that the great passion for music is a kind of "intoxication" that helps divert the devotee from performing his religious duties. It is interesting to note that the puritanical approach the Muslim purists developed incidentally received special impetus in view of the life of pleasure led during the Golden Age of Muslim civilization by the aristocratic elite and most of the caliphs, who were known as the commanders of the faithful. A similar situation can be observed during the flowering of Jewish culture in Spain. The great philosopher and Rabbinical codifier - Maimonides, who tolerated music when it served a religious purpose - formulated a negative attitude to secular music practice in radical terms because "Israel is required to be a 'sacred nation' and music provokes excitement and sensuality."[13] In both religions, one still finds ultra-orthodox minorities advocating the banning of music. Jewish extremists still identify music with joy which is incompatible with the mandated observance of grief over the destruction of the Temple.[14]

But this is only part of the intricate story. While officially Islam did not admit the development of any kind of liturgical mosque music, it is common knowledge that between the fourth and fifth century religious sung poetry - *piyyuṭīm* - began to make its appearance in the synagogue. This novelty apparently came into being as a result of the growing need for the introduction of variety, above all on Sabbath and the Holy days. Undoubtedly, the *piyyuṭ* brought a new and important musical dimension to synagogue liturgy. However, the adoption of the *piyyuṭ*, as well as the limited use of religious poems sung to enhance festive occasions in Islam, was somehow "justified" by the folk nature of the tunes to which the hymns were sung. Like the chant, folk music was not considered music; the concept of "non-music" embraced both of them. Opposition to these hymns starts to emerge as soon as art music influences begin to be mingle with the performance of the hymns. With this new development, apologetic defense also started to appear, suggesting forms of adaptive strategy to counteract radical opposition. The following response of an eminent Spanish canonist rabbi, Shlomo ben Adrat, alias Harashba (1235-1310), is a case in point. The rabbi refers to a question he was asked about a cantor with a trained voice who enjoys "showing off" his artistic talent for the purpose of impressing the worshippers, while claiming that this is his way of expressing inner devotional joy. The questioner believes that in this fashion the cantor contravenes the essence of the prayer which should express supplication. Shlomo ben Adrat argues that everything depends upon the cantor's inner motivation. If the fervor of his creative musical imagination rests on the desire to praise and give thanks to the Lord, and he stands before the divinity in fear and awe, "May he be blessed". But if his intention is to demonstrate his artistry in order to reap the praise of the congregation, his behavior is reprehensible.[15]

One can infer two new important and significant features from this example: one is the role played by the cantor as soloist who contributes towards a growing affini-

---

13 This statement is included in a responsum by Maimonides (Arabic in Hebrew characters) to an inquiry from the Jews of Aleppo concerning the singing of *muwashshaḥāt* (pl. of *muwashshaḥ*), a strophic poem established in Spain, and the practice of secular music in general. See, I. Adler, *Hebrew Writings Concerning Music*, (RISM BIX2, Muenchen: Henle Verlag), 1975, pp. 240-242.

14 Anonymous, *El Gil Ka'amim*, (Jerusalem: 1969, in Hebrew).

15 Rabbi Shlomo ben Adrat, *Responsa*, (Bnei-Braq: 1982), part one, Responsum 215, (in Hebrew).

ty for art music combined with folk musical material that largely characterizes the chanting, the solemn reading of scriptures, as well as most of the congregation's singing. The second is the conception of the musical component in ritual and worship as polyvalent, which is essential for the different ideological interpretation of music developed by both Muslim and Jewish mystic movements.

As early as the ninth century, with the emergence of the numerous mystic confraternities in Islam, the debate became increasingly heated: music and dance were doctrinally essential to the performance of the Sufi rituals which aim to enter into a closer relationship with God and realize a union with the Godhead. For the mystic, the value and nature of music and dance are chiefly determined by the virtues of listener, his degree of mystical cognition of God and His revelation. In view of the extreme importance the sufis attached to music and dance in their doctrine, most of their opponent's attacks were directed against their practices and beliefs, identifying them with polytheism and Satanic delusion.

In Judaism, a different ideological approach emerged in the sixteenth century, and involved the circle of mystics in Safed (a small town in the north of Israel). In their doctrine, singing is perceived as elevating the soul to celestial realms. Theories dealing with the power and function of song were developed extensively and given important practical application by the kabbalists of Safed. There can be no doubt that their widely accepted doctrine acted as a catalyst of prime importance in the flowering of religious poetry and song. It also served to arrest the onslaught of an extremist minority that objected to music. One of the most significant contributions is the rationalization of the borrowing of alien tunes which we touched on previously. In a way, this approach may be considered as another adaptive strategy; it reached its peak with the hasidic movements in East Europe, at the beginning of the eighteenth century. The borrowing of alien tunes was looked upon as performing a holy mission since the borrowed melodies, by implication, were thus elevated from profanity to sanctity, and the borrowers were redeemers in that they recognized the "holy sparks" embedded in the foreign folk song.

The foregoing survey has confronted us with multiple facets of the single category of religious music. Even within this limited sphere, one finds divergent approaches so conceived as to leave a de facto margin of flexibility, despite the unequivocal opposition of most extremists to music. As against the intransigent attitude of the extremists who categorically ban all forms of secular art music and all amplification of the musical component beyond rudimentary chanting, the margin of flexibility was essentially used to extend the border- line between chanting and more sophisticated music by giving more lee-way to the border-line separating the sacred and the profane. Hence, the demarcation line should not be formed on the basis of the degree of sophistication of the music, but the way the music, any music, serves the function of the prayer, consolidates and enhances religious feeling without blurring the message contained in the texts. The mind must maintain control over excessive emotion and, of course, one must avoid seeking mere aesthetic pleasure or overwhelming sensual emotion similar to that evoked by profane art music. Admittedly, the complete compliance with all these exigencies is rather difficult, so the conflicting views may have started with the early expansion of chanting toward a richer and more sophisticated state. This pertained first and foremost to the solemn reading of the Koran and Biblical scriptures. Individual talented and creative readers, particularly those living in major urban centers and attuned to art music, sought to enhance the prestige of reading and to increase the emotional impact by borrowing certain elements from art music without transgressing the basic laws and norms of the canon of works to be read.

Similarly, talented individual cantors seeking to enhance the prestige of the liturgy and increase the emotional impact of long prayers, found ways to integrate borrowed elements of art music into the dominant chant and folk singing. Although, as time passed, the borrowing embodied far-reaching consequences, especially with the adoption of the *maqām* concept and system, the walls were not breached. In most, if not all, cases, the cantors, as well as the worshippers do not consider the clear recourse to the *maqām* principles for chanting, or for metrical or improvisational pieces, as a concert performance of sorts but rather as a means for increasing the power of prayer. For this reason, any worshipper, including children, is encouraged to participate in the performance of strophes comprising long, expressive and richly ornamented sung poems. Such collective participation, which also includes many responses and the singing of entire hymns, helps to unify the spirit of the prayer and blur any suggestion of a concert in the performance of the liturgy.

In light of the foregoing summary, I wish to close with a few illustrations of the above mentioned approaches, bearing in mind that less change can be expected in religious than in social or recreational music.

1. Under the term *tajwīd* (embellishment of recitation) a remarkable system evolved regulating Koran cantillation with respect to the laws of phonetics, correct diction and rendition of the text. The *tajwīd* does not concern itself explicitly with the regulation of the musical parametre as such, because it is simply considered nonexistent. The reading became subject to divergent attitudes when it exceeded the strict role assigned to it. This happened quite early on, when the notion of *qirā'a bi'l-alḥān* (recitation with melodies)[16] evolved; this referred to the recourse of readers to a sophisticated form close to art singing. The writer and poet ibn 'Abd Rabbih (d. 940), in the section on music in his encyclopedic work *al-'Iqd al-farīd* (The Unique Necklace), recounts the case of a man who was arrested by the police because he sang in the mosque compound. A noble man from the prestigious Quraishi tribe manages to release him by testifying that he was merely reciting the Koran in a beautiful manner. Away from the mosque, the benefactor said: "I would not have lied had your singing been beautiful."[17] The adoption of art singing which becomes more and more widespread, aroused furious attacks on the part of legalists and traditionalists, but the phenomenon has not been uprooted.

2. At a *dhikr* ceremony of the mystic confraternity *al-Shādhiliyya*,[18] which I attended in the late 60s in the town of Akre, a young villager with a beautiful voice and an innate talent for music, at different moments of the ceremony performed the hymns of the order in a highly expressive and sophisticated manner. His singing however, was in perfect harmony with the usual traditional spirit characterizing such a performance. Toward the end of the ceremony the same singer recited Koran verses in the manner in which he performed the hymns. When the ceremony was over, an old man considered an expert reader of the Koran said to him: "You had better learn the rules of the *tajwīd* before such an undertaking." Once again we meet up with differences of opinion concerning the melodic recitation.

3. Two or three years later, in 1970, the Egyptian periodical *al-Hilal* published under the title of "Qur'an Cantillation: A Controversy between Art Musicians and Religious Authorities", the content of a debate dealing with the question of whether the text of the Koran may be used in composing art music much like other holy scriptures. In this debate religious authorities, a philosopher and the greatest living musi-

---

16 M. Talbi, "La qira'a bi'l-alhan", *Arabica*, 5 (1958), pp. 183-190.

17 Ibn 'Abd Rabbih, *al-'Iqd al-farīd*, Bulaq: 1876), vol. III, pp. 229-271.

18 A Sufi confraternity called after Abu'l-Ḥasan ibn 'Abdallah al-Shādhilī. It seems that the first group of adherents was formed in Tunis.

cians took part. From all the participants, only two famous musicians, 'Abd al-Wahāb, and al-Sinbāṭi, known as avid innovators, were in favor of introducing the innovation; all the rest, including the famous songstress Umm Kulthūm, who incidentally was a well-versed Koran reader in her youth, were categorically opposed.[19]

Contemplating the factors that elicited such opposition to the proposal - even though it was not meant to become part of the ritual - one can assume that the opponents may have expressed instinctive feelings of awe toward something that should be left untouched. I believe that the sacred nature bestowed on primordial traditional chanting was the source of their determination to preserve it from significant change. If we combine this interpretation with the concept that regards folk music as "non-music", we may assume that the less a musical tradition is exposed to the influence of art music, the less it is subjected to change. This is the case of ultra-orthodoxy everywhere, of Jewish and Muslim communities in rural areas and of many mystic orders.

4. In this respect I should like to cite the fascinating example of Yemenite Jews in Israel. Despite permanent exposure to Western and modernized Eastern societies for at least fifty years (the date of the mass immigration), the stability of most aspects of their liturgy is truly remarkable. Should chance bring an outsider to one of their many synagogues on the Sabbath or a holy day, he would hear a large congregation, including children born and raised in Israel, collectively performing extensive parts of the prayer by heart, with their own special accents and intonations, their own traditional tunes, and the use of various forms of plurivocality.[20] Moreover, as in days long past, the reading of the scriptures is undertaken by individual worshippers, not by a professional reader; the Aramaic translation of the Hebrew text is systematically chanted by a young boy. This is most remarkable, considering the conditions of life in modern Israel.

5. My last example concerns an interesting case of adaptive strategy. In 1969, a tiny group of fundamentalists published a booklet entirely devoted to the prohibition of music.[21] One of its first sections places blame on technical innovations in the realm of electro-acoustical equipment; a rabbinical proscription is quoted in which two famous authorities who headed orthodox Jewry decreed that the radio, phonograph and tape-recorder are in the same category as musical instruments, since they too emit music. The same group last year banned an ultra-orthodox hotel in Jerusalem because it "dared" introduce a television set into the hotel. Aside from this very tiny group, in the last decade the bulk of ultra-orthodoxy has undergone a "radical" change in this respect. Today, several pirate radio stations daily present the manifold tendencies of orthodoxy on the air waves, and quite recently, a special radio station for orthodox women was established. Cassettes are sold by the hundreds and have become the indispensable companion of drivers on the roads. Last but not least, a special cassette with songs and homilies was used in the last election campaign by more than one orthodox party. Thus, what was not long ago prohibited has today, by means of adaptive strategy, become a powerful tool for religious learning and propaganda.

In a study published in 1983, entitled "Dynamics of Change in Jewish Oriental Ethnic Music in Israel" carried out jointly by myself and the sociologist Erik Cohen,

19 Ḍiyā' al-dīn Bibars, "Talḥīn al-Qur'ān, mu'āraḍa bain ahl al-fann wā-rijāl al-dīn", *Al-Hilal*, 78/12 (1970), pp. 118-124.

20 S. Arom and U. Sharvit in collaboration with N. Ben-Zvi, Y. Mazor and E. Steinberg, "Plurivocality in the Liturgical Music of the Jews of San'a", *Yuval* V, The A. Z. Idelsohn Memorial Volume, ed. by I. Adler, B. Bayer and E. Schleifer, (Jerusalem: Magnes Press, 1994), pp. 34-67.

21 *Op.Cit.*, note 10.

we established a typology of stylistic dynamics based on four variables, two of a more musicological and two of a more sociological character. They are: Perpetuation vs. Innovation; Orthogenesis vs. Heterogenesis; Internal vs. External Audience; Spontaneous vs. Sponsored Musical Production.[22] Obviously, it is beyond the scope of this paper to discuss the details of the findings, but one thing is interesting - most of the instances mentioned here are akin to items in our nine-fold types of stylistic change which represent close relationships with the variables denoting perpetuation and orthogenesis. I believe this fact may serve as an additional asset to the thesis developed in this paper.

---

22 *Op.cit.*, in note 4.

Sacral, Secular or Sacred?
An Essay on Music and Aesthetic Emancipation

ANDERS HAMMARLUND

Ascription or Achievement

In July 1782 a spectacular première took place in the Burgtheater in Vienna. A play of a new kind, called *Die Entführung aus dem Serail*, with music by Mozart, had its first performance. Six years earlier the Emperor Joseph II had given this old court theater the official status of a National Theatre and opened it to the general public. But what kind of nation was it that this new institution was supposed to represent? Vienna was the capital of a multi-ethnic, polyglot, feudal and hierarchic empire. So the nation, in fact, was a *project*, something which now was going to be defined and implemented. The enlightened emperor and his advisers saw the nation as an association of individuals with equal rights and possibilities. The ascribed social status of the individual living in a feudal society should be replaced by personel achievement. The entrepreneur capitalist was the hero of the day - the patron, the grand seigneur, was an anachronism. The local *Gemeinschaft* of traditional society, based on personal links, communalism and patterns of protection, was going to be replaced by a national *Gesellschaft*, a mass of producers/consumers, of theoretically interchangable individuals, held together by a feeling of abstract solidarity with strangers/fellow-citizens. The central concept in this process of societal transformation was *emancipation*.

To emancipate means to liberate, to set free - originally from slavery or from paternal authority, but in a transferred sense from hierarchichal value-scales and subordinations. The emancipatory policies of Joseph II comprised not only social and religious groups such as peasants, Protestants and Jews; they also affected many different fields of social activity which hitherto had been closely interrelated and intertwined. Aesthetic activity, traditionally linked to ritual and collective social representation, now tended to be seen as belonging to a personal sphere, to be a question of individual education and expression. Art became an end, not only a means. And so music was emancipated, was given a social legitimization and did not have to refer to context or function all the time. The new National Theatre was no state-budgeted institution; it was supposed to be financed on a commercial basis, the state merely providing the venue for the staging of a new collective identity. So it was the individual citizens who were supposed to pay for their aesthetic education.[1]

On the other side of the spectrum of music production, in the church, the policies of Joseph II had an equally important impact. Here musical ostentation was seen as too dominant, as too fused with ritual, and a set of regulations was imposed on church services, marking the distinction between rational religion and rational music.

---

1 One of the best accounts of the cultural policies of Joseph II is given in Braunbehrens (Volkmar Braunbehrens, *Mozart in Wien*, München/Zürich: 1986).

It is interesting that precisely at this crucial point in the development of Central European culture a piece of musical dramaturgy was staged, in which Western, "enlightened" and emancipated characters are opposed to figures from an Islamic environment. Of course the personages depicted in Mozart's German-language *Singspiel* had very little to do with the realities of the Ottoman Empire. The "Turks" simply represent "otherness"; their function was to contrast with the values of the Westerners.

Intoning the Call

One hot summer day in 1989 I am standing in the shadow of a mulberry tree in a village in central Anatolia, waiting for the midday *ezan*. And here it comes, clear, loud and convincing, even if filtered through primitive loudspeakers. I listen, fascinated, to this sophisticated intoning of a sacred message, even if my attention is drawn mainly not to the verbal component, but to the medium of its communication - the musical aspect. I am standing here by the *cami* in the company of Mehmet, a friend of mine who was born in the village but has spent most of his life in Stockholm. As a teenager in Sweden, Mehmet started a musical career, mainly drawing on the tradition of *Türk Halk Müziği,* "Turkish folk music". One would suppose that there would be a lot of Turkish folk music in this village with a lot of Turkish folk. However, this is not the case. During our stay in the village I gradually understand that Mehmet's musical models are mainly to be found somewhere else, in the neighbourhood of national institutions and radio studios in Ankara and Istanbul.

In one of the intervals beetween the sections of the *ezan*, Mehmet whispers to me:

- He is very good singer, this Abdullah, don't you think? I really shiver when he does these wonderful melismas, you know. But, of course, he is no musician...

Abdullah is definitely no musician. But nevertheless he seems to be musically the most competent individual in the village. There are about 5000 inhabitants in this peasant settlement. But among these local residents there is nobody who would dream of claiming the title of "professional musician" - when the musical aspects of human communication are separated from a ritual context or from the recitation of sacred texts, their appropriateness becomes somewhat ambiguous. Public musical production is left to outsiders, like gypsies and other stigmatized outcast groups, who have no dignity or social status to defend in the village.[2]

But what about this Abdullah? Well, he is just a *müezzin*, a functionary who calls people to prayer by intoning the call, *ezan okumak*. And he does this with the timing and intonation of a musical virtuoso.

For Mehmet, who is trying to carve out a niche as a "Turkish immigrant musician" in Sweden, this perfect command of vocal, musical resources should be a natural source of inspiration. However, Mehmet is acting in a secular context, in which the musical expression is supposed to be emancipated from a religious content. So, when he is striving to demonstrate his cultural identity, he has to draw from traditions which have no actual roots in his village. To be acceptable, the influence from the *müezzin* can only be indirect.

---

2 See, Anders Hammarlund, *Yeni Sesler. En väg till musiken i det turkiska Sverige*, Stockholms universitet, Studies in Musicology, 1 (Stockholm: 1993).

A village mosque.

Logos and Melos

For a very long time, for almost a thousand years, the idea of aesthetic emancipation was alien to the Western church. The highlighting of verbal performance by the use of more or less standardised pitch systems and melodic formulae, i.e. the chanting or incantation of biblical texts or religious poetry, was the only fully accepted form of musical practice in the church. Since the church represented the apex of the ethical value-scale, this tradition informed western culture generally. Musical instruments had no place in the church; only in the tenth century was the organ eventually allowed to enter the house of God, but until the end of the Middle Ages, this was an expensive and uncommon asset. Where it existed, the organ was allowed only a supportive role.

There were two causes for the gradual emancipation of the musical element of the ritual which started during the high mediaeval period: the drama-like quality of the liturgy, and the evolvement of musical scripturalism. The liturgy partly consisted of a symbolic re-enacting of central episodes of the Gospels (the Eucharist is maybe the clearest example of this), and the character of staging was enhanced by the physical division in the church between lay congregation/audience and ecclesiastical functionaries/ritual actors.[3]

With the evolvement of detailed musical notation during the eleventh century, it became possible conceptually to separate the musical component of chanted liturgy from its literary and theatrical aspects. Around 1200 this led to the emergence of polyphonic music, a form of expression which comes into conflict with the verbal message and the poetic structure of the texts. At the same time, however, this intellectualisation of music production was in harmony with the rationalism of the Western church, which reached its high peak in the scholastic, theological philosophy of the thirteenth century. Religion was not a matter of personal feelings, emo-

3 The laymen were actually fenced off from the priests!

tions and beliefs - religion was firm and universal knowledge, a science. And so was music.

When mysticism became an important factor in the religious life of Western Europe, after scholasticism had been challenged by fourteenth century free-thinkers like Ockham, music did not become a main vehicle for spiritual exercise or communion. There is no tradition of mystical music in the Western sphere until the twentieth century. Musical scripturalism, a basically rationalistic phenomenon, dominated the scene.

In the Eastern churches, as well as in Judaism[4] and in Islam, the dominance of poetry was not challenged in the way it was in the West. Poetry is after all the way God speaks to man, through prophets and psalmists. Poetry is a fusion of the verbal and the musical. The irresistible poetic power of the Koran has been claimed as one of the reasons for the success of Muhammed and early Islam.[5] The breaking up of *poesis*, the effective unity of word and musical structure, therefore was always regarded as unnecessary and improper. The musical component was supposed to be subservient; it was only a *medium* of communication - not because it was seen as impotent or irrelevant; on the contrary, it was regarded as very powerful and important. But the medium was not allowed to become the message; musical aestheticism was a frequent temptation but was always condemned. Musical instruments had no place in the houses of worship and prayer.

In the East much was written about music - theoretical treatises about pitch, intervals, scale and rhythms. The music in itself, however, was *not* written. Of course the sophisticated culture of the Near East was perfectly able to develop a system of musical notation. But since the ties to oral production, to verbal communication, were so strong, a separate, full-fledged and universally accepted system of musical writing never took shape. As long as the traditional forms of education and oral transmission continued to exist, there was no great need for musical scripturalism. As a consequence, music and musical compositions were not categorized or standardised to the extent that became characteristic of Western culture. Musical extemporation, following only partly verbalized modal, *maqam* principles, became the form of music production most highly valued, from Koranic incantation through instrumental *taqsim*s to vocal *layali*s and *gazel*s. And Koranic incantation, the ultimate poetry reading, was the single point of reference for this whole musical spectrum.[6] Also, in the mosque there was no representation or re-enactment, comparable to the spectacular Christian liturgy, that could have triggered a separation of the aesthetic from the ritualistic.[7]

In Islam it was the Sufi movements which, in their efforts to overcome the limitations of naming and categorization, strove to liberate musical expression and composition from linguistic communication. Rumi's famous lines about the *nay* are very significant.[8] Instrumental music, regarded as an outflow of the verbally inexpressible

4 Concerning the Ashkenazi synagogue tradition and its relationship to the modernizing, emancipating musical culture of the West, see Eric Werner, *A Voice Still Heard*, (New York:1976).

5 Karen Armstrong, *A History of God; The 4000-Year Quest of Judaism, Christianity and Islam*, (London: 1993). Armstrong develops this theme in an interesting way, especially so in her chapter 5.

6 Lois Ibsen al Faruqi, "Music, Musicians and Muslim Law", *Asian Music, XVII / 1* (1985).

7 Liturgy means "altar service", a phenomenon alien to Islam and Judaism. In a transferred sense the ceremonies of the sufi orders often are described as a kind of liturgy. This "liturgy", however, is *not* performed in the mosque.

8 See William Stoddart, "Sufism", *The Mystical Doctrines and Methods of Islam,* (Welling-borough 1982). Under the roof of state-building, political Islam a host of different, more or less heterodox religious practices were incorporated. Sufi activities in many ways continued age-old shamanist traditions and methods of worship, formally legitimised by the acceptance of the Koran. As long as the observance of the five pillars of Islam was upheld this was not regarded as contradictory, even if the mysticists sometimes were suspected of heresy.

and intellectually inconceivable deity, now could become an important feature of the *zikr*. In Sufi and Sufi inspired vocal practice such genres that combined a fiercely regulated poetic structure with a non-metrical[9] or even improvised melodic progression came to the fore, like the *gazel*, in which the texts often seem to be more of a pretext for indulgence in purely musical expressivity.

Secular Temples of Art

As we have seen, both in Western Christendom and in Islam, the late medieval period saw the establishment of purely musical forms of expression with their own theoretical and technical concepts. In the West this was a result of a process of rationalisation, linked to scripturalism, whereas in Islam there was an opposite trend, towards orality and emotionalism. Still, however, in both traditions music was regarded basically as an outflow of collectively, universally valid principles. It emanated from sacred *ratio* or *emotio*, and did not express the whims of individuals. Even if the musical aspects of auditive communication could be conceptually separated from the verbal parameter, music was still dependent, inserted as it was in a holistic view of society and religion.

In Western society, modernisation, i.e. the breaking up of traditional social forms and the setting free of the individual, presupposed a departure from the holistic societal model.[10] Now the individual could not just "enter" music anymore, could not just attach himself to a god-given order. Music became a "cultural asset" or a commodity, to use a Marxist term. As a commodity, it was produced and consumed. During the nineteenth century the venues of absolute music, the concert halls, took over much of the symbolically co-ordinative role that traditionally belonged to the church. Simultaneously, however, these cultural establishments became temples of art - music became a kind of secular religion with its own prophets, saints and martyrs. Music in itself now represents the sphere of the numinous, the awe-inspiring and indescribable. The mystery of individual artistic creativity has replaced the mystery of revelation.

This exaltation or even "sanctification" of a phenomenon which earlier had only been a medium stood out as one of the most significant factors of modernity to those intellectuals and politicians who, in different parts of the world, strove to respond to the Western challenge. To Mustafa Kemal music apparently was one of the most important vehicles for societal transformation. Atatürk wanted to replace the traditional, holistic Islamic polity with a value-neutral, individualistic society, held together by the idea of an abstract, national solidarity. It was understood that this could not be done without emancipating the aesthetic, without letting the medium become the message.[11]

There are striking parallells between Joseph II's and Atatürk's policies. Art and

---

9 The non-metrical but composed *durak* genre is a good example of this enhancement or emancipation of the musical aspect. (In his contribution to this volume Cem Behar gives an interesting account of the structure and evolvement of the *durak*.)

10 The Austrian economist and social scientist Karl Pribram presented a very interesting and thought-provoking but nowadays almost forgotten theory on this process, which here is my point of reference (Karl Pribram, *Die Entstehung der individualistischen Sozialphilosophie*, Leipzig: 1912). Pribram regarded the challenge of Ockham's nominalism in the 14th century as a kind of watershed in Western intellectual history.

11 Erdoğan Okyay, "Türkische Musik und die geschichtliche Entwicklung der Musikerziehung in der Türkei", in *Kultur im Migrationsprozess,* ed. M. Fehr, Berlin: 1982. See also the composer A. Adnan Saygun's little book on Atatürk's views on music (A. Adnan Saygun, *Atatürk ve Musiki*, Ankara:

religion are separated and relegated to a personal sphere. Institutions of religious holism are dismantled. Outward social distinction is downplayed. Capitalism is combined with etatism. But in music, Atatürk was even more radical than the Habsburg emperor, because he discarded traditional oralism and imported alien scripturalist forms. Both the *seraglio* and the *tekke* were closed and replaced by a *national* cultural scene.

Eidos and Ethos

In 1992, I was contacted by an association in Stockholm called Iranska Kammarmusikföreningen, "The Iranian Chamber Music Association". Several times a year this association organised concerts with Iranian ensembles and musicians, who mostly belonged to the modern Iranian diaspora. In its premises in the Stockholm suburb of Akalla, the association also held courses in *dastgâh* music and gave lessons on *santur*, *setar* and *kemenche*. The artistic level of the activities was strikingly high. For the concert activities, the association could draw on a global network of exiled professional musicians. These people all seemed to be connected by way of fax and Internet. Stockholm apparently had become an important node in a world wide web of *dastgâh* specialists.

Of course, I was quite happy with this sudden enrichment of Stockholm's musical output. As a producer at the music department of the Swedish Broadcasting Corporation, I had the opportunity to co-operate with these people on several occasions. Besides the highly appreciated productions that resulted, I also got some interesting insights into their attitudes towards tradition and music-making generally.

It was quite clear that the music which these people cultivated had close links to the Fârsi-language Sufi tradition. Texts by Mevlana and other Sufi poets were almost always represented in the concert programmes. Instruments such as *nay* and *setar*, which historically have links to Sufi *zikr* contexts, featured in the ensembles. However, the religious connotations were always downplayed in the presentations of music given by the members of the association. Their *dastgâh* was explained as a purely aesthetic phenomenon: this was "art music", "classical Iranian repertoire". Talking about the texts, these Iranian Stockholmers emphasized the famous doubletalk of the Sufi poets, the religious symbolism being a way of expression which could also be given a wordly interpretation and vice versa.

Moreover, the importance of musical scripturalism was strongly emphasized. Besides its other activities the association edits and distributes printed music material. Classical repertoire as well as newly composed pieces are spread in this way.

How does this rationalistic and emancipated aestheticism go together with the emotionalistic mysticism of the the classical Sufi poets? It doesn't go together at all. Here we see an example of a re-interpretation of a musical tradition, a type of revival focusing on the form; the *eidos*. A set of musical resources which traditionally was

---

1987). Lewis' book (Bernard Lewis, *The Emergence of Modern Turkey*, London&New York: 1968) still is the classical account of the general political and societal process, for more detail see, Stanford J. Shaw and Ezel Kural Shaw, *History of the Ottoman Empire and Modern Turkey, Vol. II: Reform, Revolution, and Republic: The Rise of Modern Turkey, 1808-1975*, (Cambridge: 1988 [1977]). Rauf Yekta Bey, *Türk Musikisi*, (Istanbul: 1986), (Translation of the article "La Musique Turque" in *Encyclopédie de la Musique et Dictionnaire du Conservatoire* (ed. A. Lavignac), Vol. 5, (Paris: 1922); Suphi Ezgi, *Amelî ve Nazarî Türk Musikisi*. Vol. 1-5, (Istanbul: 1933-1953); and M. Ekrem Karadeniz, *Türk Mûsikîsinin Nazariye ve Esasları*, (Ankara: 1981) exemplifies the many (somewhat contradictory) efforts to standardize and rationalize *makam* phenomena.

linked to a specific *ethos*, the Sufi set of values, has been taken out of this context and introduced into another ideological environment. Of course, this has not been done by the Iranian immigrants in Stockholm (even if the Swedish setting probably enhances the process); rather it is a result of a cultural policy of aesthetic emancipation which was implemented by the adherents of societal modernisation during the Pahlavi regime in Iran. The introduction of Western art music certainly was an important feature of that epoch, but in the Iranian case this didn't mean an abolishment of domestic musical forms of expression. Fârsi high culture has been much appreciated among Western intellectuals since the time of early romanticism and could be seen as an important cultural asset during the period of formation of a distinctive, modern and national Iranian identity.[12]

But this identity-building also presupposed a separation of form and content and a subsequent switch of *ethos* - the *dastgâh* was now conceptualized as an emancipated musical phenomenon in the terms of the Western enlightenment tradition and consequently had to be scripturalised, rationalised, and standardised. The *ethos* cultivated and transmitted by Iranska Kammarmusikföreningen in Stockholm is basically identical with the spirit mainained by the *Gesellschaft der Musikfreunde* in early nineteenth century Vienna.[13] Not the immanence of God Almighty, but the transcendence of Art!

Ethos and Ethnos

Recently I was invited to a conference on the theme "Music Education and Religious Minorities", which was organized by the University and Music Conservatory in Göteborg in Sweden. The background for the conference was a feeling of disorientation described by many music teachers in ethnically and religously mixed schools in Sweden. Not only have the teachers been given very scanty insights into non-Western music traditions during their education: for many of them it has become clear that their unreflecting way of conceptualising and evaluating music as a social phenomenon is not universally valid. It has become important to learn something about *ethos*, not only about *eidos*.

As part of the conference, representatives from various "minority" religious communities presented their respective music. Lectures were given on Koranic incantation, Syrian-Orthodox music, Torah incantation etc. A series of workshops gave the participants some practical experience. I took part in a workshop on Syrian-Orthodox music. Four young men performed on the *ud, baǧlama, ney* and *darbuka*. A sheet with a printed version of a liturgic melody was distributed among the audience. As an introduction to the workshop, a long and detailed presentation was given, stressing the antiquity of the music of the Syrian-Orthodox church. But it also became clear in an indirect way that the instrumental performance was something very untraditional and innovative. When there were questions from the audience concerning the traditional roles of the instruments, the young spokesman of the ensemble answered very carefully, but it was also clear that he was a little bit reticent and uncertain. He was careful to refer to a person, about thirty years older, who was also

---

12 See Ella Zonis, *Classical Persian Music. An Introduction*, (Cambridge, Mass: 1973).

13 It can be mentioned as an example that the collection *Le repertoir-modèle de la musique iranienne*, commented and notated by Jean During "Introduction et notation", in *Le Repertoire-modele de la Musique Iranienne. Radif de Tar et de Setar de Mirza 'Abdollah. Version de Nur 'Ali Borumand*, (Teheran: 1991) is used by Iranska kammarmusikföreningen, for teaching and external information.

present during the presentation - the cultural spokesman of the Assyrian association, to which this musical ensemble was affiliated.

Understandably, most of the participants in the workshop did not grasp the actual complexity of the situation. To me, however, who could draw on experiences of ethnomusicological fieldwork among the Christian population of Tur Abdin in south-eastern Anatolia (the region of origin of most of the Syrian-Orthodox people in Sweden), and in the corresponding immigrant community in Sweden, the whole communication became somewhat overstated and almost too illustrative.[14]

Deeply embedded in the complex historical fabric of the "fertile crescent", this cradle of cultures, the Christian minorities shared the general *ethos* of monotheistic Middle Eastern culture. The group-specific traits that marked their identity were linked to their particular versions of monotheism, to forms of worship and ritual. Their specific forms of musical practice were all components of liturgy.[15] The idea of musical group representation outside the church walls was completely alien. Music was not an ethnic marker. On the contrary - music did not exist as an emancipated field of activity! So what happened when these people settled in an European environment is the following: in order to be communicable, the collective identity now has to be re-formulated on the lines of the ethnic and national categories which are basic to secularized, Western societies. A sacral and holistic tradition, in which the verbal and the musical, *logos* and *melos*, were inseparable components of *poesis* is taken as the source of expressive resources for an emancipated music. This new aesthetic category which comprises the musical *eidos* of the old *poesis* then is linked to a new *ethos*, which in many ways stands out as a negation of a traditional *ethos*. This new *ethos* serves *ethnos*, or rather *ethnogenesis*, a project which is handled by a political elite, eager to interact and communicate with the authorities of the new environment. Emancipated music is a ticket to modernity.

We see that the Syrian Orthodox case is even more extreme than the Iranian one. In Iran the process did not start from zero, since the musical *eidos* had already begun to free itself because of the Sufi emphasis on the emotional, non-verbal and "unspeakable" experience of God's presence. In the Syrian-Orthodox community a corresponding tradition of mysticism and emotionalism does not seem to have evolved. Poesis remained united.

Knitting these various empirical and theoretical threads of different colours into a kind of conclusive pattern, I would like to stress the complexity and ambiguity of such phenomena that are subsumed under terms such as 'revival' or 'renewal'. What we very often see is *re-interpretation*, i.e. the documenting, codification and cultivating of a specific musical *eidos*. This obsession with the form, with the details of a repertoire, presupposes a switch of *ethos* and also a disruption and discontinuity of tradition. It is often paired with an idea of pureness and authenticity, meeting new demands for symbolic distinction.

Then there is another phenomenon which often is not so demonstrative and obvious as what I have called re-interpretation. This should rather be called *survival* instead of revival (a term that presupposes the preceding death of something). Survival implies the *continuity* of an *ethos*. But it is important to understand that the

---

14 See Anders Hammarlund, "Från Gudstjänarnas Berg till Folkets Hus. Etnicitet, nationalism och musik bland assyrier/syrianer", *Musik och Kultur*, in ed. Owe Ronström, (Stockholm: 1990); for the anthropological and historical background, also Ulf Björklund, *North to Another Country. The Formation of a Suryoyo Community in Sweden*, Stockholm Studies in Social Anthropology, 9, (Stockholm: 1981); and Bengt Knutsson, *Assur eller Aram*, (Norrköping: 1982).

15 Heinrich Husmann, "Die ostkirchlichen Liturgien und ihre Kirchenmusik", in *Geschichte der katholischen Kirchenmusik 1*, ed. K. G. Fellerer, (Kassel: 1972).

maintenance of *ethos* does not presuppose the preservation of *eidos*. On the contrary, we often see that social groups or societies which seem to have a strong cultural and historical cohesiveness have a rather lax attitude towards the purity and stability of *eidos*. An example from the Jewish sphere comes to my mind: maybe it is not the revivalists of Eastern European *niggunim* who preserve the *ethos* of hasidism. The noisy and trivial forms of syncretic rock music used by some highly vivid hasidic communities seems to be a more typical expression of a vital or truly revived *ethos*. To preserve the content, the form must continuously be changed.

Maybe, Sufi rock music can become a vehicle for *zikr* in the future, rather than staged *sema* shows of so-called whirling dervishes.

PART III

STRUCTURE AND EVOLUTION

Structure and Evolution of the Mevlevî Ayîn: The Case of the Third Selâm

WALTER FELDMAN

Probably somewhat earlier than the appearance of the courtly *fasıl*, the Mevlevî dervishes had developed a liturgy employing a cyclical concert format. While sharing a general function with the *semâ'* of medieval Sufis and the general cyclical (suite) principle and a few items with the Ottoman courtly *fasıl*, the Mevlevî *âyîn* has developed into a musical structure of such originality that it must be discussed as a sui generis phenomenon.

The early history of the two genres - courtly fasıl and Mevlevî *âyîn* - is quite divergent. While courtly music seems to have received considerable patronage in fifteenth century Anatolia, the imperial conquests of Selim I and of Süleyman I inaugurated an era of musical stasis and even decline as the Ottoman court attempted to pattern itself on the music of the Safavids, excluding indigenous instruments and preventing the development of indigenous musical genres. It is only in the last third of the sixteenth century that Ottoman instrumental music shows new independent development, through expansion of the *peşrev* form and the creation of the *taksîm*. At the beginning of the next century the characteristic Ottoman vocal compositional forms, the *beste* and *semâ'î*, make their appearance, in a cyclical format, employing Turkish-language texts, composed by Ottoman composers and performed on distinctively Ottoman instruments, such as the *tanbûr* and the new form of *ney*.[1]

The importance of the Mevlevî order within Ottoman Turkish music must be assessed from several points of view. An organized ritual, known as *âyîn* or *mukabbele*, based on musical compositions emerged in the fifteenth century under the direction of Pîr Adil Çelebi (1421-1460).[2] Mevlevî tradition, which will be discussed below, offers some compelling evidence that the basic structure of the *âyîn* was already in place at some time prior to the seventeenth century. This musical structure, while adopting the essential modal and intonational principles of the contemporaneous art music, resisted the adoption of all the composition forms, either of sixteenth century Iranian art music or of the nascent Turkish art music of the seventeenth century. When an independent Anatolian Turkish art music emerged again in the early seventeenth century, the Mevlevî dervishes interacted in several significant ways with this newly developing music. By the middle of the century Mevlevî *neyzen*s constituted more than half of the master flutists named by Evliyâ Çelebi, and by the turn of the century they occupied an equally prominent position at the court. Furthermore, their instrument, the reed-flute *ney* becomes the second instrument of the courtly ensemble, a unique development within Islamic art music.[3]

---

1 This paragraph summarizes the argument presented in Walter Feldman, *Music of the Ottoman Court: Makam, Composition and the Early Ottoman Instrumental Repertoire*, (Berlin: 1996), ch. 1, pp. 45-64.
2 Ekrem Işın, "Mevlevîlik", *İstanbul Ansiklopedisi*, vol. 4, 1994, p. 423.
3 Feldman, *Music of the Ottoman Court*, pp. 136-142.

Most of the constituent items of the *fasıl* and the *âyîn* have different lineages, but during the sixteenth century a degree of mutual borrowing seems to have occurred - those structural features held in common by *fasıl* and *âyîn* must predate the seventeenth century. During the later seventeenth century, the composers of *âyîns*, such as Mustafa Dede, Osman Dede and Mustafa Itrî, were also composers of the courtly fasıl, but the courtly fasıl and the Mevlevî *âyîn* were already two distinct musical structures.[4] After this period the only major borrowing from one genre to the other is the rhythmic transformation of the third *selâm* and adoption of the new form of *peşrev* in the new *usûl devr-i kebîr* and the introduction of some secular *semâ'î* melodies into the Mevlevî repertoire, which seem to have occurred at the end of the eighteenth century.

The Sufi origin of the term *semâ'î* also reinforces the likelihood that the *semâ'î* may have been borrowed by the court musicians from the Mevlevî *âyîn*. The sections (*selâms*) of the *âyîn* exhibit a fixed succession of rhythmic cycles but these do not follow the cyclical principles of the *fasıl*, and of most other courtly Islamic cyclical formats, i.e. acceleration of tempo and shortening of the rhythmic cycles.

Sources and Formal Structures of the Ayîn

Although it is possible and desirable to analyze the structure of the surviving *âyîn* repertoire synchronically, a diachronic analysis is hampered by the absence prior to the turn of the nineteenth century of written documents comparable to the *Mecmûa-i Saz ü Söz* of Ali Ufkî Bey (ca. 1650) or the collection of Prince Cantemir (ca. 1700). Despite this caveat, the situation is not as discouraging as it might appear. A close look at the form in which the *âyîns* exist today reveals a practice of transmission differing in several respects from that of the secular fasıl which may facilitate some diachronic research.

The situation of sources is the following. The earliest document of the *âyîn* is found in the *Tahrîrîye* of Abdülbaki Nâsir Dede written in 1795 in a form of notation similar in principle, although differing in detail, from those of Cantemir and Osman Dede. Abdülbaki Nâsir transcribed only a single *âyîn*, the Sûzidilârâ of his patron Sultan Selim III. This *âyîn* has been transcribed and published quite scientifically by Rauf Yekta Bey in an interlinear transcription with the form of the *âyîn* current at the beginning of this century.[5] The next known transcriptions of the *âyîns* date from approximately 1875 in the form of a Hamparsum manuscript, formerly belonging to Mahmut Celaleddin Paşa (1848-1908) and now in the library of Ankara University.[6] Rauf Yekta Bey and his collaborators published a series of Mevlevî Ayînleri in the 1930s, basing them not on any written source but rather on the musical practice of his own Yenikapı Mevlevîhâne and of his teacher, Zekâî Dede (d. 1896). A single otherwise unrecorded *âyîn* (by Sermüezzin Rif'at Bey 1820-1896?) in Ferahnâk was transcribed in Western notation and published in 1902 by P.J. Thibaut, and recently edited by Bülent Aksoy (1992).[7]

Although the earliest notated Mevlevî *âyîn* dates only from 1795, several *âyîns* are ascribed to well-known musical figures of the seventeenth and eighteenth centuries, including Itrî, and Osman Dede. The earliest known composer was Köçek

---

4 *Ibid*, pp. 50 and 93-99.

5 Rauf Yekta Bey, *Mevlevî Ayînleri*, (Istanbul: 1935), vol. V, pp. 486-511.

6 Owen Wright, "Aspects of Historical Change in the Turkish Classical Repertoire", in Richard Widdess (ed.), *Musica Asiatica* 5, (Cambridge: 1988), p. 62.

7 Bülent Aksoy, *Sermüezzin Rifat Bey'in Ferahnak Mevlevî Ayini*, (Istanbul: 1992).

Mustafa Dede (d. 1683). The identified mecmûa (lyric anthology) documentation of the âyîns dates only from the early eighteenth century.[8]

Three earlier ayîns prior to the Beyatî Ayîn of Köçek Mustafa survive today and are known collectively as the "beste-i kadîmler" or "ancient compositions". The three *beste-i kadîmler* are in the makams Pençgâh, Hüseynî and Dügâh (the ancient Dügâh = modern Uşşak). Of these only the first is complete, having all four sections (selâm). The Dügâh Ayîni has three sections and the Hüseyni only one. It is highly significant that the Mevlevî tradition did not invent composers to go along with the "ancient" âyîn composition. While pseudographia was a common phenomenon in the Ottoman secular musical tradition, evidently the Mevlevî dervishes were able to tolerate the existence of compositions by unknown composers, and even to allow them to remain fragmentary, without composing appropriate second, third or fourth sections. These facts, coupled with some internal evidence, suggest that the Mevlevî attribution of these ancient compositions to a period prior to the seventeenth century must be taken seriously.

Another distinctive feature of the Mevlevî *âyîn* is the attribution of each *âyîn* to a single composer. Beginning with Mustafa Dede, every *âyîn* in the repertoire is the work of only one musician. This applied to the vocal *âyîn* proper - the introductory peşrev and closing peşrev and semâ'î were taken from other, often non-Mevlevî sources. The composition of the four selâms of an *âyîn* by one individual meant that the *âyîn* became the largest arena in which a Turkish composer could expend his skill. It was the longest and most demanding of all Ottoman compositional forms. Thus, from the point of view of the development of composition, the Mevlevî *âyîn* in the seventeenth century had already reached a level of sophistication which the secular music was only to approach over a century later.

During the later eighteenth century the *âyîn* had the following structure:

1) Na'at-i Şerîf: a pre-composed rubato form.
2) a taksîm on the ney
3) a peşrev in usûl muza'af devr-i kebîr (56/4).
4) Selâm-i Evvel in usûl devr-i revân (14/8) or düyek (8/4)
5) Selâm-i Sânî in usûl evfer (9/4)
6) Selâm-i Sâlis beginning in usûl devr-i kebîr (28/4) and continuing in usûl semâ'î (6/8)
7) Selâm-i Râbi' in usûl evfer
8) a taksîm on the ney
9) a son peşrev in usûl düyek
10) a son yürük semâ'î (6/8)

The notated *âyîn*s as they exist today constitute a rich field for stylistic and structural analysis. It is also possible to make some general observations on their characteristics as a genre, and on certain features of the process of musical transmission, according to the principles of Ottoman musical transmission as enunciated by Wright (1988) and Feldman (1996). This process is discussed in some detail by these two authors, but only in relation to instrumental music. From their discussion it is evident that the instrumental repertoire atttributed to musicians prior to the end of the eighteenth century must have undergone fundamental recomposition in the course of oral transmission, so that a musical item known in the nineteenth and

---

8 Mecmua, Konya Müzesi no. 1295. Dated Zilhicce 1114 (=1704).

twentieth centuries may have only a very tenuous link with any possible sixteenth, seventeenth or eighteenth century piece. However the following discussion of the *âyîn* would suggest that these conclusions cannot be generalized to cover the entire Ottoman repertoire.

The first, and perhaps most obvious, point is that the *âyîn* is a vocal genre - the instrumental peşrev preceding it (used now for the Sultan Veled devri procession), the final peşrev and the final yürük semâ'î are less integral to the genre. The peşrevs used in the processional share only a single characteristic - they must be composed in the usûl devr-i kebîr. Most of these peşrevs have been in use in the *âyîn* since the end of the eighteenth century or since the second half of the nineteenth century. Some, but not all, were composed by Mevlevî musicians for the *âyîn*. A few were composed by earlier musicians, such as Nayî Osman Dede. But the peşrevs could be, and were, replaced with relative ease. For example, in Rauf Yekta's edition the Beyâtî *âyîn* of Mustafa Dede is preceded by a peşrev attributed to the sixteenth century mehter musician Nefîrî Behrâm, but by the time of Heper's edition it had been replaced by the famous peşrev by Emin Dede, one of the few major Mevlevî musicians of the mid-twentieth century. Attributions of the early peşrevs rest on shaky evidence, as several of the peşrevs atttributed to Osman Dede in the nineteenth century were not known to be his in the seventeenth century. In addition, the expansion of the devr-i kebîr usûl, and the fivefold increase in the melodic material in each line, demonstrated at great length by Owen Wright (1988) renders these atttributions almost meaningless as the form of the peşrev known today bears very little resemblance to anything Osman Dede might have composed. The soñ peşrevs and semâ'îs show a rather different pattern of transmission, as their usûl basis has not altered since the seventeenth century, both remaining a simple düyek (8 beats) and semâ'î (6 beats) respectively. A few of the existing pieces in this category, such as the famous Hicaz semâ'î and the Neva soñ peşrev named "Bülbül-i uşşak" can be traced through various transformations back to seventeenth century originals in the secular repertoir.[9] It is at present not known when the custom of the Sultan Veled Devri arose, but it is difficult to conceive of such a procession being performed to the quick 14/4 rhythm of the seventeenth century devr-i kebîr usûl, unless it were executed somewhat like a dance movement. The fact that the soñ peşrevs and semâ'îs do demonstrate evident links with the music of the seventeenth century indicates a rather conservative pattern of transmission for these genres whichs is not paralleled in the instrumental music of the secular courtly repertoire. Thus the transmission of the opening peşrevs and the final peşrevs and semâ'îs constitute different processes, and this fact should allow us to view the process of transmission of the entire *âyîn* with greater scrutiny.

The rhythmical structure of the first, second and fourth sections of the *âyîn* employ short rhythmic cycles which were common in the kâr and naqsh genres of the late sixteenth-early seventeenth centuries. This fact indicates the courtly genres must have been a model for the Mevlevî composers at the period when the *âyîn* was formed. These particular rhythmic cycles (*devr-i revân, evfer*) do not seem to have been in common use prior to the sixteenth century. Neither of them are mentioned by Mârâghî, and only an usûl named *rawân* (but not *evfer/ufâr*) makes its appearance in the fifteenth century treatise of Ladikî. This fact would suggest that the *âyîn*, in the form in which it is known today, could not have been created prior to the early sixteenth century. The second selâm of the Pençgâh and Dügâh *âyîns* are in the usûl evfer, using nine beats. The second selâm is considerably shorter than the first. Evfer

---

9 See, Feldman, *Music of the Ottoman Court*, pp. 485-486, and 423-426.

was considered a lighter usûl, and it was commonly used in the nakş. After the end of the seventeenth century evfer was no longer used in the courtly fasil at all, thus its permanent position in the second selâm indicates that the model had to have been created before, and, in all likelihood, considerably before that time. The third selâm is always created out of two large usûl movements, the first usually in a form of devr-i kebîr in 14 or 28 beats, then changing, sometimes with a short transition to the ancient semâ'î usûl in 6 beats. In some early âyîns, such as the Hicaz by Osman Dede, the second selâm commences in the 8 beat düyek. The fourth selâm always returns to evfer.

Third Selâm: Devr-i Kebîr

Although the Ottoman courtly repertoire developed along the lines of "rhythmic retardation" and increasing "melodic elaboration" as described by Wright, the vocal core of the âyîn did not undergo a similar process to the same degree. Thus the first part of the third selâm, which is usually in the usûl devr-i kebîr, provides very significant material to follow the evolution of usûl and melody within the âyîn repertoire.

The key to understanding this process was provided by Rauf Yekta Bey in a footnote in the second volume of his *Mevlevî Ayînleri*, published in 1934. Here he writes out the 14/4 usûl pattern for the 3rd selâm of the anonymous Dügâh and observes that: "As can be understood from the the peşrevs written 250 years ago in the Cantemir notation - the era when these peşrevs were composed in the quick meter called vezn-i kebîr - the devr-i kebîr usûl was written in the oldest form comprised of 14 beats, as I have written it."[10]

In this statement Yekta anticipates the discovery, elaborated on more recently by Owen Wright (1988) and Feldman (1996), of the process which led to the rhythmic-melodic relations of modern Turkish music. As Wright has shown, this process led to the total transformation of all the peşrevs in devr-i kebir employed in the Mevlevî âyîn, as well as the peşrevs of the general secular Ottoman repertoire.[11] When we go through the 3rd selâm sections of the âyîns prior to those of Ismail Dede Efendi (d. 1846), we come up with the following pattern:

1. Pençgâh: 3rd selâm in 14/4, melody follows the internal subdivisions of the usûl, and each devir of the usûl concludes on a significant total center of the makam. There is no melodic linkage between devirs. The Heper edition obscures this structure by writing out the section in bars of 4/4 under the signature of 28/4.
2. Dügâh: same structure.
3. Hüseynî: no 3rd selâm.
4. Beyâtî (Mustafa Dede d. 1683): same.
5. Segâh (Itrî d. 1712): same.
6. Rast (Osman Dede d. 1730): Frenkçin (12/2).
7. Uşşak (Osman Dede): very short 3rd selâm (7 1/2 devirs). 14/4 with internal subdivisions, but the 5th and 6th devirs are joined by the held 6th degree (f#).
8. Çârgâh (Osman Dede): 3rd selâm 7 1/2 devirs. 14/4 with joining of 5th and 6th devirs on the 6th scale degree (f).
9. Hicaz (Osman Dede): düyek.
[Gap of fifty odd years in the surviving âyîn repertoire.]

---

10 Yekta, *Mevlevî Âyînleri*, p. 285.
11 Wright, *op.cit.* pp. 71-75.

10. Irak (Abdürrahman Şeyda Dede, d. 1804): 14/4 devr-i kebîr, clear subdivisions and no linkage, but longer than previously (19 devirs).

11. Hicaz (Musahhib Seyyid Ahmed, d. 1794): 14/4 devr-i kebîr, no linkage (11 1/2 devirs).

12. Nihavend (Seyyid Ahmed): Same.

13. Suzidilârâ (Selim III d. 1808): Frenkçin.

14. Acem-Bûselîk (Abdülbaki Nasir Dede d. 1804): 3rd selâm, new devr-i kebîr in 14/2 (24/4).

15. Hicaz (Abdürrahman Künhi Dede d. 1831): 3rd selâm, new devr-i kebîr.

This chart reveals some crucial information: the old devr-i kebîr was employed right up until the turn of the nineteenth century. Two *âyîn*s of the later eighteenth century continue to use it while the newer form appears only in the Acem-Bûselîk *âyîn* of Abdülbaki Nasir Dede at the end of the century. After that it was continued by his brother, Abdürrahman Künhi Dede, and then became standard in the *âyîn*s of Ismail Dede Efendi and his sucessors until the present day. Both Abdülbaki Nasir and Abdürrahman Künhi were sheikhs of the Yenikapı Mevlevîhâne in Istanbul, so it would appear that the new form of devr-i kebîr was used first within the *âyîn* in the Yenikapı tekke. We may also note the gradual expansion of scope in the 3rd selâm sections by the later eighteenth century, a process in accord with the general tendency of Ottoman music. Of extreme interest as well is the close structural correspondece between the 3rd selâms of the Uşşak and Çârgâh *âyîn*s by Osman Dede. Such a correspondence would suggest a high degree of stability in the transmission of these pieces, even without any written form. Viewed as a whole, this data from the devr-i kebir sections of the 3rd selâms demonstrates that the transmission process for the *âyîn*s was far more stable than it was for instrumental music, or, probably, for secular vocal compositions. While the peşrevs attributed to Osman Dede have been recomposed in succeeding generations to the point of utter unrecognizability, his vocal *âyîn*s display many of the structural characteristics of the early eighteenth century, in which he lived, as well as internal isoglosses linking them to the style of a single composer. Thus general conclusions about the nature of the oral transmission of the composed repertoire of Ottoman music cannnot be based on the instrumental peşrev and semâ'î alone, or even on the secular vocal fasıl items, but must take into account the Mevlevî *âyîn*, which demonstrates a markedly divergent pattern.

Third Selâm: Semâ'î

Following the devr-i kebîr section, the third selâm continues and concludes with a lengthy series of melodies in the usûl semâ'î, which gradually increases in tempo, being in fact the only section of the * âyîn* where acceleration is permitted. This semâ'î is a member of a broad group of Ottoman musical genres which had employed this simple usûl, and which all retained the named "semâ'î" - namely the vocal semâ'î of the fasıl, the vocal semâ'î of the Bektaşi aşıks, and the instrumental semâ'î of the fasıl and of the mehter, as well as the structurally divergent soñ semâ'î of the *âyîn*. As I have attempted to demonstrate elsewhere, all of these genres seem to have developed out of an early Anatolian Sufi genre with probable Central Asian Turkic origins.[12]

The persistant association of the rhythm semâ'î with Sufi genres lends weight to

---

12 See, Feldman, *Music of the Ottoman Court,* pp. 460-465.

the etymological derivation of the name from the *semâ'* (Ar. *samâ'*), the spiritual "audition", or concert of the medieval Sufi's (*semâ'* < Ar. *sami'a:* "to hear"). While *semâ'*, which had been borrowed into a great many Muslim languages, is a venerable term in Sufism, 'semâ'î' has a much more limited diffusion. It is possible that the term may have been used for Sufi genres in several portions of the Muslim world, but its known documention is principally within Ottoman Turkey, in seventeenth century Iran, and possibly in modern Central Asia.[13] The only source for the Iranian semâ'î are some verbal remarks in Cantemir's treatise. Unlike the peşrev, which, as a musicological term appears as early as the fourteenth century, and, as a musical genre, can be traced to the *tarîqa*, an instrumental version of the *ṣawt*, mentioned by al-Farabî in the tenth century, semâ'î is not documented prior to the seventeenth century.

The rhythmic pattern of the seventeenth century semâ'î is highly distinctive in Anatolia and the rest of the Middle East. At present it is extremely rare in Anatolian folk music of any region, nor is it well known in the Arab Levant. Where it does appear there, it is clearly a reflex of the urban semâ'î. The entire Iranian region is rich in triple meters, but almost all of the triple rhythmic patterns found in various genres of Iranian music are foreign to Turkish music, and differ signficantly from the semâ'î. The geographical area where a rhythmic pattern closely resembling the semâ'î is most widespread today is Khwarezm, (in the western part of former Soviet Uzbekistan) including the adjacent desert areas, formerly ruled by the Khwarezmian Khanate, and now part of the Turkmen Republic. In both Khwarezm and Bukhara an usûl known as ufor has a pattern which is expressed with drum mnemonics identical to or closely resembling the Ottoman semâ'î. In Khwarezm this is expressed as gul tak tak gul tak (i.e. the same pattern as Harutin's düm tek tek düm tek), and in Bukhara as bum bum bak bum bak, i.e. with a substitution of a bass for the first treble stroke. Various triple meters are common throughout Uzbekistan, but the ufor is the hallmark of Khwarezmian, more than of other Uzbek regional musical idioms. The centrality of this rhythmic pattern is evident is many Khwrezmian musical genres, including the *ufor*, which closes the instrumental section of the maqom, and in the dutar maqoms (e.g. "Ali Qämbär"), which are considered emically to be among the most ancient musical genres of Khwarezm.

The name *ufor* (<Ar. *awfar*) means "most abundant, numerous"and this may refer to the ubiquitousness of the rhythmic pattern in Oghuz Turkic music. Despite its Arabic name, this usûl does not appear in any Arabic or Persian musicological source prior to the sixteenth century, when it is found in the Bukharan treatise of Najm al-Dîn Kaukabî.[14] There is thus little cause to doubt that the *ufor/evfer/semâ'î* usûl pattern is of Central Asian origin. This usûl name is also known in Turkey, where it is pronounced *evfer*. However, in most early Turkish sources, and in the later tradition, evfer is an usûl in nine beats, not six beats, apprently reflecting the popularity of another Turkic rhythmic pattern, the nine beat aksak pattern of the Yörüks of western Anatolia and adjacent regions of the Balkans, which in its turn has analogues in modern Bukharan and Western Kazakh music (usûl-i lenk in Bukhara). Thus the

---

13 In the instrumental portion (certim yoli) of the Khwarezmian maqom-i Näva, and in the corresponding section of the Bukharan maqom-i Dugah, there is a genre termed *säma*. Like the Ottoman semâ'î, it is a quick, short instrumental piece, played toward the end of the cycle. Unlike the former, it is in 4/4, rather than 6/8. The name säma is not identical to semâ'î, and at present the relationship of the Uzbek säma to the Ottoman semâ'î is unclear.

14 Angelika Jung, *Quellen der traditionellen Kunstmusik der Usbeken und Tadshiken Mittelasiens: Untersuchungen zur Entstehung und Entwicklung der sasmaqam*, (Hamburg: 1989), p. 132.

semâ'î/ufor usûl may actually furnish a relatively rare connection between Central Asian Turkic and Ottoman music.

The aura of sacred ecstasy that continued to adhere to the semâ'î usûl may be seen in a marginal note in the Cantemir Collection, where an anonymous semâ'î melody in the Irak makam is labeled "Sultan Veled, qadîm semâ'î" ("Sultan Veled, ancient semâ'î") indicating that in the seventeenth century there had been a tradition linking this semâ'î melody to Rûmî's son and one of his successors.[15] The association of Sultan Veled with the semâ'î is also strengthened by the appearance of one of his Turkish verses at the beginning of the semâ'î section of the third selâm in all early and late âyîns, the well-known "Ey ki hezâr âferîn bu nice sultan olur", which in the pre-nineteenth century âyîns is the sole example of Turkish in the entire libretto. The use of this text at the start of the semâ'î section is evidently a tradition of the Mevlevî âyîn, which was documented by European travellers as well.[16]

The earliest surviving complete âyîn, the anonymous Pençgâh, features this text and it reappears in the Beyâtî âyîn of Köçek Mustafa Dede (d. 1683). Here this section of the third selâm modulates into the makam Acem-Aşirânî, a makam of the seventeenth century concluding on the note F (acem-aşirân). It is also noteworthy that the relation of rhythm, melody and text for this part of the Beyâtî âyîn corresponds very closely to that of the Pençgâh âyîn, although the actual makams are quite different. In fact these early âyîns seemed to form the pattern for which all later âyîns - that is the Turkic verses at the semâ'î section of the third selâm - always follow the identical rhythmic, melodic and metrical pattern, even in the nineteenth century âyîns of Ismail Dede Efendi.

This structure suggests that such a melody could well have been composed in the eras of these early âyîns and that at that period the semâ'î section of the third selâm was already associated with Sultan Veled and, moreover, with the use of Turkic Sufi verse. It should not be ruled out that even the sixteenth century Pençgâh *âyîn* may be following a pattern set by a now lost semâ'î hymn sung during, or shortly following, the lifetime of Sultan Veled, and that this became enshrined in this section of all later Mevlevî âyîns.

Conclusion

The third selâm presents very rich material with which to study both the evolution and the transmission of the Mevlevî âyîn repertoire. Within this third selâm the devr-i kebîr and the semâ'î sections present divergent strategies.

In the devr-i kebîr section we can observe a clear diachronic development, whereby the melodic element gradually frees itself from the constraints imposed by the concept of the rhythmic cycle, forcefully extending the latter as it expands. In the secular repertoire (as in the peşrevs of the âyîn itself) this process led to the total

---

15 Owen Wright (ed.), *Demetrius Cantemir: the Collection of Notations, Part 1: Text*, (London: 1992), p. 253.

16 Jean Antoin de Loir, *Les voyages du Sieur du Loir*, (Paris: 1654), p. 154. While the break-up of the text given in this source (with a ceasura between each 7 syllable unit) agrees with some of the early âyîns, e.g. the Dügâh, de Loir renders the semâ'î as a binary rhythm. Thus the treatment of the text, as well as the modality of the melody, suggest that de Loir was attempting to render a melody he had actually heard. In light of the argument presented here it would seem unlikely that the semâ'î of the third selâm could have been performed to a binary rhythm in the 17th century. In that case we can only conclude that 1) de Loir misheard or miswrote the rhythm of the semâ'î, or 2) this extract is not from the third selâm, but rather represents another usage of this text, perhaps as an ilâhî.

recomposition of the older pieces in the repertoire, while in the âyîn, on the other hand, a number of compositions were preserved which faithfully record the stages in this musical evolution.

In the semâ'î section of the third selâm, an ancient compositional nucleus has been preserved, and this fragment of antiquity is constantly repeated in every composition of whatever historical period, and used as the introduction to an increasingly complex and sophisticated musical development. This melodic and modal sophistication is not allowed to interfere with the fundamental primitiveness of the structure of the semâ'î - for example, the development of the ancient semâ'î in 6/8 time into the more relaxed and expansive 10/8 time (aksak semâ'î) is not permitted in the semâ'î section proper, but only as a transition from the devr-i kebîr section. It is very likely that the retention of the ancient form of the semâ'î, plus the most archaic form of these melodies, which are always performed to a very early poetic text in the Turkish language, is a gesture toward the basic ecstaticism of this culminating section of the âyîn as a whole. This ecstasy is further aestheticized and legitimated spiritually by being cast in the musical, poetic and linguistic form of the earliest Sufis of the Mevlevî order.

In these areas two points stand out: the zeal of the Mevlevî musicians to preserve much earlier musical forms and to use them as the basis for new and expanded composition; and their interest in transmitting specific musical compositions of earlier musicians with the express intent of retaining their peculiarities rather than effacing them through the process of modernization and standardization common to the oral transmission process. This much is of great interest for musicology. For general Ottoman cultural history the broader question remains: why did the Mevlevîs adopt such an attitude?

At this stage in our understanding of the relation of the Mevlevîye to general Ottoman culture any conclusions must be tentative at best. But it cannot be coincidental that the earliest attempts by Ottoman Muslim intellectuals to develop an indigenous musical notation and to use it to preserve musical repertoire emanates from the Mevlevîye. While it is known that several court musicians of European origin (the most famous of whom is the Pole Bobowski/Ali Ufkî Bey) had put parts of the Ottoman repertoire into staff notation, and that Prince Cantemir had done the same with an Islamic cypher notation, among the Turks proper it was only Cantemir's contemporary, Osman Dede (d. 1730), who created a musical notation. Furthermore, another Mevlevî dervish, Mustafa Kevserî, copied and developed the Cantemir notation, while in the following generation, Osman Dede's grandson, Abdülbaki Nasir Dede, reformed the Islamic notation and used it to notate an âyîn composition. Thus, throughout the eighteenth century, musical notation among the Muslim Turkish part of the Ottoman intelligentsia was confined to Mevlevî dervishes. While it is true that none of the three Mevlevî variants of their musical notation system ever acquired much currency among any segment of Ottoman society, and that the Mevlevîs themselves used both seventeenth century notation systems only for the secular repertoire, the fact that notation was developed at all suggests that influential elements among the Mevlevîs of the capital felt a need to preserve musical repertoire in a manner distinct from the continually changing forms of oral transmission. Until the time of Selim III none of the Mevlevî experiments had been patronized by the Ottoman court, so they must have been created in response to a need felt by the Mevlevîs themselves.

This very preliminary analysis of features of the structure of the Mevlevî âyîn suggests that later generations of Mevlevî musicians invested their musical compositions with a value beyond general musical form - the specific musical features of individual compositions of the past still had relevance to the present, not only in a general mythological/symbolical sense of the validation of current praxis but as phenomena in themselves. Although we can be sure that modernization of musical detail, especially intonation, and probably aspects of modulation certainly occurred as the *âyîn*s were transmitted across a span of up to four centuries, the Mevlevî present did not feel entirely free to reshape the Mevlevî past in its own image. For example, according to principles governing the Ottoman secular repertoire in general, there would have been no need to preserve fragmentary versions of the "ancient compositions" (beste-i kadîmler); new second or third parts (selâms) would have been composed and then the whole strucuture refashioned to suit the then current musical style. The fact that the Mevlevî musicians took no such step emphasizes the difference in their musical goals.

In seeking to characterize this attitude we lack a developed language - it is all too facile to employ either the Islamic discourse of *feyz* and *baraka* or the post-romantic Western discourse of art and genius. Our task at this point is either to discover or to reconstruct an appropriate discourse to characterize the Mevlevî attitute toward musical artistic creation.

Through much of the Islamic Middle Ages the 'Ilm al-Musiqa, the Science of Music, constituted a legitimate interface of human science and art, without the necessary interpretation of a specifically Islamic religious dogma. It was for this reason that the Jewish and Christian minorities were able to adopt so much of both the theory and practice of the 'Ilm al-Musiqa.

Evidently the Mevlevîs seized on the practical, not just the theoretical, application of the 'Ilm al-Musiqa as a way of granting a degree of autonomy to musical art, similar in this respect to the autonomy long granted in Islamic societies to poetry, while at the same time enrolling it within an obstensibly spiritual discipline, with the whole complex built upon an orthodox, Sunni Muslim foundation.

Thus the Mevlevîs adopted an approach toward the role of music in religious devotion which is unique among the surviving forms of Sufi liturgy. While it is not unlikely that various Sufi groups had been tending in a similar direction in their semâ practices in the medieval period, before tasawwuf had developed into the tarikat mass phenomenon, its particular history seems to have allowed the Mevleviye to develop these tendencies among the more elite Sufi elements to reach a very high technical and conceptual level. The examples presented here from the third selâm of the *âyîn* ceremony suffice to demonstrate that the Mevlevîye of the seventeenth century and thereafter viewed the purely artistic, musical aspect of their ceremony, with its particular human, historical compositions, as being worthy of preservation. That is, while the semâ was a devotional act taking place in the present moment, part of the inspiration for this devotion was the musical compositions of the past. Although parts of the semâ could be performed to improvised music, which was also highly valued, after the seventeenth century there was increasing emphasis upon musical composition. At present we cannot be certain whether this attitude commenced essentially with Pîr Adil Çelebi in the fifteenth century, who organized the nucleus of the *âyîn* ceremony, or whether it emerged with the establishment of hereditary sheikhly lineages in later seventeenth century Istanbul.[17]

It is possible that the reasons for this preservation of individual musical compositions may be connected with the veneration of the Mevlevîye as a founding patron who was a well-documented historical figure and whose charisma was based, not primarily on miracles and legends documented only in much later hagiographical literature, but in works of written literature accessible to any member of the literate classes

---

17 Işın, *op. cit.*

(and by extension, even to many of the illiterate) within the Islamic world. While many other Sufi thinkers created literary monuments, there is no real analogue to the conjunction of literature, specific mystical praxis, hierarchical Sufi organization, sacred lineage and well-known quasi-historical hagiography represented by Jallal al-Din Rûmî and the later Mevlevî tarikat. Within this cultural complex, human artistic creation held a highly significant role, a point emphasized by every modern discussion of the Mevlevîye. In this context it would appear that the Mevlevî leadership, primarily within Istanbul, began to invest the early musical compositions of the *âyîn* with certain qualities that demanded their preservation and their employment as models for the future.

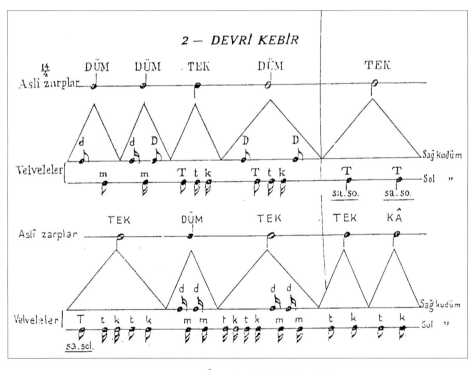

Devr-i kebîr after Rauf Yekta Bey, *Mevlevî Âyinleri*, vol 1 (1934), p. 303.

ÜÇÜNCÜ SELÂM

(Pençgâh, Dügâh)

[1] *Kantemir oğlu* notası ile 250 sene evvel yazılmış Peşrevlerden anlaşıldığına göre —bu peşrevler o tarihte (Vezni kebir) denilen *yürük vezinde* bestelendiği vakit — (Devri kebir) ikinin burada yazdığımız gibi 14 zarptan mürekkep olan *en eski şeklile* yazılıyordu. Görülüyor ki 600 senelik birer musiki abideleri olan (Pençgâh), (Dügâh) ve (Hüseyni) Âyinlerinin üçüncü Selâmları da *Devri kebirin* en eski *yürük veznile* ve bu gün (Hafifi evvel) dediğimiz tavrı ile bestelenmiştir. Şimdiki notamızla ¹⁴/₄ olarak yazdığımız bu *Devri kebiri.* Mevlevilerin kudümle nasıl vurduklarını 268 inci sahifede göstermiştik. Son iki asrın klasik Türk bestekârları, bu ikai (Hafifi sani) tavrına naklederek iki misli ağırlaşdırmışlar ve bundan dolayı bittabi *asli zarpların* arasına bir takım (Velveleler), ve daha ilmi tabirile (Taz'if) ve (Ter'it) ler katarak Murabba'lar ve Peşrevler yapmışlardır ki ¹⁴/₂ hesabile yazdığımız (Devri kebir) in bu şekli de 280 inci sahifedeki Peşrevin altına işaret edilmiştir. Mevlevilerin kudümlerde vurdukları üçüncü bir (Devri kebir) leri daha vardı ki iki *Devri kebir* mecmuuna müsavi olan bu ikin şeklini de 262 inci sahifeye kaydetmiştik.

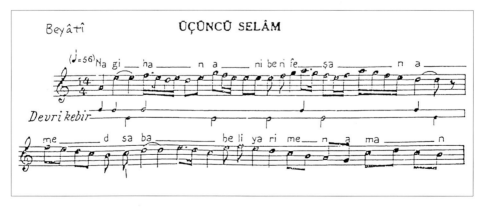

Opening of the third selâms of Pençgâh, Dügâh, and Beyâtî ayîns according to Yekta, including Yekta's long note on devr-i kebîr, in Yekta, *Mevlevî Âyinleri*, vol. I, p. 285 and vol. II, p. 316.

ÜÇÜNCÜ SELÂM

Third selâm of the Uşşak Âyîn by Osman Dede showing the linkage of the 5th and 6th measures, after Yekta, *Mevlevî Âyinleri*, vol. II.

Third selâm of the Çargâh Âyîn by Osman Dede showing the linkage of the 5th and 6th measures, after Yekta, *Mevlevî Âyinleri*, vol. II, p. 405.

Relation du Voyage

NOTA 3 MEVLEVÎ AYÎNÎ, III. Selam'dan, *Du Loir, 1639-1640*.

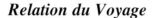

J ki hezar a feryn, ay ay, J ki hezar

a feryn bou nidge Sultan olur dgia-num

Kouli olan Kıchiler, dgianum ,hufreu-u hha-

kan olur.

Ey ki hezar aferin bu nice sultân olur
Kulu olan kişiler (cânım) husrev-u hakân olur

Semâ'î from third selâm in Jean Antoin du Loir, *Les voyages du Sieur du Loir*, Paris: Gervais Clovzier, 1654.

Opening of the semâ'î section of the third selâm of Pençgâh, Dügâh, and Beyâtî ayîns after Yekta, *Mevlevî Âyinleri*, vol. I, pp. 269-270, p. 286, and vol. II, p. 318.

Music and Samā' of the Mavlaviyya in the Fifteenth and Sixteenth Centuries: Origins, Ritual and Formation

İLKER EVRİM BİNBAŞ

Mavlavī music and *samā'*, with their originality and highly ceremonial composition, have an undeniable importance within the tradition of Turkish Sufi music. Towards the end of the nineteenth century and during the twentieth century, some scholars reflected on the problems of the evolution of the Mavlavī ceremony which is called *muḳābele* on the basis of their observations.[1] Since Mavlānā lived in the thirteenth century, but the ritual itself came into being in the fifteenth century and the said scholars made their assessments on the basis of observations within the last hundred years, it is difficult to trace the evolution of the Mavlavī ceremony into *muḳābala*. In this study, I will try to explore the evolution and development of the Mavlavī *samā'* in the historical context of the fifteenth and sixteenth centuries when our sources do not, as yet, mention the *muḳābala*.[2]

Although the inner tradition of Mavlaviyya attributes the organization of *muḳābala* to Sultān Valad (d. 1312), son of Mavlānā Jalāl al-Dīn Rūmī, neither the writings of Mavlānā and Sultān Valad, nor the other early sources of the Mavlaviyya[3] written in the fourteenth century, give a detailed picture of the *samā'* comparable with the *muḳābala*. It is generally assumed that the Mavlavī *muḳābala* gradually evolved during the fourteenth and fifteenth centuries and reached its final form in the sixteenth and seventeenth centuries. According to Abūlbâki Gölpınarlı, the *muḳābala* in its present form was established by Pīr Ādil Çelebi (d. 1460) in the first half of the fifteenth century. The *na't* (which is now part of the *muḳābala*) by Itrî (d. 1712) was added to the beginning of the *muḳābala* in the late seventeenth or early eighteenth century.[4] Gölpınarlı adds that Pīr 'Ādil Çelebi took the title of *pīr*, which is a title

---

1 The most detailed and reliable description of Mavlavi *muḳābala* was recorded by Abdülbaki Gölpınarlı in his *Mevlevî Âdâb ve Erkânı*, (İstanbul: İnkılap ve Aka, 1963), pp. 78-94.

2 The terminology is very confusing even in our sources. Different terms such as *samā'*, *muḳābala*, *davr* need to be explained in order to avoid any confusion. *Samā'* generally indicates the whirling in a Mavlavī ceremony. On the other hand, *muḳābala* covers the whole occasion including the recitation of Koran, and the *Mesnevī-i Ma'nevī* of Mavlānā. *Devr*, or *Sulṭān Veled Devri* means the circular movements of dervishes around the *samā' hāne* (samā' hall) three times during the *muḳābala*.

3 We have two important hagiographic works written soon after the death of Mavlānā. The first one is *Risāla-i Sipahsālār* and the second one is *Manāḳib al-'Ārifīn*. Ferīdūn bin Aḥmed Sipahsālār, *Risala-i Ferīdūn bin Aḥmad-i Sipahsālār-Ahvāl-i Mawlāna Jalāl al-Dīn Mawlavī* , (ed.) Sa'id Nafīsī, (Tehran: 1325). Aḥmed al-Aflākī, *Manāḳib al-'Arifīn*, 2 vols., (ed.) Tahsin Yazıcı, (Ankara: Türk Tarih Kurumu Yayınları, 1976-1980). Tahsin Yazıcı translated both of them into Turkish. Ferīdun bin Ahmed-i Sipahsālār, *Mevlânâ ve Etrafındakiler-Risâle*, (Istanbul: 1977). Ahmet Eflâkî, *Âriflerin Menkıbeleri*, 2 vols., (Istanbul: Milli Eğitim Bakanlığı Yayınları, 1995). I have cited both Persian and Turkish editions in this article.

4 The addition of Itrî's *na't* to the begining of the *āyīn-i şerîf* was not a spontaneous act; it was initiated by the order of the *dergâh* of Konya which had been the formal center of Mavlaviyya. Ömer Tuğrul İnançer, "Mevlevi Musikisi ve Samā'", *İstanbul Ansiklopedisi*, vol. 5, p. 420.

generally given to the founder of a dervish order, for having established the *muḳābala* ritual.[5] Recent scholarship tends to confirm this view. Walter Feldman stressed the emergence and evolution of Ottoman Court Music and proposed that the Mavlavī *muḳābala* could not predate the sixteenth century. According to him, the *āyīn-i şerīf*, the musical genre played during the *muḳābala*, is the first example of the cyclical form of music that emerged in sixteenth and seventeenth centuries.[6]

In fact, none of the early sources of Mavlaviyya include any clear description of *samā'*, but other sources may give some clues about the origin of the Mavlavī *samā'*. Mavlānā's father, *Sulṭān al-'Ulamā'* (Sultan of the Scholars) Bahā' al-Dīn Valad, had a neutral attitude towards *samā'* and *zikr*, i.e. remembrance of God. According to him, music and *samā'* are right for an emotional moment, but they are not necessary in order to feel God in the inner world or to reach the truth.[7] Mainly, he opposes the music and *samā'* as an institutionalized means to bring about ecstasy. Najm al-Dīn Kubrā, who was the mentor of Bahā' al-Dīn Valad, and followed the Kubravī tradition, engaged in *samā'* or *zikr-i jahrī*, i.e. vocal *zikr*.[8] Sayyid Burhān al-Dīn Muḥaḳḳiḳ-i Tirmizī, the disciple of Bahā' al-Dīn Valad and the mentor of Mavlānā, also approved the *zikr*.[9] Probably, Mavlānā received and continued some of his father's practices. *Risāla-i Sipahsālār*, on the other hand, gives special attention to Shams-i Tabrīzī as a major factor in the change of Mavlānā's way of life from that of a scholar to that of a mystic and poet. According to *Risāla-i Sipahsālār*, Mavlānā followed Shams-i Tabrīzī's way of performing the *samā'* (*ṭarī ka-i samā'*).[10]

Mavlānā's *Fīh-i mā Fīh* [Discourses] and Sulṭān Valad's *Ma'ārif* [Gnostic Sciences] include some chapters on *samā'*, but these chapters, like many other sufi treatises, were written for the purpose of defending *samā'* against the criticisms coming from the ulama.[11] The earliest description of Mavlānā's *samā'* can be found in the *Risāla-i Sipahsālār* of Farīdūn bin Aḥmad-i Sipahsālār (d. ca 1312). According to *Risāla-i Sipahsālār*, Mavlānā's *samā'* includes these different movements or figures:[12]

> All the movements emanating from mystics during the *samā'* symbolize a point or a truth. For instance, whirling (*charḥ zadan*) is a sign of unity and this is a station of saints ['*ārifān-i muvaḥḥid*] who [stand in that station] see the beloved and the desired

---

5 A. Gölpınarlı, *Mevlevî Âdâb*, pp. 75-77. Balım Sultan, who was the real founder of the Bektaşiyye and organizer of Bektaşi rituals in the sixteenth century, carries the title of *pîr-i sânî* (second pîr). John K. Birge, *The Bektaşi Order of Dervishes*, (London: Luzac & Co. Ltd., 1965), p. 56.

6 Walter Feldman, "Cultural Authority and Authenticity in the Turkish Repertoire", *Asian Music*, 22/1, (1990-91), 78.

7 Fritz Meier, *Bahâ-i Walad-Grundzüge Seines Lebens und Seiner Mystik*, (Leiden: E.J. Brill, 1989), pp. 45, 82. According to Gölpınarlı, Bahā' al-dīn Valad used to perform *zikr* but it was not so crucial for him. A. Gölpınarlı, *Mevlevî Âdâb*, p. 122.

8 See Muhammad Isa Waley, "A Kubravî Manual of Sufism: the Fuṣuṣ al-adab of Yaḥyā Bākharzī", *The Legacy of Medieval Persian Sufism*, (London, NY: Khaniqahi Nimatullahi Publications, 1992), pp. 301, 307. For the Najm al-Dīn Kübra's *samā'* see Jāmī, *Nafaḥāt al-Uns min ḥaḍarāt al-ḳuds*, (ed.) Mahdi Tawḥīdīpçr, (Tehran: 1337), pp. 421-422. Muhammad Isa Waley, "Najm al-Dîn Kubrâ and the Central Asian School of Sufism (the Kubrawiyyah)", *Islamic Spirituality-Manifestations*, (ed.) Seyyed Hossein Nasr, (London: SCM Press, 1991), pp. 83, 85.

9 A. Gölpınarlı, *Mevlevî Âdâb*, p. 122. See *Manāḳib al-'Ārifīn*, vol. II, pp. 997, 998 for the Mavlavī chain of *zikr* going back to Hz. Ali.

10 *Risāla-i Sipahsālār*, p. 24; *Mevlânâ ve Etrafındakiler*, p. 35.

11 Sultan Valad, *Ma'ârif* [Gnostic Sciences], (trans.) Meliha Ü. Anbarcıoğlu, (Istanbul: 1984), pp. 10-19.

12 *Risāla-i Sipahsālār*, pp. 66-67; *Mevlânâ ve Etrafındakiler*, p. 72. This passage was translated from the Persian original. I am indebted to Dr. Hootan Shambayati from Bilkent University for his corrections of this translation.

Mevlevi ayini
Drawing by van Mour in Charles de Ferriol, *Recueil de Cent Estampes*, Paris, 1714.
(This and the other pictures in this chapter are reprinted in Bülent Aksoy, *Avrupalı Gezginlerin Gözüyle Osmanlılarda Musiki*, Istanbul, Pan Yayıncılık, 1994).

everywhere and in all directions and they attain divine grace wherever they turn. To jump (*jahādan*) and to stamp the foot (*pā kūftan*) denote two things: the first one denotes the joy of connecting with the spiritual world. To stamp the foot denotes that the sufi, in that position, subordinates his self and with that strength he treads upon everything except God. Opening the arms (*dast afşāndan*) denotes several things: the first is related to the joy of the honour of attainment and to the conferral of the degree of perfection. Secondly, it is a victory over the army of inordinate appetites of the self (*nafs-i ammāra*), and the greatest holy war (*jihād*) consists of defeating these. Embracing a saint (*'azīz*) during the *samā'* and dancing together happens at that time, when the dervish (*fakīr*) becomes completely void of himself, i.e. spends all of his self. At the moment when he is recovering in the midst of that gathering, in whose inner mirror he observes himself with full pleasure, he takes hold of that holy person and with the image of his own beauty (*jamāl*), he plays "the lover and the beloved" with that holy person. To draw people into *samā'* and to instigate them to move is the duty of the sober people (*ahl-i şahv*), and the benefits of [such an act] are spread on all those present and convey God's compassion in a public manner on all.

We do not see some of these figures such as jumping or stamping the foot in Mavlavī *mukābala* as it is known to us. Moreover, the *Risāla-i Sipahsālār* does not allow us to visualize a strictly structured ritual. Many examples given by *Manākib al-'Ārifīn* by Aḥmed Aflākī support the description of *Risāla-i Sipahsālār*.[13]

Dīvāne Meḥmed Çelebi who was one of the major propagandists of the sixteenth century Mavlaviyya, describes the *samā'* in a poem. In this poem, *samā'* is divided into three sections named *devir*, that is, cycles. If this is a genuine reflection of a real Mavlavī ceremony, we can assume that this is the forerunner of *mukābala* and that, during the first part of the sixteenth century, there were three sections in the Mavlavī *samā'*.[14]

---

13 Passages in *Manākib al-'Ārifīn* were compiled and summarized by Tahsin Yazıcı. Tahsin Yazıcı, "Mevlânâ Devrinde Semā'", *Şarkiyyat Mecmuası*, 5, (1964), pp. 135-150.
14 Abdülbâki Gölpınarlı, *Mevlânâdan Sonra Mevlevîlik*, (Istanbul: İnkılâp ve Aka, 1983), pp. 473-476.

An important couplet of this poem allows us to construct a symbolic relationship between Mavlavī *samā'* and the popular *samā'* conceptions as elaborated below. This couplet is as follows:[15]

İstedi kim biline evsâf ile
Emredüp halketti nûn-u kâf ile
With His qualities He desired to be known,
So commended and created with [the letters] *nûn* and *kâf*

This part of the poem is an explanation of the creation of the universe. God utters *kun* (be!), an Arabic word consisting of two letters *kaf* and *nun*, in order to create the universe.[16] There is a more detailed picture of this view in an anonymous *risâla*, i.e, a small treatise about *samā'*, the earliest copy of which dates from the fifteenth century. This treatise was attributed to 'Āshık Pasha, the famous sufi poet of the fourteenth century and the grandson of Baba İlyas-ı Horasanī, who was a sufi and a political activist in the thirteenth century. This small treatise was presumably written for the popular audience and for the legitimization of the *samā'*, music and "dance". These are described in relation to the creation of the universe as an emergent divine melody (*nağamat-ı ilahī*). According to this treatise, this divine melody is said to stop in twelve pitches (*oniki perde*). From these twelve pitches four movements (*dört oyun*) emerge. These are *çarḫ* (circling), *raḳs* (vibrating), *mu'allak* (hanging) and *pertâv* (jumping). Then a mystic clad in blue (*ṣūfī-i azrāḳ-pūsh*) enters this eternal "dance". These four types of movement mean four elements (*'ānāṣır-i arba'a*) and the seasons.[17] As we read this anonymous treatise, we can say that Mavlavī and popular religious perception share a common understanding of *samā'* as an imitation of the cosmic universe.

For the same period we have one more record about the Mavlavī *samā'*. This is *Vāḥidīs Menāḳıb-ı Ḫvoca-i Cihān ve Netīce-i Cān*, which contains descriptive information about contemporary religious groups: Ḳalandarīs, Abdals of Rūm (*Abdalān-ı Rūm*), Haydarīs, Camīs, Bektashīs, Shams-i Tabrīzīs, Mavlavīs, Edhemīs, 'Ālims, Ṣ -ufīs. Except for the 'Ālims, which presumably represent the ulama, other groups denote the mystic groups of the sixteenth century. As the author ascribed the *ẕikr* to the Ṣufīs, this term seem to refer to all of the Sunni *ṭarīḳat*s, such as Naḳshbandiyya and Ḥalvatiyya. Actually Vāḥidī's book is a critical work in which he approves some

---

15 A. Gölpınarlı, *Mevlânâdan*, p. 474.

16 Theory of *bazm-i alast* in the perception of *samā'* has been used since *Risāla-i Sipahsālār* (p. 66) in the Mavlavī written culture. According to this theory, God asks the human being (Koran: Araf, 172): "Am I not your Lord?" and he answers "Yes, you are (*Alastu bi-Rabbikum-Kâlu-balâ*)". After the creation, when they (i.e. human beings) listen to a beautiful melody or hear a nice word, they remembered this beautiful voice. But, only sufis can perceive the exact meaning and gnosis of any sound or word. For a detailed description of this theory see Süleyman Uludağ, *İslam Açısından Musiki ve Semâ'*, (Bursa: Uludağ Yayınları, 1992), pp. 331-342.

17 There are two known manuscript copies of this *risâla* and both of them were analysed independently by Agâh Sırrı Levend, and by Ahmet Kutsi Tecer. See, Agâh Sırrı Levend, "Âşık Paşa'ya Atfedilen İki Risale", *Türk Dili Araştırmaları Yıllığı-Belleten*, (1955), 153-173. Ahmet Kutsi Tecer, "Oyun Rakıs Hakkında Mühim Bir Eser", *Türk Folklor Araştırmaları* (1958-59), 106-118. The Ankara manuscript used by Ahmet Kutsi Tecer is to be found at the end of a *Ğaribname* which is a well known mystic poem of 'Âşık Paşa. Perhaps, the attribution to 'Âşık Paşa is due to the fact that a later copyist used this fifteenth century copy and regarded the author of *risâla* as 'Âşık Paşa. Fuad Köprülü speaks about another treatise on *samā'* which is also attributed to 'Âşık Paşa and is preserved in Manisa Muradiye Library, its name being *Risâle fî beyân al-samā'*. This manuscript was not available to me during the preparation of this article. Fuad Köprülü, "Âşık Paşa", *İslam Ansiklopedisi*, vol. I, pp. 701-706 [I used the reimpression of the same article: *Edebiyat Araştırmaları*, 2 vols., (Istanbul: Ötüken Yayınları, 1989), vol. 2, p. 512.]

groups, such as the last four groups, and criticizes others. The section about the appearance of Mavlavīs can be summarized as:[18]

> Beards grown and moustaches trimmed in accordance with the law and traditions. Eyes kohled. Wearing seamless, one-piece caps, over the length of which appear green lines in the shape of the letter *elif*. The lappets of the turbans wrapped over the caps reach down to the waist. Dressed in tunics and black robes with scarfs around the neck. Playing tambourines, drums and reed flutes. Chanting hymns and prayers and engaged in *semâ'*.

Pīr 'Alī Ḳonavī who is the fictive shaykh of the Mavlavīs in Vāḥidī's work, says:[19]

> Sema is occasioned by the efforts of the Mevlevi to return to his father, who is the sky, itself also in constant rotation (the mother is earth). The decree that obliges the Mevlevis to dance is issued to them through the sound of the reed-flute and the spirit, which is intoxicated by this sound, then ascends to the sky.

From Vāḥidī, we learn that Mavlavīs used to play *ṭabl* (tambourine), *ney* (reed-flute) and *def* (small drum) and that they engaged in *samā'* after dinner.[20] This text contains, unfortunately, very little information about the details of Mavlavī *samā'*. Rather Vāḥidī gives special attention to the legal definition of the *samā'*. According to Vāḥidī, the Mavlavī *samā'* is permissible because it is a medium for reaching the truth.

The earliest description of Mavlavī *samā'* which corresponds to nineteenth and twentieth centuries practices was recorded by Ṣāḳıp Dede (d. 1735) in *Safīna-i Nafīse-i Mavlaviyān*. This is the first book that claims to cover the whole history of Mavlaviyya after Aflākī's *Manāḳib al-'Ārifīn* (ca. 1353). Ṣāḳıp Dede records a small risâle named *Işārat al-Başāra* about *samā'* and attributes it to Jalāl al-Dīn Erġūn Chelebi (fourteenth century).[21] In this *risâla*, Mavlavī *samā'* is divided into four *selâm* in accordance with the twentieth century practice and *muḳābala* is explained according to the movements of the planets (*sayyāra*). Ṣāḳıp Dede tries to incorporate the principles of Naḳshbandiyya, whose basic ritual is *ẕikr*, into the Mavlavī *samā'*.[22] At about the same time we observe a trend to combine Naḳshbandī and Mavlavī *silsile* (chain of spiritual ancestors).[23] These are clearly signs of Naḳshbandī influence over the Mavlaviyya.

But we do not see any considerable Naḳshbandī influence on Mavlavī *samā'*. Although Mavlavīs practice *ẕikr-i ḥafī* (silent *ẕikr*) in repeating the name of God, *Allah*, while whirling,[24] Mavlavīs have never accepted *ẕikr* as the basis of their ritual. But they allowed other *ṭarīḳat* members to perform *ẕikr* after *muḳābala*. Sadettin Nüzhet Ergun says:[25]

---

18 Ahmet T. Karamustafa, *Vāḥidī''s Menāḳıb-ı Ḫvoca-i Cihān ve Netīce-i Cān*, (Harvard University Printing Office, 1993), pp. 11, 15. The summaries quoted in the text belong to Ahmet T. Karamustafa, editor of the Vāḥidī's book.

19 A. Karamustafa, *Vāḥidī's*, p. 11.

20 A. Karamustafa, *Vāḥidī's*, pp. 174-166 (fols. 89a-90b).

21 Ṣāḳıp Dede, *Sefīne-i Nefīse-i Mevleviyān*, (Matbaā-Vehbiyye, 1283), p. 77-83.

22 Ṣāḳıp Dede, *Sefīne-i*, p. 81. These principles are *hūsh dar dam* (awareness while breathing), *naẓar bar qadam* (watching the steps), *safar dar vatan* (journeying to the homeland), *khalvat dar anjuman* (solitude in the assembly), *yād-kard* (remembrance), *bāz-gasht* (restraint), *nigāh-dāsht* (watchfulness), *yād-dāsht* (recollection). See, Kāshifī, *Rashāḥāt-i 'ayn al-ḥayat Tercümesi*, (Istanbul: 1279), p. 25. The translations are those of Bo Utas quoted by İsenbike Togan (see below n. 29).

23 A. Gölpınarlı, *Mevlânâdan*, pp. 319-320.

24 A. Gölpınarlı, *Mevlevî Âdâb*, p. 88.

25 Sadettin Nüzhet Ergun, *Türk Musikisi Antolojisi I-Dini Eserler*, (Istanbul: İstanbul Üniversitesi Edebiyat Fakültesi Yayınları, 1942), p. 124.

If it is suitable for the *zikr*, it was possible to sing some parts of a Mavlavī *âyîn* (*âyîn-i şerîf*), in other ṭarīkat *âyîn*. In fact, Mavlavīs did not sing *ilâhî* (hymns). This was not because they despised the *ilâhîs*, but because of the requirements of their *âyîn*. Moreover, on the special days when *mevlîd* or *mirâciye* was sung, they might invite members of other ṭarīkats and after Mavlavī *semâ'*, they might leave the conduct of the meeting to the oldest *şeyh* (head of a tarikat) who is present in that meeting; and they might be allowed to sing hymns and to perform *zikr-i ḳiyāmī* (*zikr* performed standing) or *zikr-i ḳu'udî* (*zikr* performed sitting).

By the same way, Mavlavīs might attend rituals of other *ṭarīkat*s and they would perform *samā'* during *zikr* ceremonies.[26] It seems that rituals were not dividing factors among the *ṭarīkat*s in the Ottoman Empire. Similarly, the music of these rituals was shared by different *ṭarīkat*s. S. N. Ergun points to this issue:[27]

> A musician attached to the Mevlevi tarikat would compose lines for a verse by a Halveti poet, a Sa'di could hear a Celveti work, a Bayrami could hear a Kadiri's ilahi with its own tune in the tekke to which he belonged. Fundamentally the works, because they were created with an eye for the type of ceremony, were distinguished not according to tarikat but only according to the type of zikir. There was no tradition that "this ilahi is sung in the Rufai tekkes; it is not sung in the Kadiri tekkes."

This attitude was not common in the medieval Islamic World. For example, different types of *zikr* were seen as a reason for conflicts, as exemplified by the *zikr-i ḥafî* (silent *zikr*) and *zikr-i jahrī* (vocal *zikr*) among Naḳshbandiyye.[28] But in the inclusive politics of the Ottomans, we do not encounter such a conflict nor a discussion of it among different *ṭarīkat*s and all *ṭarīkat*s found the ability to perform their own rituals in this environment.[29]

Mavlavī Music and Ancient Compositions (*Beste-i Kadimler*)

A further question concerns the type of music that was played in the *samā'* of Mavlānā. Unfortunately, it is impossible to know with precision which type it was. But we know that Mavlānā employed a *neyzen* (reed-flute player), and that there were many musicians around him.[30] Although his famous Maṣnavī starts, "listen to the reed, how it tells a tale", the *rabāb*, a bowed-string instrument, seems to have been more important than the *nay*, and, in fact, Mavlānā himself was a *rabāb* player. According to a problematic passage in *Manāḳib al-'Ārifîn*, he himself made

---

26 A. Gölpınarlı, *Mevlevî Âdâb*, pp. 100-101.

27 S. N. Ergun, *Türk Musikisi*, p. 124 [This translation is quoted from Walter Feldman, "Musical Genres and Zikir of the Sunni Ṭarīkats of Istanbul", in Raymond Lifchez (ed.), *The Dervish Lodge*, (Berkeley: University of California Press,1990), p. 189.

28 For a general outline of this discussion see, Hamid Algar, "Silent and Vocal Dhikr in the Naqshbandî Order", *Akten des VII. Kongresses für Arabistik und Islamwissenschaft, Göttingen, 15. bis 22. August 1974*, (Göttingen: Vandenhoeck & Ruprecht, 1976), pp. 39-46.

29 İsenbike Togan, "The Khafî, Jahrî Controversy in Central Asia Revisitied", in E. Özdalga (ed.), *The Naqshbandis in Western and Central Asia. Change and Continuity*, (London: Curzon Press, 1998), pp. 17-45. I am indebted to Professor İsenbike Togan for her comments on the draft of this paper.

30 *Manāḳib al-'Ārifîn*, I-231, 255, 394; *Ariflerin Menkıbeleri*, I-422, 450, 612.

Mevlevi ayini
From: Aubrye de la Mortraye, *Voyages du Sr Aubrey de la Mortraye en Europe, Asie, et Afrique*, Lahey 1727.

some changes to the body of the *rabāb*. This passage is sometimes interpreted as an addition of strings to the *rabāb* by Mavlānā.[31]

The text is:[32]

> ....and he ordered them to make the *rabāb* as a six *khāna* instrument. Because, the Arabic *rabāb* consisted heretofore of four *khāna*. Mavlānā said that the purpose of a *rabāb* with six *khāna* is to explain the six sides of the world (*'ālam*) and the *alif* like strings show that the spirits are in union with the *alif* in the name of God.

Mavlānā attributed the highest mystic values to the *rabāb* and this was a subject of conflict with the ulama.[33] Such a mystical value ascribed to the *rabāb* is not peculiar to the Mavlaviyya. A fifteenth century source in Chagatai, *Sazlar Münāzarası* (Conversation of the Instruments) written by Ahmedī, reflects the same attitude towards the *rabāb*. Ahmedī symbolizes social groups or positions through the instruments. For example, the *rabāb* speaks as a dervish and the *ūd* imitates a scholar. The *chang*, a harp-like instrument, reflects a picture of pleasure.[34] This leitmotif can also be found in Aflākī's *Manākib al-'Ārifīn* in which the *chang* is described as the instrument of the prostitutes.[35] Another fifteenth century Anatolian source, Aḥmad-i Dā'ī's *Changnāma*, continues this image of the *chang* on the more complex level. We see the *chang* as an instrument which symbolizes man indulging in joyful entertainments.[36] By the seventeenth century, the *rabāb* seems to have disappeared from the Mavlavī *samā'*. In the early seventeenth century, we do not see any mention of the *rabāb* in the official documents of the Konya Lodge.[37] Moreover, the Maṣnavī com-

---

31 Yılmaz Öztuna, *Büyük Türk Musikisi Ansiklopedisi*, 2 vols., (Ankara: Kültür Bakanlığı Yayınları, 1990), pp. II-221.

32 *Manākib al-'Ārifīn*, I-88; *Āriflerin Menkıbeleri*, I-259.

33 *Manākib al-'Ārifīn*, I-295-296; *Āriflerin Menkıbeleri*, I-496-497.

34 Gönül Alpay Tekin, "XV. Yüzyılın İlk Yarısında Yazılmış Bir Münâzara: Sazlar Münâzarası", *Araştırma-Dil ve Tarih-Coğrafya Fakültesi Felsefe Araştırmaları Enstitüsü Dergisi*, X (1972), 99-132.

35 *Manākib al-'Ārifīn*, I-375; *Āriflerin Menkıbeleri*, I-590-591.

36 Aḥmed-i Dā'ī, *Çengnāme*, Gönül Alpay Tekin (ed.), (Harvard University Printing Office, 1992), pp. 57-98.

37 Suraiya Faroqhi, "Agricultural Crisis and the Art of Flute-Playing: The Worldly Affairs of the Mevlevî Dervishes (1595-1652)", *Turcica*, 20 (1988), 56.

Semazen
Drawing by van Mour, in Charles de Ferriol, *Recueil de Cent Estampes*, Paris, 1714.

mentator, İsmail Ankaravî (d. 1631), wrote a treatise about the *samā'* and in this *risâla*, he counts the *rabāb* as among the forbidden instruments and adds that this instrument was not used in the Mavlavī *muḳābala*.[38]

The oldest musical examples of Mavlavī music are the Panchgāh, Dugāh and Ḥusaynī *Beste-i Kadīm*s that are "ancient compositions" by unknown composer(s). Oral traditions of Mavlaviyya attribute these three compositions to Sulṭān Valad.[39] As the musical features of these *Beste-i Kadīm*s reflect sixteenth century characteristics, this attribution is generally not taken into consideration by scholars.[40] Although their composition is fully compatible with the Mavlavī *muḳābala*, they do

---

38 İsmail Ankaravî, *Ḥuccet al-Samā'*, Süleymaniye Kütüphanesi-Pertev Paşa Kitapları 255/2, p. 18 (My pagination; I have used the microfilm preserved in Milli Kütüphane-Ankara, MFA 1994 A 4396).

39 A. Gölpınarlı, *Mevlânâdan*, p. 456.

40 Rauf Yekta Bey, *Mevlevî Âyinleri-I*, (Istanbul: 1934), p.V; Sadettin Heper, *Mevlevî Âyinleri*, (Konya: 1979), p. 534.

have any recurring parts. For example, the Dugāh *āyīn-i şerīf* shares half of the third *salām* and the fourth *salām* with the Panchgāh *ayīn-i şerīf*. For that reason, Mahmut Ragıp Gazimihal suggested that these *āyīn*s might not originally have been composed as *āyīn-i şerīf*s, but that they might be an arrangement of different pre-existing hymns.[41] Although it is impossible to know exactly, we have evidence that the repertoire of the Mavlavī music in sixteenth and early seventeenth centuries contained additional compositions. For example 'Alī Ufkī's (1610?-1675) *Majmū'a-i Sāz ü Söz* [Collection of Notations and Lyrics] includes a notated piece in the *Muḥayyar* section under the name of *Davarān-i Darvīshān-i Ẕavī al-Shān* (the whirling of renowned dervishes) which may be an example of the Mavlavī music of the period.[42] The words of this song, which starts *Ey ki hezar aferin bu nice sultan olur*, belong to Aḥmed Aflākī Dede (d. 1360). But 'Alī Ufkī does not provide us with the context of this piece. As we have seen above, it was possible that a *ṭarīḳat* might use a hymn of another *ṭarīḳat*. So, 'Alī Ufkī's record may be a hymn of another *ṭarīḳat*. The second notation example, which is more precise than the previous one, can be found in a European source. Du Loir, a French traveller who visited İstanbul in 1639-1640 and attended a *muḳābala* at the Mavlavī lodge of Galata, notated a small section of an unknown *āyīn-i şerīf*.[43] The present Mavlavī music repertoire does not include his notated piece, either.

Aflākī Dede's poem was composed in the Bayâti makam by Köçek Mustafa Dede (d. 1689) and started to be used in the third section of the *āyīn-i sharīf*s. This is the first *āyīn-i sharīf* by an identified composer. After Köçek Mustafa Dede's *āyīn-i sharīf* in the Bayâti makam, the next composed āyīns were Segâh by Itrî and Çargâh, Hicaz, Uşşak and Rast by Nāyī Osman Dede (d. 1729). These demonstrate an internal melodic, rhythmic and formal structure which is known today. So it may be postulated that these *āyīn*s served as final models for all subsequent compositions. Moreover, Mavlavī *peşrev* as a genre came into being at the beginning of the eighteenth century.[44] We can therefore say that the Mavlavī musical ritual may have acquired its nearly final structure at the beginning of the eighteenth century.[45]

Mavlaviyya in Historical Change

Mavlānā's spiritual and intellectual eminence, along with his political influence, was the most crucial factor in the early history of the Mavlaviyya. It is obvious that this influence and reputation, spreading from Anatolia to Central Asia, meant intel-

41 Mahmut Ragıp Gazimihal, *Konya*, (Ankara: 1947), p. 28.

42 This piece stands in the Muhayyer section of the *Mecmûa*. Ali Ufkî, *Mecmûa-i Sâz ü Söz*, Şükrü Elçin (ed.), (İstanbul: Millî Eğitim Basımevi, 1976), p. 84. Gültekin Oransay assumes this piece to be part of a forgotten âyîn-i şerîf. See, Gültekin Oransay, "*Ali Ufkî*", Unpublished Dissertation for Associate Professorship. Ankara University Faculty of Divinity, 1975, Ankara Üniversitesi İlahiyat Fakültesi Kütüphanesi. Y: 16566 (p. notation 5).

43 Bülent Aksoy, *Avrupalı Gezginlerin Gözüyle Osmanlılarda Musiki*, (İstanbul: Pan Yayıncılık, 1994), pp. 37, 287. For illustration, see Walter Feldman's article p. 64 this volume.

44 Walter Feldman, *Music of the Ottoman Court,* (Berlin: Verlag fur Wissenschaft und Bildung, 1995), p. 97.

45 If there are any notable persons in the Mavlavī *āyīn* as visitors, the *muḳābala* may be extended and an additional *Niyaz Ayīni* could be played. But these notable persons should make some donations to the musicians. During this *āyīn*, *Niyaz İlahileri* are played and these *ilâhî*s show the musical features of late eighteenth century. This century was the peak of Mavlaviyya in terms of their prestige in the eyes of the bureaucracy and the ruling class, especially those of Sultān Selim III who was a initiated Mavlavī. So, because of excessive demand, *Niyaz Ayīni* might have started to be played at this time and, probably, this was the final stage in the development of Mavlavī *āyīn* (I am indebted to Prof. Cem Behar from Boğaziçi University for this remark.)

lectual power for his descendants and followers who wanted to make a place for themselves within the Mavlavī tradition.[46] But, perhaps more important than this power, the reverence shown for the descendants of Mavlānā provided self-esteem and self-awareness for them. This reverence, on the other hand, has been more significant for the inner evolution of Mavlaviyya itself.

Obviously, this self-awareness was the main reason for the compilation of the stories told within Mavlavī circles in two hagiographic works written in the first half of the fourteenth century. The first one, *Risāla-i Sipahsālār*, was written approximately 39 years after Mavlānā's death (1273).[47] Its author, Ferīdun b. Aḥmed-i Sipahsālār (d. 1312), 'had probably seen Mavlānā in his lifetime. The second one was *Manāḳib al-'Arifīn* written by Aflākī between 1318 and 1353. In other words, within a century after Mavlānā's death, these two hagiographic works had already been completed. The important point is that during the fifteenth to seventeenth centuries, when hagiographic literature flourished in Ottoman lands, Mavlavīs chose to be silent[48] and did not produce any hagiographic work comparable to these early books until the beginning of the eighteenth century.

Mavlavīs were consistent in establishing a policy of good relationships with the major centers of political power in every period. Mavlānā had intimate relations with the sultāns of Konya, and, as far as we can understand from his *Mektūbāt*,[49] he had a considerable influence over the governors. Later, his descendants continued this attitude.[50] *Çelebi*s, as spiritual and administrative heads of the Mavlaviyya, expanded the *ṭarīḳat* in Anatolian principalities such as Germiyanoğulları and Aydınoğulları.[51] In the fourteenth century, Mavlavīs opened numerous lodges at the important political or cultural centers of Anatolia: Kütahya, Amasya, Denizli, Afyon, and even to the east in Sultaniye. A further interesting point is that Mavlavīs were not involved in Ottoman politics until the reign of Murad II who reigned during the years 1421-1444 and 1444-51.[52] Murad II founded a Mavlavī convent in Edirne[53]

---

46 I should note here that, at present, my studies are limited to Anatolian sources. Any discovery in other regions especially about Bahā' al-Dîn Valad may change this argument. Moreover, I am not aware of the influence of Alim Çelebi who went to Central Asia (*dasht-i Turkistan*) in the middle of fourteenth century, on the spread of Mavlavī culture. See, *Manāḳib al-'Ārifīn*, II-980-981; *Āriflerin Menkıbeleri*, 579-580.

47 The original compilation of this book includes only the biographies of Mavlānā and his father. The son of Ferīdun bin Aḥmad Sipahsālār extended the scope of the book through additional biographies including those of descendants of Mavlānā.

48 I should mention here the sixteenth century poet Şâhidi's several works such as *Gülşen-i Esrār* in which he mentions in part the life of Dīvane Mehmed Çelebi. But his works can be regarded as exceptions for several reasons. First, *Gülşen-i Esrār* is not a hagiographic work; Şâhidi gives only some fragments about the life of Dīvane Mehmed Çelebi at the end of his poem. Secondly, Dīvane Mehmed Çelebi was not a member of mainstream Mavlaviyya of the sixteenth century. He was, in fact, a Şams-i Tebrīzī, which is a division of Mavlaviyya shaped by strong Kalenderî influences. Lastly, Şâhidi's books was prohibited by the shaykhs of Mavlaviyya. See, A. Gölpınarlı, *Mevlânâdan*, pp. 104, 137.

49 Mevlânâ Celâleddîn, *Mektūbāt*, Trans. by Abdülbaki Gölpınarlı, (Istanbul: 1963).

50 A typical example can be found in the *Maârif* of Sultān Valad: in the 18th section of *Maârif*, he praises the sultān for his services to the Mongols. See, Sultān Valad, *Maârif*, p. 63.

51 *Manāḳib al-'Ārifīn* includes many passages on relationships between these principalities and the Konya *çelebi*s. For example, Yakub I., ruler of the Germiyan principality, was a disciple of Ulu Arif Çelebi, son of Sultān Valad (*Manāḳib al-'Ārifīn*, II-945-947; *Āriflerin Menkıbeleri*, II-542-543). Moreover, Süleyman Şah, who reigned between 1361 and 1387, married the daughter of Sultān Valad, Mutahhara Hâtun. See Mustafa Çetin Varlık, *Germiyan-oğulları Tarihi (1300-1429)*, (Erzurum: Atatürk Üniversitesi Yayınları, 1974), p. 63. See also A. Gölpınarlı, *Mevlânâdan*, pp. 267-278, 330-340.

52 Early Mavlavī texts do not include any information on or give any sign of a relationship occurring between Mavlavīs and Ottoman governors. According to Ahmet Yaşar Ocak, this may be because of the fact that the Ottomans were not an important enough center of power to attract the notice of Mavlavīs. See his "Türkiye Tarihinde Merkezi İktidar ve Mevleviler (XIII-XVIII. Yüzyıllar) Meselesine Kısa Bir Bakış", *Selçuk Üniversitesi Türkiyat Araştırmaları Enstitüsü Dergisi*, 2/2 (1996), 20.

53 Halil İnalcık, *Ottoman Empire-The Classical Age*, (London: Phoenix, 1995), p. 201.

and facilitated the first translation of *Meṣnevī-i Ma'nevī* under the title of *Meṣnevī-i Murādiyye*.[54]

Although its early consolidation started soon after the death of Mavlānā under his supreme spiritual and poetic authority, the actual formalization of Mavlaviyya occured towards the end of the fifteenth and beginning of the sixteenth centuries when the real center of the order shifted to Istanbul where the first Mavlavī convent had been opened in the fifteenth century. By this formalization, Mavlaviyya acquired a form that was more centralized, and an organization that was well defined. For example, before this transformation, the term of Mavlavī was used only for those who had been initiated directly by Mavlānā himself. Others who had been initiated by Sulṭān Valad or Ulu 'Ārif Çelebi were named Valadī or 'Ārifī.[55] After the establishment of Mavlaviyya as a *ṭarīḳat*, the importance of individual shaykhs decreased and organizational affiliation rather than personal attachment became the leading norm.[56]

It may be postulated that the Ottomans supported the Mavlaviyya with the aim of making use of their spiritual influence over their Muslim subjects. Besides, the Ottomans would have seen the Mavlaviyya as a catalyst for the Shī'ī or there *bāṭinī* movements as in the case of Bektaşīs.[57] But this view does not consider the inner evolution of sufism and the general transformation which the state and society underwent during the fifteenth and sixteenth century. In a different context, Dewin DeWeese introduces an interpretation of the development of the *ṭarīḳat*s with the following words:[58]

> In suggesting a later formation of actual "orders" than is usually supposed, there is no denying the existence and growing social importance of organized sufi communities in the thirteenth and fourteenth centuries; rather, I want to distinguish such communities, marked in those centuries by organizational patterns based on local and regional traditions and shrines, on hereditary lineages of shaykhs, or on the individual charisma of particular teachers or wonder-workers from the actual Sufi *tariqah*s organized around specific *silsilah*s, and conscious of themselves as distinct spiritual communities based upon a particular "way" of doctrine and practice that lent charisma to the "order" itself, and not just to an individual shaykh. The emergence of the "orders" naturally rested in part upon the cultivation of political patronage in the centuries following the Mongol conquest, and that cultivation itself, in many cases, presupposes a pattern of actual, historical influence wielded by Sufi shaykhs among the khans and *amîr*s of the western Mongol successor states. But I believe that that influence belonged originally to the shaykhs who, although they may have established local communities of their followers and enjoyed considerable esteem among particular villages and/or tribal groups, nevertheless did not understand themselves as representing an "order" ; such shaykhs were suitable for "adoption" several generations later, however, by individuals and "orders" - which may, in fact, have had familial or *silsilah* links with those shaykhs, or, on the other hand, may have shared only the earlier shaykh's prominence in a particular locality-eager to

---

54 Mevlânâ, *Meṣnevī-i Murādiyye,* Kemal Yavuz (ed.), (Ankara: Kültür ve Turizm Bakanlığı Yayınları, 1982).

55 Abdülbaki Gölpınarlı, *Mevlânâdan,* p. 151.

56 This formalization seems not to be exclusive to the Mavlaviyya. During the same period, many of the Bektaşīs, who had been living as one of the various Kalenderî groups, formed their own *ṭarīḳat*. Ahmet Yaşar Ocak, *Kalenderîler,* (Ankara: Türk Tarih Kurumu Yayınevi, 1992), pp. 214-215.

57 A. Gölpınarlı, *Mevlânâdan,* p. 269.

58 Dewin DeWeese, *Islamization and Native Religion in the Golden Horde,* (Pennsylvania: The Pennsylvania State University Press, 1994), pp. 138-139.

show to a sixteenth-century ruler both the importance of paying attention to Sufi shaykhs, as the ruler's thirteenth-century predecessor would be portrayed as observing, and also the traditional ties between the "order", now "founded" by that earlier shaykh, and the heritage of rulership that linked the thirteenth- and sixteenth-century sovereigns.

The brief history of Mavlaviyya explained above, does not, I think, show any considerable diversity from the general schema drawn by Dewin DeWeese. But like any other historical issue, this transformation in the structure of the sufi communities needs to be put into a larger framework which will enable, especially for the subject in this article, an interdisciplinary analysis to be established. In this regard, İsenbike Togan used the following perspective: [59]

> Retribalization in the thirteenth and fourteenth centuries [is credited] with decenlization away from the "imperial yoke" and the re-emergence of localism in the form of steppe tribes and Sufi orders (urban tribes), a development under which mer chants operated in collaboration with the Sufi orders and brought the markets to the steppe tribes.

In the fifteenth century, we see the decline of the universalist claims of the states and ideologies. During this time, the Ottomans in the West, the Safavids in Iran and the Uzbeks in Central Asia, emerged as regional dynasties. Culturally, Ottoman Turkish in the West and Chagatai in the East became literary languages and Persian lost its privileged position. The Ottomans, in this localist atmosphere, were successful in using diverse intellectual traditions to legitimize their authority.[60] In this way, it became possible for each tradition to have a place within the Ottoman system. Hagiographies of the fifteenth century were written after these different traditions had secured for themselves a place in the Ottoman system.[61] Therefore, different *ṭarīḳat*s such as Mavlaviyya, Bektashiyya and Naḳshbandiyya could later flourish at the same place and time.

Within an atmosphere of decentralisation and localism similar to that in which the Mavlaviyya came into prominence, they also developed their own hagiographies during this period and were able to carry them into later centuries. If we look at other *ṭarīḳat*s, we see the rise of *manāḳıbnāme* literature. For example, the Bektaşī *manāḳıbnāme*s started to be written in the fifteenth century. Since Mavlaviyya already had such a literature written in Persian in the fourteenth century, they did not need to establish a written culture. Instead, they introduced highly ceremonial rituals such as the *muḳābala*, and then followed the mentality of their time by outlining the borders of the Mavlaviyya.

---

59 İsenbike Togan, *Flexibility and Limitations in the Steppe Formations*, (Leiden: E.J. Brill, 1998), p. 7.

60 İsenbike Togan explains this success of the early *beylik* period as follows (Togan, *ibid.*, p. 7).

> In West Asia, it was in this atmosphere that the Ottomas competed with the other beyliks in Anatolia by drawing the merchants, as well as the ulama and the Sufi orders, into their own inclusive system, their world order.

61 Yet we need to understand how and why the two early hagiographic works of the Mavlaviyya were able to sustain themselves as symbols of legitimacy well into the eighteenth century, when others were only establishing their legitimacy in the fifteenth century. Such a question can only be pursued in a comparative approach, both in terms of the structure of the respected tarikats and in terms of the discourse of the hagiographies.

Concluding Remarks:

The transformation of the Mavlavī ritual towards a highly regularized form can be understood from the point of view which emphasizes the rituals as a reflection of communality. Localist tendencies of the fifteenth century resulted in the definition or re-definition of the borders of the communities. As recently noted by Dewin DeWeese in the Central Asian context, the transformation of religious practices denotes not only a change in ritual patterns, but also a change in communal self-identity.[62] Mavlavī ceremony, from that point of view, is one of the most important spheres in which the Mavlavīs defined themselves.

If we look from the perspective of music, unlike the situation in Central Asia, *samā'* and *zikr* never became a subject of a debate among different *ṭarīkat*s. Although some scholars such as Ṣāḳıp Dede, tried to combine the Naḳşbandī *zikr* and the Mavlavī *samā'*, not at the practical level but at least in definition, these views were absorbed in a flexible environment. In this way, we can understand that, while the practice of *zikr* was purging the *samā'* practice from the *ṭarīkat* rituals in other regions, in the Ottoman sphere these two practices found it possible to co-exist.

---

62 Dewin DeWeese, *Islamization*, p. 37.

From the Court and Tarikat to the Synagogue: Ottoman Art Music and Hebrew Sacred Songs

EDWIN SEROUSSI

The involvement of Jews in Ottoman art music, whether in the secular forms of the court or in the religious traditions of the Sufi orders, emerges nowadays as a major issue in the research of Jewish culture in the Ottoman Empire. Until recently, this phenomenon was given only sporadic attention, mainly by Jewish intellectuals who were active in the performance of this music or who knew about the role of Jews in it. This is the case of the poet and journalist, Isaac Eliyahu Navon (Edirne, 1859 - Tel Aviv, 1952),[1] the historians Abraham Galante[2] and Salomon Rozanes,[3] the synagogue cantors Isaac Algazi[4] and Moshe Vital,[5] both originally from Izmir, a Jewish reporter from Bosnia[6] and others.[7] To these sources we may add the contribution by Abraham Zvi Idelsohn[8] to the study of music among Oriental Sephardi Jews and the impact of the concept of the Arabic *maqam* on this tradition. However, Idelsohn had only a superficial knowledge of Ottoman art music. His main sources for the study of the *maqam* were Arab and Syrian Jewish musicians residing in Palestine, where Idelsohn worked between 1908 and 1921. These musicians were proficient in the Arabic musical styles that by that time had become clearly different from the Ottoman style.

In recent years, we were able to expand dramatically our extant knowledge about Jewish music and musicians in the Ottoman Empire.[9] The search for primary sources

---

1 Isaac Eliyahu Navon, "Music among the Near Eastern Jews", *Hallel*, 3 (1930), 55-57 (in Hebrew); M. Geshuri, "The Road Pavers (On the Luminaries in the Song of the Sephardi Jews)", *Hallel*, 2 (1930), 39-41 (in Hebrew); Edwin Seroussi, "The Peşrev as a Vocal Genre in Ottoman Hebrew Sources", *Turkish Music Quarterly*, 4/3 (1991), 1-9.

2 Abraham Galante, "Les juifs dans la musique turque", *Historie des juifs de Turquie*, vol. 7, (Istanbul: 1985), pp. 66-73.

3 Salomon Rozanes, "The Poet R. Israel Najara", *The History of the Jews in Turkey and the Levante*, vol. 3, (Sofia: 1936-1938), pp. 405-414 (in Hebrew).

4 Edwin Seroussi, *Mizimrat Qedem, The Life and Music of R. Isaac Algazi from Turkey*, (Jerusalem: Renanot - Institute for Jewish Music, 1989).

5 Moshe Vital, "Lecture at the first convention of ḥazzanim and conductors in Palestine, Jerusalem", *Die Shul und die Chasanim Welt* (June 1938), p. 3 (in Hebrew).

6 Theodor Fuchs, "Prilog Muzici Sefardskih Zidova u Turskoj", *Oumanuth*, 1 (1936/7), 157-164 (Zagreb).

7 Shabetay Dinar, "Shemtov Chiquiar, maestro compositor de música oriental", *Voz Seferadí*, 2 (1967), 40-42 (Mexico City).

8 A. Z. Idelsohn, "Die makamen in der hebräischen Poesie der orientalischen Juden", *Monatschrift für Geschichte und Wissenschaft des Judentums*, 57 (1913), 314-325; idem., *Hebräisch-orientalischer Melodienschatz*, vol. 4 (*Gesänge der orientalischen Sefardim*), (Jerusalem, Berlin, Wien: 1923).

9 Paméla Sezgin Dorn, "Hakhamim, Dervishes, and Court Singers: The Relationship of Ottoman Jewish Music to Classical Turkish Music", *The Jews of the Ottoman Empire*, ed. with an introduction by Avigdor Levy, (Princeton, New Jersey: 1994), pp. 585-632; Edwin Seroussi, "The Turkish *Makam* in the Musical Culture of the Ottoman Jews: Sources and Examples", *Israel Studies in Musicology*, 5 (1990), 43-68

led us to the study of unknown written documents and of the oral traditions still extant in Turkey, Israel and the Americas.

Evidence of the proficiency and deep involvement of Jewish musicians in Ottoman art music can be now dated back to the mid-sixteenth century, i.e. from the period when the identity of this music was emerging out of its previous forms of Persian origin. The geographical span of Jewish musical activities in the Ottoman Empire which centered at the beginning of our research on two cities, Edirne and Istanbul, can now be extended to Izmir, Saloniki,[10] Aleppo, Jerusalem[11] and even to Egypt. New evidence further confirms that the close relations between Jewish Ottoman musicians and their Muslim and Christian colleagues in both the court and the *tarikat* continued throughout the Ottoman era. To summarize, the documentation available now reveals that the historical study of the relation between Ottoman Jews and Ottoman art music has been scarcely given its full scope.

At the outset, we shall point out that the Turkish *makam* system has permeated to all contexts of religious musical performance among the Ottoman Jews. We must distinguish, however, between music of the normative liturgy and all other types of religious rituals such as midnight devotions or events related to the life cycle. The music of the Jewish liturgy in Ottoman lands deserves a special treatment which is beyond the scope of this presentation. Therefore I shall focus here only on non-liturgical contexts, which are closer in their form and content to Ottoman art music.

A main source for a comprehensive historical study of this topic are manuscripts and printed collections of Hebrew sacred songs (*piyyutim* and *pizmonim*) which contain indications pertaining to their musical performance, such as the names of *makams*, *usuls* and musical genres, and/or a reference to the opening line of songs in Turkish or Persian, all provided in Hebrew characters. These manuscript compilations containing Hebrew sacred songs, classified according to the Turkish *makams* dating from the seventeenth to the early twentieth centuries, can be truly called *mecmuas*, as their Turkish counterparts.[12]

These manuscripts were overlooked by scholars of both Ottoman Jewish culture and sacred Hebrew poetry. Scholars from these fields were incapable of evaluating these documents because they ignored their crucial musical background. The growing influence of music was detrimental in terms of the literary quality of sacred Hebrew poetry in the Ottoman Empire after the early seventeenth century. As a result of the submission of the poem to musical composition, the *piyyutim* very often have awkward forms, e.g. stanzas with a different number of lines, lines of a different number of syllables within the same stanza, different rhymes in one stanza and many stanzas of nonsense syllables or sentences (*terrenüm*). This awkwardness can be now explained by an interdisciplinary approach which considers the musical context of these Hebrew compositions.[13]

The context for the performance of most of these religious songs in Hebrew are

---

10 David A. Recanati, "Sacred Poetry and its Singing in Saloniki", *Zikhron Saloniki: Grandeza i Destruyicion de Yerushalaim del Balkan*, ed. David A. Recanati, vol. 2, (Tel Aviv: 1986), pp. 337-347 (in Hebrew); Edwin Seroussi, "Ottoman Classic Music among the Jews of Saloniki" in Judith Dishon and Shmuel Refael eds., *Ladinar: Meḥkarim ba-ṣifrut, ba-musika ube-historia shel dovrei ladino*, (Tel Aviv: 1998), pp. 79-92 (in Hebrew).

11 Edwin Seroussi, "On the Beginnings of the Singing of Bakkashot in 19th Century Jerusalem", *Pe'amim*, 56 (1993), 106-124 (in Hebrew).

12 Owen Wright, *Words without Song: A Musicological Study of an Early Ottoman Anthology and its Precursors*, (London: 1992).

13 Tova Beeri, "Ḥidushe tavnit ba-shirah ha-ivrit ba-mizraḥ ba-me'ot ha-shesh-esre ve-ha-sheva-esre", *Proceedings of the Eleventh World Congress of Jewish Studies*, Division C, Volume 3, (Jerusalem: 1994), pp. 29-35. (Structural innovations in the Oriental Hebrew poetry of the sixteenth and seventeenth centuries.)

special religious gatherings held in the synagogue or at private homes, usually in the early morning hours of the Sabbath. These gatherings, first developed in kabbalistic circles in Upper Galilee, had a mystical background. They indeed bear some common characteristics with the Sufi *sema*'14 with two important differences: first, the Jewish tradition is purely vocal, and includes solo and choral singing, even in the performance of instrumental genres; and second, there is no dancing or any other type of body movement as an integral part of the performance. The mystic rationale of these gatherings has eroded since their heyday in the late sixteenth century. Singers who carry on this tradition in the contemporary period usually deny any mystical intentions in their performances. What fuels continuity is the deed of preserving a venerable religious tradition (*minhag*), and the aesthetic pleasure provided by the music to performers and listeners as well.

The thousands of Hebrew poems composed to be performed to Ottoman music remained unpublished until the early twentieth century. Moreover, only a very small fraction of these songs composed throughout the centuries remained alive in oral tradition. The living repertoire is reflected in the most important, and practically only, printed Hebrew *mecmua* called *Shirei Israel be-Eretz ha-Qedem* (Istanbul, 1921). This collection reflects the repertory of the choral society called "Maftirim" from Edirne. This prominent Jewish institution of Ottoman art music was probably established as early as the first half of the seventeenth century and continued its activities without interruption until World War I, when many of its members moved to Istanbul after 1918. The Ottoman Hebrew songs performed until the present by Turkish Jews in Istanbul and Israel derive from the specific repertoire of "Maftirim" with some additional pieces composed by contemporary musicians from Istanbul and Izmir.15

The earlier records of Hebrew sacred poems sung to Turkish music are found among Romaniote (Byzantine) Hebrew poets such as Shlomo Mazal Tov16, who were influenced by the Spanish style of Hebrew poetry in the early sixteenth century. In his collection *Shirim ve-zemirot u-tushbaḥot* (Constantinople, 1545), Mazal Tov assigns to several of his poems a "laḥan turki" (a "Turkish melody"), without any further specification. This practice reflects an early involvement of Ottoman Jews with Turkish music.

Following the expulsion of the Jews from Spain in 1492 and from Portugal in 1497, and their resettlement in Ottoman lands in impressive numbers, there is an influx of Andalusian Jews, who had mastered the Western style of Arabic music. A pertinent anecdote related to this issue appears in *Seder Eliyahu Zuta* by Rabbi Eliyahu b. Elkanah Capsali (1483-1555).17 This story tells about a Jewish musician from Spain who is discovered by the Sultan during one of the monarch's clandestine visits to his Jewish subjects. Eventually this Andalusian Jew becomes the chief musician of the court (see appendix to this article). Even if apocryphal, this story is symptomatic of the early involvement of Spanish Jews in the music of the Ottoman court.

The real initiator of the Jewish tradition of Ottoman music is Rabbi Israel Najara (ca. 1555-1625). Considered by scholars today as the most outstanding poet of Sephardi Jewry in the Eastern Mediterranean in the late-sixteenth and early-seven-

---

14 Paul Fenton, "Les *baqqašot* d'orient et d'occident", *Revue des Etudes Juives*, 134 (1975), 101-121; Amnon Shiloah, "The Symbolism of Music in the Kabbalistic Tradition", *The World of Music*, 20/3 (1978), 56-69.

15 The literary repertoire of a similar choral association from Saloniki was published in 1879. See, Seroussi, "Ottoman Classic Music", *ibid.* (note 10).

16 Tova Beeri, "Shelomo Mazal Tov", *Pe'amim*, 59 (1994), pp. 65-76 (in Hebrew).

17 *Seder Eliyahu Zuta*, by Rabbi Eliyahu b. Elkanah Capsali (1483-1555). *The History of the Ottomans and Venice and Chronicle of Israel in the Turkish Kingdom, Spain and Venice*. Published for the first time from four manuscript versions, Jerusalem: the Ben Zvi Institute and The Institute for the Diaspora Research, (Jerusalem: 1976), vol. 1, p. 91ff.

teenth centuries,[18] Najara's novelty consisted of adopting the then new Ottoman makam system to Hebrew poetry.[19]

A close examination of the two compendia of religious poems written by Najara, *Zemirot Yisrael* (published in three different editions: Safed 1587, Saloniki 1599/1600 and Venice 1600) and *She'erit Yisrael* shows his progressive involvement with Ottoman music.[20] This tradition was in its formative stages during Najara's lifetime. [21] It is still a matter of conjecture how he managed to be so "updated" on this music while he carried on his activities in the Damascus-Safed axis.

Najara achieved the following accomplishments:

a) He established a tradition of Ottoman Hebrew music. This tradition is reflected in the compilation of his Hebrew sacred poems following the Turkish pattern, i.e. according to the *makam*s. During the first stages of his work, his models were Turkish songs from two sources: the coffee houses, particularly those of the Janissaries with whom the Jews had close ties in Syria, and, in some cases, from the Sufi sects, as testified by the mention of songs by poets such as Pir Sultan Abdal of the Bektasi order in Najara's *mecmua*.[22] Later writings by Najara show his awareness of more modern musical forms. In *She'erit Yisrael*, his last, and mostly unpublished, collection of religious poems, he mentions, in addition to the *makam*s, a few *usul*s (cyclic rhythms) and instrumental musical genres (particularly the *peşrev*) which compose the compound form of Ottoman court music, the *fasıl*. *She'erit Yisrael* can thus be considered as the first truly Hebrew *mecmua*, and as a model and inspiration for Jewish composers and poets throughout the Ottoman Empire.

b) He assigned specific religious contexts for the performance of this Ottoman Hebrew vocal music, such as the early Sabbath morning vigils.

c) He had disciples who continued to compose Hebrew sacred poetry set to Ottoman art music and even refined the musical aspect of this tradition according to the latest developments in the Ottoman court. This musical refinement was usually at the expense of the level of the poetry which had been in constant decline since the peak achieved by Najara.

Three important facts should be pointed out in the development of the singing of *piyyutim* according to Ottoman art music after Najara:

1) Constantinople and Adrianople became the centers of Hebrew music creativity after the seventeenth century;

2) Since the second half of the seventeenth century Jewish poets and composers became closer to Muslim and Christian musicians serving at the seraglio and at the Mevlevi *tarikat*;

---

18 W. Bacher, "Les poesies inedites d'Israel Nadjara", *Revue des Études Juives*, 58 (1909), 241-269- 59 (1910), 96-105; 60 (1910), 221-234; Meir Benayahu, "Rabbi Israel Najara", *Asufot*, 4 (1990), 203-284 (in Hebrew); Moshe Gaon, "R. Israel Najara and his songs", *Mizraḥ uma'arav*, 5 (1930-1932), 145-163 (in Hebrew); A. Z. Idelsohn, "Israel Najara and his Poetry", *Hashiloaḥ*, 37 (1921), 25-36, 122-135 (in Hebrew); Salomon Rozanes, "The Poet Israel Najara", 1936-38; Joseph Yahalom, "R. Israel Najarah and the Revival of Hebrew Poetry in the East after the Expulsion from Spain", *Pe'amim*, 13 (1982), 96-124 (in Hebrew).

19 See my lecture "The singing of the *piyyut* in the Ottoman Empire after Israel Najara", delivered at the Twelfth World Congress of Jewish Studies, Jerusalem, August 1997 which will be published in the proceedings of this conference.

20 Published in a very partial version under the title *Pizmonim* by M. H. Friedlander, Vienna 1858; mostly still in manuscript.

21 Walter Feldman, *Music of the Ottoman Court: Makam, Composition and the Early Ottoman Instrumental Repertoire*, (Berlin: 1996), (Intercultural Music Studies 10).

22 Andreas Tietze and Joseph Yahalom, *Ottoman Melodies, Hebrew Hymns, A 16th Century Cross-Cultural Adventure*, (Budapest: 1995).

3) Jewish musicians served the Jewish community and at the same time appeared before non-Jewish audiences.

Najara's closest disciple was Avtaliyon ben Mordecai Avtaliyon. The precise dating of Avtaliyon's life span is still problematic. In the colophon of one of the most important manuscript copies of *She'erit Yisrael* by Najara, which was in the possession of the Jewish community of Sarajevo, Avtaliyon refers to Najara as "my master". This colophon was copied and published by the historian Salomon Rozanes but regretfully this manuscript was lost. While Avtaliyon appears to have been a few years younger than Najara (in one source the year 1577 is mentioned for his birth), the musical terminology used by him reflects the state of Ottoman court music in the second half of the seventeenth century. We have located so far three copies of Avtaliyon's impressive *mecmua* which is titled *Ḥadashim la-bqarim*.[23] The most complete version of this collection is Ms. Sassoon, no. 1031, the only copy that contains the introduction by the poet.[24] We assume this manuscript to be an autograph.[25]

Even a superficial examination of Avtaliyon's work shows that his involvement with the courtly tradition is far deeper and more advanced than that of his master Najara. He uses a larger number of *makam*s (including compound ones), his compositions usually bear in their title their correspondent *usul* and the musical forms employed by him are the standard ones at the Ottoman court. While Najara composed only vocal *peşrev*s and very few *semai*s, Avtalyion's collection includes, in addition to many *peşrev*s and *semai*s, pieces from genres such as the *beste*, *kâr*, *nak*s, *yürük semai* and the *peşrev semai*, a form mentioned only in Jewish sources since the late seventeenth century. Moreover, his pieces were apparently intended to be performed in cycles, like the courtly *fasıl*, based on one *makam*.

In the footsteps of Najara and Avtaliyon, a school of Ottoman Jewish musicians developed in Constantinople and Adrianople. Some of these musicians attained fame in non-Jewish circles and are mentioned in Turkish sources of the late seventeenth and eighteenth centuries.[26] Among them are instrumentalists such as *miskali* Yahudi Yako and *tamburi* Yahudi Kara Kaş and composers such as Çelebiko (a teacher of Cantemir), Moshe Faro (known also as Musi or *tamburi ḥakham* Muse, d. 1776) a leading musician in the court of Sultan Mahmud I, Aharon Hamon (known as Yahudi Harun, who died after 1721)[27] and Isaac Fresco Romano (Tanburi Izak or Ishak, 1745-1814), a musician at the court of Sultan Selim III. The Hebrew *mecmua*s show that almost all these Jewish masters composed *piyyutim* too.

Other prolific composers appearing in the Hebrew *mecmua*s of the late seventeenth and eighteenth centuries who are not mentioned at all in Turkish sources are Isaac Alidi, Aharon Alidi, Moshe Shani, Yaakov Amron, Eliyah Walid, Moshe Yuda Abbas, Shelomo Rav Huna, Eliyahu Falcon and many others. Almost no biographical details about these musicians are extant. We may attribute their absence from Turkish sources to the fact that they only composed Hebrew pieces.

In the nineteenth century we witness the development of two other important Jewish centers of musical activities in the Ottoman Empire: Izmir, following the leadership of the composer Rabbi Abraham Ariyas (late eighteenth century) and

---

23 "[They are] new every morning", after Threni 3:23, a reference to the fact that the poet wrote a new poem for every Sabbath.

24 David Salomon Sassoon, "Ohel David", *Descriptive Catalogue of the Hebrew and Samaritan Manuscripts in the Sassoon Library*, vol. 2, (London: 1932), p. 818.

25 For Avtalyon see now: Tove Beeri, "Avtalyon ben Mordekhai: An Hebrew poet from early-seventeenth century Turkey", Lecture delivered at the Twelfth World Congress of Jewish Studies, August 1997, to be published in the proceedings of this conference.

26 Feldman, *Music of the Ottoman Court*, pp. 48-50.

27 Jefim Hayyim Schirmann, "Hamon, Aaron Ben Isaac", *Enyclopedia Judacia*, 7 (1972), col. 1249.

Saloniki, founded by Aharon Barzilay (second half of the nineteenth century). In the late nineteenth century Jewish Ottoman composers split into two groups: those who wrote songs in Turkish and instrumental compositions, such as Missirli Ibrahim (Abraham Levy Ḥayyat) and Isaac Varon, and those who wrote Hebrew pieces, such as Moshe Cordova in Istanbul. This split reflects a break between secular and religious Jews in the sphere of music. Only in Izmir did Jewish musicians compose both secular instrumental music and Hebrew sacred songs. The most outstanding among the Jewish musicians from Izmir was Shem Tov Shikiar (Santo Şikiar, 1840-1920).

The close relationship between Jewish musicians and the music of the Ottoman court and tarikat, even by those whose activities were limited to the synagogue, is testified by the mention of contemporary musical works by composers from the court in Hebrew manuscripts from the late seventeenth- and early eighteenth centuries. We uncovered several Hebrew manuscripts in which Ottoman musicians are mentioned. Two of them, Ms. no. 1214 of the Jewish Theological Seminary (JTS) in New York and Ms. Heb. no. 3395 of the Strassbourg municipal library, are a particular rich source of information on this matter. Ottoman compositions mentioned in them can be identified with precision in the manuscript collections of Ali Ufqi and Prince Cantemir.[28] Ottoman composers whose compositions mentioned in Hebrew sources we can not yet identify are Mehmed Kasim (d. ca. 1730), Osman Dede (1652-1730), Baba Zeytun, Aga Mumin, *mişkali* Solakzade (d. 1658) and the Greek *tamburi* Angelos. There are other musicians mentioned in Hebrew sources whom we have not yet been able to identify in Ottoman sources: Selim-zade Aga, Aga Reza and Husni Hoca.

I would like to examine an Ottoman Hebrew piece that is still extant in oral tradition. This is the *peşrev semai* set to the poem *Avo el mizbeaḥ elohim simḥat gili* (I shall come to the altar of God, my joy) by a composer named Aharon, probably Aharon Hamon or Aharon Alidi. The transcription is based on a notation by *kanuni* David Behar from Istanbul (who resides now in Tel Aviv) and on a performance by the Reverend Samuel Benaroya (born in 1910), a native of Edirne, who has lived in the United States since 1951. This composition was recorded by Benaroya in Seattle in 1990.[29]

The piece consists of five *hane* corresponding to the five stanzas of the poem. Each stanza has a different rhyme, but all the stanzas close with a line ending on the same word: *elohenu*. The *hane* have irregular forms, consisting of four to seven musical phrases. Each phrase covers two cycles of the *usul semai*, except for four of them which cover only one cycle. The last two musical phrases of the opening hane (x+y) serve as a musical ritornello at the end of each of the other *hane* (except for hane IV, whose end resembles phrase y only vaguely). Phrase y corresponds to the literary refrain (*elohenu*). The piece ends with a "coda" (phrase z) based on the refrain (phrase y) but leading to the ending note (*karar*) of the *makam*.

The table on page 91 summarizes the formal structure of this piece.

---

28 Examples of Ottoman compositions mentioned in these two Hebrew manuscripts are: *Nevah laḥan peşrev Şerif usul zarbufet* (Strassbourg 3395, fol. 44a, correponding to the *Peşrev Şerif neva - muhammes*, cf. Cantemir 1992, no. 66); *Hüseyni peşref Şah Murad degeşmeş ve-yeş lo ḥamişah usules genber düyek fehte [merefşan] semai* by Aharon Alidi (JTS 1214, p. 10, corresponding to *Peşrev Şah Murad hüseyni degişme*, cf. Cantemir 1992, no. 73); *Besteni giyar peşref Kantemir merefşan* by Aharon Hamon (JTS 1214, p. 170, corresponding to *Kantemiroglu bestenigar - berefşan peşref* , cf. Cantemir 1992, no. 281); *Sultani 'irak peşref Kantemir devr-i kebir* by Aharon Alidi (JTS 1214, p. 335, corresponding to *Kantemiroglu sultani irak - devr-i kebir*, cf. Cantemir 1992, no. 290). Theoretically one can try now to reconstruct some of these old Hebrew compositions by adapting the text to the music of those pieces which have been identified in notated Ottoman sources or were preserved in oral tradition.

29 See the CD *Ottoman Hebrew Sacred Songs Performed by Samuel Benaroya*, Anthology of Music Traditions in Israel no. 12 (AMTI 9803), (Jerusalem, 1998).

Hüseyni pešrev semai by Aharon

חוסיאיני פישריף סמהי סימן אהרן

I

אבוא אל מזבח אלהים שמחת גילי
שמה חנון אערוך לך צורי וגואלי
את שיר מהללי, הרימה קולי
כפאולי שיר חדש תהלה לאלהנו.

II

הט אזניך לאמרתי, שמע תפילתי
האזינה שעותי, אלהי ישועתי
השיבה את שבותי כי אותך קויתי
וגם לדבריך דודי חי הוחלתי
תחיש גאולתי, פדני מגלותי
כי גדול ומי צור זולתי אלהינו.

III

רחם בחסדיך כרחם אב על בנים
האל הגדול אדון האדונים
וזכור עדתך קנית קדם הזרוויים
בתוך גוים עניים ואביונים
וחדש ששונים בגילות ורננים
ויודו כל המונים לה׳ אלהינו.

IV

נר לרגלי דבריך ואור לנתיבתי
ואתהלכה ברחבה תוך נותי
עיר ציון במדינות שרתי
ואשתעשע אז ואגיל
בבית ה׳ בחצרות אלהינו.

V

לבי ובשרי ירננו אל חי
ולשוני תהגה את שיר רנני
פי ושפתי הללו הודו לה׳
וגם כליותי הבו גודל לאהלינו.

Full text of *Hüseyni peşrev semai* by Aharon.

Transcription of *Peşrev Semai* in *makam* Hüseyni by Aharon according to Samuel Benaroya.
Roman numbers designate the *hanat*; letters designate musical phrases. Notes (parts III to V)
continue on pp. 89-90.

hane	phrase	stanza	line (rhyme)
I	a	1	a (li)
	b		a (li)
	x		a (li)
	y		x (elohenu)
II	a	2	b (ti)
	b		b (ti)
	a1		b (ti)
	b1		b (ti)
	Ib + x		b (ti)
	y		x (elohenu)
III	a	3	c (nim)
	a+b		c (nim)
	c		c (dem)
	IIb1 + Ib		c (dem)
	d (1 usul)		c (dem)
	Ib + x		c (dem)
	y		x (elohenu)
IV	a	4	d (ti)
	a+b		d (ti)
	c		d (ti)
	d		d (gil)
	y? (1 usul)		x (elohenu)
V	a	5	e (hay)
	b (1 usul)		e (hay)
	x		e (nai)
	c (1 usul)		e (nay)
	y		e (tay)
			x (elohenu)
	z ["coda"]		e (tay)
			x (elohenu)

Conclusion

We may state that research into the Hebrew branch of Ottoman art music is still in its infancy. The importance of this tradition is becoming clearer as historical facts revealed by Hebrew *mecmua*s continue to expand our views on this subject. The relations of the Hebrew Ottoman tradition to those of the Ottoman court and the Mevlevi *tarikat* appear to be closer than was thought until now. For example, we find Hebrew compositions based on music by Mevlevi composers, such as Ismail Dede Effendi. Contemporary testimonies show that the bond between Jews and Sufis continued well into the twentieth century. A personal communication by Reverend Samuel Benaroya concerns the mutual visits of Jewish singers to the Mevlevi *tekke* in Edirne and of Mevlevi singers to the synagogue (interview held in Seattle, 23/10/1992).

To expand the research on the Hebrew Ottoman tradition, we have to engage in further efforts to retrieve old commercial and archival recordings in order to gather a comprehensive corpus for stylistic analysis. Despite the erosion of the oral tradition, one can still find singers like Isaac Maçorro in Istanbul, whose performances may help us to understand better the Ottoman Jewish music tradition.

Three main issues await future research in this field: 1) the use of the *makam* and other aspects of Ottoman art music in the Jewish liturgy and in other types of Jewish music in the Ottoman Empire, such as the songs in Ladino (Judeo-Spanish); 2) the study of the historical Hebrew sources in light of the contemporary practice revealed by commercial, archival and field recordings; and 3) the comparison between the

Jewish and non-Jewish Ottoman traditions in terms of performance practice, style and genres. This last issue is related to a larger question: to what extent is the Jewish identity within the Ottoman social fabric reflected in music.

Appendix

Translation from *Seder Eliyahu Zuta* by Rabbi Eliyahu b. Elkanah Capsali (1483-1555): *The History of the Ottomans and Venice and Chronicle of Israel in the Turkish Kingdom, Spain and Venice.* Published for the first time from four manuscript versions, Jerusalem: the Ben Zvi Institute and The Institute for the Diaspora Research, Jerusalem, 1976. Volume 1, p. 91ff.

And the King [Sultan Bayazid II, 1481-1511] went from neighborhood to neighborhood... And it so happened that the King passed by the people and there was one of the Spanish Jews who came to live in this land after the expulsion from Spain and his name [was] Abraham Shondor [chantor? or perhaps sündir, player of a folk lute, cf. Feldman, p. 171], and he was called like this after his art, because he was the only one of his generation in his art, one "who is skilled in music, a stalwart fellow and a warrior, sensible in speech and handsome in appearance" [Samuel I 17:18]... His listeners would say that he was "the ancestor of all those who play the lyre and the pipe" [Genesis 4:21]. And on that day the man was performing his art at his home playing "the drum and the lute and revelling to the tune of the pipe" [Job 21:12]. And the King passed by and he heard the tune and he liked it, and he descended from his chariot and entered the house of that Jew and asked the Jew: "May I sit for a while in your home and listen to the voice of male and female singers as well as the luxuries of commoners - coffers and coffers of them." [Ecclesiastes 2:8] And Abraham replied to the King and said: "Sit as long as you wish." Then Abraham ran to the lyres [paraphrase of Genesis 18:7, nevalim meaning the herd] and he took "the melodious lute and the lyre" [Psalms 81:3] and started to play again and again "as the musician played" [Kings II 3:15] and the king was pleased...

And the King arose in order to leave, and the Jew held him and played for him another tune on instruments of different kinds...

And the Jew did not know that the [man was the] King, [he] only thought that he was one of the ministers because he paid "no attention to his appearance or his stature" [Samuel I 16:7] and from his face it was obvious that he was a minister and an official, but no one could imagine that he was the King.

And the day after, the King was seated eating... and the musicians stood up each one with his instrument on his hand, "the horn, lyre, psaltery, bagpipe and all other types of instruments" [Daniel 3:5], and they played as customary. And the King said: "spare me the sound of your hymns, and let me not hear the music of your lutes" [Amos 5:23] because from the day I heard the tune of the Jew I have not tasted the flavor of a beautiful tune, there is not one like it in the country. And the King said to the clerk upon whom he was leaning: Hasten to me the Jew who plays and he will play for me and I will be pleased.

And the couriers left hastily and arrived and took the Jew and placed him in front of the King and the Jew prostrated himself on the ground. And the King said to the Jew: "I have heard that you are a player and a singer; now play before me, sing to us from your songs, play to us with your hands, rejoice us with your art, take in your hands the sweet lyre and the lute because I have heard about you"... [Gittin 88:1]. At that moment the Jew tried to play as always and he had no power, and he tried "to do his work, strange is his work, and to perform his task, astounding is his task" [Isaiah 28:21]... And the King was surprised by what happened and said: ...one night he was a supreme artist but "he perished overnight" (Jonah 4:10) and he became [like] an apprentice of all apprentices. Who ever heard the like? "Who ever witnessed such events?" (Isaiah 66:8)

And the King thought he was drunk. And the King said to him: Until when are you going to get drunk?... And Abraham prostrated himself before the King and said: "No, my Lord, I am sober and I have drunk no wine or other strong drink, but I have been pouring my heart out to the Lord" (Samuel I, 1:15), to rejoice him with my actions... but I saw you my Lord, my King, as if I were seeing an angel of God, and a great anxiety fell upon me and I was too anguished to play and too frightened to sing" [Isaiah 21:3]... "Look away from me, that I may recover" [Psalms 39:14].

And the King spoke to him softly and said: "Why are you afraid, what I have done to you? Go and play, and go and sing..". And the Jew replied to the King and said: "Why my Lord, my King, should I not be frightened by your presence, why should I not tremble when confronting you? I had heard [about] you with my ears but now I see you with my eyes" [Job 42:5] When I was in Andalusia "I learned of your renown; I was awed, O Lord, by your deeds" [Habakkuk 3:2], we were scared and frightened... And when we heard about your strength and might "we lost heart, and no man had any more spirit left because of you" [Joshua 2:11] so mighty was your arm as perceived by the inhabitants of Spain... And why should I not now be afraid, "when my eyes look forward, my gaze be straight ahead" [Proverbs 4:25] "fear and trembling invade me; I am clothed with terror" [Psalms 55:6].

And the King heard these words and he was pleased; his heart was happy and his honor rejoiced when he heard that from one edge of the world to the other people trembled at his presence and were in awe. And he comforted the heart of the Jew, and the Jew started to strengthen gradually and then he played a little, "murmur upon murmur" [Isaiah 28:10], on that day. And on the next day the King permitted the Jew to leave and to come back before him. And so the Jew did and Abraham woke up early in the morning and went to the place where he had stood [the day before] and he played with his hands and so he did, day after day...

And Abraham attained great honor, and the King put his chair on a high level, overlooking the rest of the singers and players that played with him, and he performed his melodies in honor of the King for the rest of his days... And the King ordered, and so it was written in the book of chronicles, that this Jew should receive an award of thirty coins each and every day. "His prison garments were removed and... a regular allotment of food was given him at the instance of the king - an allotment for each day - all the days of his life" [II Kings 25:28-30].

PART IV
CHANGE AND CONTINUITY
IN THE MODERN ERA

The Technical Modernization of Turkish Sufi Music: The Case of the Durak

CEM BEHAR

The rationalization, theorization and subsequent standardization of traditional Ottoman/Turkish music was a vast enterprise, initiated towards the end of the last century by Rauf Yekta Bey (1871-1935), and brought to fruition in the 1940s and 50s by two of his colleagues and contemporary composers and musicologists: Hüseyin Sadettin Arel (1880-1955) and Dr. Subhi Zühtü Ezgi (1869-1962). Pitch, scale, intervals and makams were standardized and adapted to western staff notation. Rhythmic patterns (*'usûl*s), musical genres and pieces were classified and systematized. Large portions of the orally transmitted repertoire were transcribed, new treatises and books were written for the teaching and transmission of traditional music, new teaching methods were devised etc., etc.

The timing, the unfolding and the various details of this purposeful program of "westernization" need not bother us here. The Arel-Ezgi program was, however, on the whole, much more successful than that which for instance, their contemporary Ali Naki Vaziri (1886-1981) and his students and followers tried to implement for Persian music.[1] Nowadays, just about all formal teaching of traditional Ottoman/Turkish music is based on what later came to be called the Arel-Ezgi system. What, in real musical life, seems not to fit these two authors' system is, in most cases, perceived by musicians of the younger generations either as an exception or as an unexplainable deviation from the norm.

There is no aspect of traditional Ottoman/Turkish music that really escaped the homogenizing thrust of the Ezgi-Arel enterprise. We shall try here to examine briefly the impact of this modernizing venture, at a strictly technical level, on the fate of one very particular genre within Turkish religious/Sufi music: the *durak*.

The Durak: Form and Structure

The durak, for all we know, a specifically Ottoman/Turkish genre, is part of a family of liturgical vocal genres that are pre-composed but are non-metrical. In other words, these genres totally lack a fixed rhythmical pattern; they have no *'usûl*. They are entirely pre-composed, though, and do not allow for any kind of improvisation. Neither do they allow, in principle, for any performance-generated variants.

The other members of the same family of pre-composed ametrical genres are the *na't*, the *mevlut*, the *temcit-münacaat*, and the *miraciye*. Coincidentally, these are all religious/Sufi genres. The pre-composed *mevlut* has been lost and forgotten and

---

1 See, for instance, Hormoz Farhat, *The Dastgah Concept in Persian Music*, (Cambridge: Cambridge University Press, 1990).

today the text of the mevlut is sung in a quasi-improvised manner. The text itself, written in Turkish by Süleyman Çelebi (d.1409), celebrates the birth of the Prophet and is chanted on various occasions. As to the temcit and the na't, these two genres have become virtually extinct.

The only member of the family, indeed, which was not consigned to oblivion is the durak. Our main historical source on the texts of the duraks (Sadettin Nüzhet Ergun's fundamental and unavoidable *Anthology of Turkish Music*) was published in 1943. It lists the texts of no fewer than a hundred composed duraks. These run in a continuous line from about the middle of the seventeenth to the very end of the nineteenth century.[2]

Of these hundred duraks whose texts are given by Sadettin Nüzhet Ergun, only around forty have been notated and have, therefore, survived as musical pieces, but only about half of this number are effectively sung today. A number of duraks have also been composed in the twentieth century. The official biographer of the musical reformer and composer, Hüseyin Sadettin Arel, attributes to him no less than 108 duraks, most of them composed in the late 1940s. But that is quite another matter. We shall return to it shortly.

Contrary to the na't and the münacaat, which might use texts in Arabic or in Persian, the durak always uses texts in the Turkish language. It is invariably sung *a capella*, without any instrumental accompaniment and, as far as we can surmise, by only one performer at a time. The texts of the duraks are notable for their expression of mystical fervor and enthusiasm rather than for their orthodox piety. The lyrics are mostly taken from gazels and other poems of various well-known Turkish mystical poets such as Yunus Emre, Aşık Paşa, Aziz Mahmud Hüdai, Nasuhi, Niyazi-i Mısri, Eşrefoğlu Rumi etc.

The verses that have been selected for composing a durak are indifferently metrical (*arûz*) or syllabic. The sung texts are of varying lengths and of various poetical forms. The number of lines that are to be sung are also highly variable. Two or three lines, one or two stanzas, a quatrain or two of the same poem may have been put to music.

The number of lines put to music as a durak may therefore vary. Some of the duraks have a refrain, and some do not. Some of the duraks use some of the attributes of Allah (Hû, Hayy, Kayyûm etc.) as syllables for purposes of melodic elaboration and embellishment, but others do not. Apparently, therefore, no single type of lyric, no pre-set poetic form seems to have really prevailed and to have been taken as a standard textual form for the composition of a durak.

More or less the same thing can also be said of the internal melodic structure of the duraks in the repertoire. Some of the duraks are longish and repetitive pieces, but others are quite short. Some of them have a *meyanhane*, that is, a middle section which modulates into a different makam. But many of the duraks do not have that middle section and only have one or more very short modulating passages. A few of them, however, have a full double *meyanhane* modulating successively into two different *makam*s. For some duraks, apparently the introductory section, or even a short motivic sequence, may function as a sort of ritornello. But this is not the case for some other duraks. Besides, there seems to be no standard relationship between the lengths of the introductory section (*zemin*), that of the middle section, if any, and that of the concluding melodic phrases, or of the ritornello (*nakarat*), if any.

---

2 Sadettin Nüzhet Ergun, *Türk Musikisi Antolojisi-Dini Eserler,* 2 vols., (Istanbul: 1942-1943). For the list of Duraks, see pp. 719-723.

All these elements are highly variable. Pending more detailed historical, textual and musical analyses, of course, this great variability induces me to think that it is difficult to speak either of a uniform textual or of a more or less stable musical structure for the durak. Had the durak had an *'usûl*, a fixed rhythmical pattern, this rhythmical entity, this fixed and stable configuration of strong and weak beats might well have served as a unit of compositional measurement and a means of comparing the respective lengths of each of its parts, as it does in many of the religious or secular pieces of the répertoire of Ottoman/Turkish music.

This is, indeed, a function that the *'usûl*s perform in many other genres of Turkish music, whether secular or religious. Partitioning pieces into sections, relating these sections to each other and thus giving these compositions a further element of structuring is, in Ottoman/Turkish music, an important function of the rhythmic cycles, especially of the longer ones. We have here, therefore, an *a contrario* argument pointing to the non-metrical structure of the durak. The few duraks that we know for sure were composed in the late nineteenth century, though, and notwithstanding the fact that they, too, are non-metrical, seem to have a more balanced internal structure. Apparently they have an introduction, a middle and a final section of comparable, though not necessarily equal lengths.

The absence of any discernibly uniform textual or musical structural characteristics in the duraks must, therefore, be considered as an important piece of circumstantial evidence speaking in favor of the fact that this absence of a fixed rhythmical pattern was really an original attribute of the genre. This fundamental structural "anarchy" plaguing such a highly prestigious musical genre did, as we shall see, certainly deeply disturb the self-appointed modernizers and rationalizers of Ottoman/Turkish music, Arel and Ezgi.

Of the origin of the durak, nothing is really known. Neither do we have any precise information on its liturgical place and function in the earlier periods. Ali Ufkî's collection of notations, dating from about the middle of the seventeenth century, contains a number of religious and Sufi hymns (İlahi, Tesbih etc.), but none that is entitled 'durak'. The earliest known duraks are the ones composed by Sepetçizade Mehmet Ağa (d.1694), Hafız Post (d.1693), and Ali Şirügani Efendi (d.1714). These composers are contemporaries of Itrî (d.1712) and of Yusuf Çelebi (d.1728?), the composers of the oldest known two na'ts (another non-metrical genre of Ottoman/Turkish music).

Walter Feldman has suggested that the duraks "seem to display a deep and old relation to certain chants of the Greek Orthodox Church".[3] That statement, however, is just a very interesting hypothesis which, of course, needs to be substantiated. If it were so substantiated, however, this idea would probably change our understanding of the formation of the specific Ottoman/Turkish Sufi musical tradition. Besides, the relationship of the durak and na't performance style to the vocal improvisations (*taksim, gazel*) of Ottoman/Turkish music has not yet been made the object of any serious study.

---

3 See Walter Feldman "Musical Genres and Zikir of the Sunni Tarikats of Istanbul", in Raymond Lifchez (ed.) *The Dervish Lodge-Architecture, Art and Sufism in Ottoman Turkey*, (Berkeley: California University Press, 1992), pp. 187-202. As stated by Walter Feldman, the structural principles of the Durak were also used, at least once, to create a religious work of larger dimensions. This is the Miraciye of Osman Dede (1652-1730). The Miraciye was considered as an inimitable composition and remained as the only example of this genre.

The Durak: Liturgy, Style and Transmission

The liturgical place and function of the durak is also significant. What we know of it, however, mostly relates to the nineteenth century practices.

The singing of duraks at particular points within the *zikr* ceremony of the Halveti and Cerrahi tarikats seem to have marked a period of particular solemnity, concentration and deep meditation. The duraks were chanted, according to Ekrem Karadeniz, in a period of total silence just after the *kelime-i tevhid zikri* and before the beginning of the circular standing *zikr*.

The duraks were, in fact, sung during the *zikr* of most of Sunni tarikats in Istanbul, except the Mevlevi. In the course of the eighteenth century, the duraks were also accepted in mosques outside of the dervish *tekke*s. Ekrem Karadeniz tells us that in the nineteenth century they were especially chanted just before Friday prayers in mosques that had a *vakıf*.[4] Nowadays, the duraks are also sung to mark particular resting points, stopping points during the recitation of the Mevlut.

The word *durak* itself means "a stopping point, a rest or a pause". What we know of nineteenth and twentieth century practices seems to suggest that the genre itself was, perhaps from the very beginning, conceived as an insert of particular significance set to mark points of special concentration within a wide and diversified Sufi liturgical framework. But there is also an alternative, and quite pedestrian, explanation. The durak, sung by a single person, might simply have been used to provide a period of well-deserved physical and mental rest for the numerous dervishes participating in a long and sometimes exhausting *zikr* exercise. If that were true, the liturgical function of the durak would, then, be not that of a climax but quite the opposite.

Duraks were composed not only by the *zakir*s of Sufi orders of whose liturgy the durak was a part, but also by other Sufi musicians and even by totally secular composers. A court musician and singer of the last century, Hacı Arif Bey (1831-1885), a composer of hundreds of light songs (*şarkı*) for instance, is also the author of a well known durak in the makam Hicaz.

Although the genre never was part of the Mevlevi ritual, such eminent Mevlevi musicians as the great İsmail Dede Efendi (1777-1846) and his pupil Zekâi Dede, a Mevlevi musician, too, also composed a few duraks and were also probably familiar with the repertoire of duraks. A well known durak performer of the late nineteenth century, Behlül Efendi (c.1830-1895), for instance, was a pupil of İsmail Dede Efendi and had received his musical education in the Mevlevi tekkes of Istanbul. But he was also one of the most famous durak performers of his time. He used to chant the durak during the *zikr* in two different Halvetî *tekke*s in Üsküdar as well as attending to the singing of *ayin*s in the Mevlevi lodge of Yenikapı. Many Mevlevi musicians were, therefore, themselves part of the chain of transmission of the repertoire of duraks, although these were basically performed in other Sufi orders.

Apparently, the durak and the na't were always considered as highly sophisticated and very prestigious forms of Sufi music. Writing in the 1950s and 1960s, for instance, Ekrem Karadeniz describes them as "the highest works of art in Turkish music". He also complains about the fact that there are very few good performers of the durak left. A beatiful voice and a good musical education, we are told by Karadeniz, are not sufficient conditions for performing the duraks correctly. The vocalist should also have learned well the special "Durak style"[5] (*durak tavrı*).

---

4 Ekrem Karadeniz, *Türk Musikisinin Nazariye ve Esasları*, (Istanbul: İş Bankası Yayınları, 1983), p. 166.

5 *Ibid.*, p. 166.

The na'ts and duraks were indeed perceived as having to be performed in a special style and manner, different from that which would apply to any other type of religious, Sufi or secular music. This style, as far as we can judge from existing sources and recordings, involved freely-flowing but nevertheless carefully balanced, slow and solemn singing. This singing could be so ponderous and heavy that it would, at times, be awkward to the point of being disregardful of some of the basic prosodic rules of the Turkish language.

This style of chanting is, in many sources, named *durak tavrı*. This particular Durak style was most probably transmitted, together with the repertoire of duraks itself, from one zakir or müezzin to another. The singing of the na'ts, it seems, required more or less the same style. There is, today, in Turkish musical circles, a general consensus as to the fact that Hâfız Kâni Karaca (born 1930) is the best performer of the various ametrical genres of Turkish Sufi music.

There certainly is some historical documentation showing that there was, in the second half of the nineteenth century a particular line (we wouldn't go so far as to say a school) of performers who were specialized in and famous for their rendering of the na'ts and of the duraks. Kâzım Uz (1872-1938) writes:

1308'de suzidil makamında bestelemeye çalıştığımız na't-ı Mevlanayı Zekâi Dede'ye arzettiğimde beni... Behlül Efendi'nin yanına götürüp na't ve durağın tavrını bu zattan öğren diyerek elini öptürdü.[6]

When, in 1308 (1893), I was trying to compose, in the makam Suzidil, a na't in honour of Mevlânâ and I presented it to Zekâi Dede...he took me to Behlül Efendi, made me kiss his hand and told me to learn the style of the na't and of the durak from him.

Behlül Efendi (c.1830 - 1895) was indeed one of the most famous performers of the durak of his time. Even a very important composer of liturgical and Sufi music such as Zekâi Dede (1824-1897), author of a large output of religious music and composer of a number of duraks himself, clearly recognizes the particularity of performing - and hence of composing - na'ts and duraks.

Another well-known zakir and singer of Sufi music of the second half of the nineteenth century was Hacı Nafiz Bey (1849-1898), who officiated as *zakirbaşı* in many Halvetî dervish lodges of Istanbul. He was so appreciated for his singing of the durak that he was nicknamed "Durakçı (singer of duraks) Nafiz bey". Nafiz bey had a number of pupils to whom he transmitted the whole of his repertoire of na'ts and duraks as well, presumably, as the particular style necessary for their rendering.

One of the better known of Nafiz Bey's pupils was Hoca Fehmi Efendi (d. 1938), the zakirbaşı of both a Halvetî-Şabanî and of a Sünbülî tekke in Istanbul. He, in turn, taught all or most of the duraks he knew to Dr. Subhi Ezgi and to Abdülkadir Töre (1873-1946). Both of these musicologists did transcriptions of these duraks. Abdülkadir Töre's notations, though only very few were ever effectively published, are reputed to have been more accurate.

As for Dr. Subhi Ezgi, he first published, in 1933 and 1935, a few of the duraks and na'ts in his five-volume work as examples of notation, to illustrate makams and 'usûls. Then, in 1946, he collected them in a small volume containing notations of thirty-nine duraks and of a small number of na'ts.[7] We shall return to it shortly.

---

6 İbnülemin Mahmud Kemal İnal, *Hoş Sada*, (Istanbul: Maarif Basımevi, 1958), p, 105. For Behlül Efendi, see also Sadettin Nüzhet Ergun, *op. cit.*, pp. 443-444.

7 Suphi Ezgi, *Türk Musikisi Klâsiklerinden Temcit-Na't-Salât-Durak*, (Istanbul: Istanbul Konservatuarı Neşriyatı, 1946).

Suphi Ezgi

Saadettin Arel

"The Taming of the Shrew"

As early as 1700 Demetrius Cantemir wrote in his treatise on music:

İlm-i musıkide cümlesinden lâzım olan ilm-i 'usûldür... usulsüz nağme mücerred musıki nağmesi değildir...'usûl musıkinin terazisi ve endazesidir.[8]
In the science of music, the science of rhythmic patterns is most indispensable...a melody without a rhythmic pattern is not music...the usuls are the scales and the proportions of music.

Ironically enough, Kantemiroğlu was a contemporary of the period which witnessed the birth of the non-metrical genres such as the na't and the durak. Besides, he had great respect for and spoke very highly of the *taksim* (improvisation) and clearly acknowledged its non-metrical structure It may also well be that Cantemir was, perhaps, mostly thinking in terms of instrumental and secular music. However that may be, there is no doubt that his theoretical work would have difficulty in admitting this type of an anomaly: music which was ametrical, had no usul, but was nevertheless entirely pre-composed and not at all improvised. This type of music would not fit anywhere in his system.

Kantemir, too, in his time, was a "systematist" and also a modernizer of sorts. In large portions of his treatise on Turkish music he stresses firmly the opposition between "les anciens" (*kavl-i kadîm*) and "les modernes" (*kavl-i cedid*), thereby giving himself the role of a musical reformer. On the question of the durak, however, Cantemir had a great advantage over Ezgi and Arel. Cantemir could easily afford, in the late seventeenth century, simply to ignore such newly emerging vocal genres as the na't and the durak.

---

8 Demetrius Cantemir (Kantemiroğlu), *Kitab-ı 'ilm-ül musıki 'alâ Vech-i Hurufat,* İstanbul Üniversitesi Türkiyat Enstitüsü Kütüphanesi, Manuscript [Y.2748], p. 78.

From the seventeenth to the twentieth century, however, the problem has basically remained the same: how can Turkish musical theory account for the non-metrical structure of some important religious/Sufi compositions? In other words, how can it accept the existence and the persistence of several religious/Sufi vocal genres whose rhythm does not conform to any of the established rhythmical cycles? Ezgi and Arel seem to have found a way out of the dilemma.

What they did, in reality, was simply to invent a tradition, or rather a small technical segment of a tradition, in order to fit their needs. Arel and Ezgi's enterprise in the rationalization and uniformization of traditional Turkish music was to suffer no exceptions and could, therefore, not tolerate such an important lacuna as the anomalous na'ts and duraks.

Therefore, the supposedly "inherent" but unfortunately "forgotten" rhythmic cycle of the durak had necessarily to be "rediscovered" by Dr. Ezgi - hence a new 'usûl called "Durak Evferi". If the new Arel-Ezgi system did not fit the music, then the music had to fit the new modern system. We shall now try to trace the path followed by this "technical modernization" process. In a sense, the whole attempt can be called a "taming of the shrew".

The invention of a "technical tradition" by Ezgi and Arel

The 'usûl Durak Evferi, first put forward by Ezgi in 1935, as having the following form, with eight basic weak and strong beats, and a total of twenty one time units:[9]

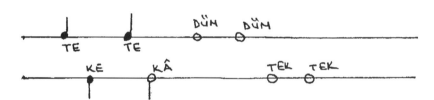

As defined by Ezgi, this Durak Evferi has a rather unusual structure. First of all, this new rhythmic pattern starts witk a a weak beat, a "tek". This is highly unusual because the beginning of a rhythmical cycle is normally marked with a strong beat, a "düm". Indeed, from among nearly a hundred 'usûls known and used in Ottoman/Turkish music, barely a couple start with a weak beat.

Secondly, Ezgi defines this 'usûl as a "compound [*mürekkep*] 'usûl", that is, as a longer rhythmical cycle made up of a succession of shorter and simpler usuls. This constitutes a parallel to Arel and Ezgi's new taxonomy of Turkish makams. Indeed, Arel and Ezgi classified all the modal entities of Ottoman/Turkish music as either "simple", "compound", or "transposed" *makams*.

According to Ezgi, the composition of the 21 time-unit Durak Evferi is 5 + 4 + 4 + 4 + 4, that is, a succession of five short 'usûls. The first 'usûl is a Türk Aksağı and has five time-units, and then we have four *sofyan*s, with four time-units each. The definition of a long and complex rhythmical pattern not as a particular, *sui generis*, arrangement of strong and weak beats of variable durations, but necessarily, as a succession, a chain, a fixed sequence of a number of shorter and simpler 'usûls is, again,

9 Dr. Suphi [Ezgi], *Nazarî ve Amelî Türk Musikisi*, (Istanbul: Istanbul Konservatuarı Neşriyatı, vol. II, 1935), p. 56 (where the *'usûl* is first exposed).

a novelty introduced by Arel and Ezgi. Arel and Ezgi systematically tried to decompose longer 'usûls into smaller constituent parts. Each of the longer 'usûls is then defined by them as a particular arrangement of the two- and three-time unit basic building blocks.

Thirdly, this 21 time-unit Durak Evferi has a beat-density which is unusually low. It has only a total of eight strong and weak beats, covering a duration of 21 time-units. The average duration of each of the beats is therefore quite long. By opposition, Fahte, another 'usûl of comparable length (twenty time-units) has no less than fourteen beats. Çenber, a slightly longer, 24 time-unit 'usûl, has a total of seventeen strong and weak beats. This low beat-density makes the Durak Evferi a very compliant and flexible 'usûl, if we may say so. This is so because fewer beats for a given tempo means greater adaptability of the rhythmic cycle to melodic structures of quite variable notational densities. This structural flexibility of the Durak Evferi greatly facilitates its adaptation to the repertoire of duraks.

Finally, Ezgi does not even try to explain why the durak notations of his have so many rests and "pointsd'orgue", which are sprinkled all over the pieces, thereby often interrupting the regular flow of the rhythmical pattern. Nor does the 'usûl durak Evferi account for the unmeasured syllable, "Ah" or "Dost", of variable duration, with which all the duraks invariably start.

The fitting of the duraks to a fixed rhythmical cycle took the form, for Arel and Ezgi, of a search for authenticity. Arel and Ezgi were looking for an 'usûl which really existed but which was, somehow, "lost and found". Their idea was that all of the duraks must necessarily have been composed with an 'usûl, but that this particular 'usûl had somehow been forgotten. The duraks were therefore to be subject to an operation of "restoration". No reason is given as to why it is that the 'usûl durak Evferi is, from among almost a hundred different rhythmic cycles, the only one which has, disappeared after the seventeenth century without leaving any trace.

The first question which must be answered is, therefore, whether Ezgi's search for the authentic and genuine rhythmical structure of the durak rested on sound historical and musical evidence.

About ten years before Suphi Ezgi started publishing his five-volume work on Turkish Music,[10] in 1922 Rauf Yekta's well known book-size article, "La Musique Turque", appeared in Lavignac's *Encyclopédie de la Musique*. In this first systematic study of the theory and practice of Ottoman/Turkish music,[11] by one of its foremost authorities, are carefully described no less than forty-five different rhythmic cycles, and all of them are illustrated with musical examples. Ezgi's Durak Evferi, however, is not to be found among them.

Neither is this 'usûl Durak Evferi (or anything approaching or having a resemblance to it, for that matter) to be found in any of the known seventeenth, eighteenth or nineteenth century Turkish manuscript or published sources.

Ali Ufkî (that is, Wojciech Bobowski), in one of his as yet unpublished manuscripts, probably dating from the 1640s, gives the strong and weak beat patterns of about thirty different usuls.[12] Writing about half a century later, Demetrius Kantemir, in his treatise on Turkish music, describes, with the help of the traditional circles used

10 Dr. Suphi [Ezgi], *Nazarî ve Amelî Türk Musikisi*, (Istanbul: Istanbul Konservatuarı Neşriyatı, 5 vols., (I/1933, II/1935, III/n.d., IV/1940, V/1953).

11 Rauf Yekta Bey "La Musique Turque", in A. Lavignac (ed.), *Encyclopédie de la Musique et Dictionnaire du Conservatoire*, vol. 5, (Paris: Delagrave, 1922), pp. 2945-3064.

12 Ali Ufki *Mecmua*, Paris, Bibliothèque Nationale de France, Manuscrits Orientaux [Turc 292], folios 51b, 103a, 121a, 131a, 136a, 136b, 149a, 149b and passim. Most of the Ottoman/Turkish authors, up to the early twentieth century, described the various *usûls* either by placing the succession

for explaining makams and their transpositions as well as the usuls, about twenty different rhythmic cycles.[13] Ezgi's Durak Evferi is not among them.

There are a number of eighteenth-century manuscript sources containing 'usûl descriptions. Hızır Ağa's manuscript, *Tefhim ül makamat fi'ttevlid ün nagamât* probably dating from the 1740s, gives a list of twenty five 'usûls.[14] A contemporary of Hızır Ağa, the Armenian tanbur-player Arutin, gives, in a treatise on music written in Armenian characters, a list of twenty eight different beat patterns.[15] Charles Fonton, a dragoman of the French Embassy, in his *Essai sur la Musique Orientale*, written in Istanbul and dated 1751, lists the beat patterns of no less than thirty different 'usûls.[16] Towards the end of the eighteenth century, Abdülbaki Nasır Dede, a Mevlevi sheikh and a protégé of Sultan Selim III, in his *Tedkik ve Tahkik* dating from 1794, describes twenty-one different 'usûls.[17]

None of these seventeenth and eighteenth-century basic manuscript sources mention any 'usûl named Evfer other than the well known 'usûl in 9/4 or 9/8 often used in Mevlevi music. Not only is no trace to be found of Ezgi's Durak Evferi, but none of these sources even mention any other usul having twenty-one time-units.

A perusal of the nineteenth century's important printed sources is not more productive of any Durak Evferi. The first printed song - text collection of Turkish music - in Arabic characters, for "Karamanlı" publications using Greek characters predate these by about a quarter of a century - is Haşim Bey's *Mecmua*, published twice, in 1855 and 1864. It contains descriptive figures of thirty-five 'usûls. Durak Evferi is not among them. Bolahenk Nuri Bey (1834-1910), one of the famous music teachers of his time, published in 1873 a song-text collection. This "Mecmua" lists, in its introductory section, thirty-two 'usûls, among which Durak Evferi is not to be seen. Another well-known Mecmua, Şeyh Edhem Efendi's collection of lyrics, is named "Bergüzar-ı Edhem" and was published in 1890. It lists only fifteen 'usûls but, again, there is in it no sign of Durak Evferi.

Ahmet Avni bey (1871-1938), scholar, musician and composer, published in 1899 a song-text collection named *Hanende*. This is, perhaps, the most famous printed song-text collection of the whole nineteenth century. This thick 600-page volume is still much appreciated for its supposed exhaustivity and for its very systematic listing of the various types of lyrics. It is often considered as a sort of catalogue of the late nineteenth century repertoire. Besides, Ahmet Avni bey was Dr. Ezgi's close friend, his colleague, and life-long music companion. *Hanende* contains, in its introductory sec-

---

of beats within circles (hence the name Edvar given to their works) or by just giving a flat listing of strong and weak beats (*Düm*s and *Tek*s) for each *usûl*. Ali Ufki is indeed a very notable exception in this matter. For him, rhythmical beats are represented by notes of various durations. Ali Ufki represents each *usûl* by placing notes of various durations on a horizontal line. The duration of the notes correspond to the duration of the beats. The tails of the notes are turned up or down according to whether they represent a strong or a weak beat. The names of each of the beats appear below the line and the total number of time units of the usûl is put to the left of the same line.

13 Demetrius Cantemir (Kantemiroğlu), *op.cit.*, pp. 80-86.

14 Hızır Ağa, *Tefhim ül makamat fi'ttevlid ün nagamât*, Paris, B.N.F., Manuscrits Orientaux [Supplément Turc 1495], folios 25b-27a.

15 Tanburist Arutin, *Rukovodstvo po Vostochnoi Muzika*, N. Tahmizian (ed.), (Yerevan: 1968).

16 Charles Fonton, *Essay sur la Musique Orientale comparée à la Musique Européenne* (1751), Paris, B.N.F., Manuscrits Français, [Nouvelles Acquisitions 4023]. For a modern edition of this important manuscript see Eckhard Neubauer "Der Essai sur la Musique Orientale von Charles Fonton mit Zeichnungen von Adanson", *Zeitschrift für Geschichte des Arabisch-Islamischen Wissenschaften*, vol. 2 (1985), pp. 277-324 and vol. 3 (1986), pp. 335-376. For an introduction to and Turkish translation of Charles Fonton's manuscript see, Cem Behar, *Onsekizinci Yüzyılda Türk Müziği*, (Istanbul: Pan Yayıncılık, 1987).

17 Abdülbaki Nasır Dede, *Tedkik ve Tahkik*, Istanbul, Süleymaniye Library, Nafiz Paşa Manuscripts [1242/1].

tion, the description of no less than thirty-seven different 'usûls. But nowhere is Dr. Ezgi's Durak Evferi to be seen. Neither is it to be found in any other late nineteenth and early twentieth century published source on Ottoman/Turkish music.

A contemporary of Suphi Ezgi, the composer and music teacher Kâzım Uz (1872-1938), published in 1893 a small Dictionary of Turkish Musical Terms (*Musıki Istılahatı*), the first of its kind. Among a total of five hundred and thirty entries of this Dictionary are thirty-nine different 'usûls. Durak Evferi is not one of them.

We are left with no possible alternative but to conclude that Dr. Ezgi has, when writing the first volume of his book in the early 1930s, simply created, made up, invented a new 'usûl to suit his needs.[18] Besides, Doctor Ezgi's Durak Evferi apparently bears no resemblance to any of the usuls listed in any of the basic eighteenth and nineteenth sources we have covered. There is no way we can say, therefore, that this 'usûl might have been born as a derivative of or have evolved as a variant of a pre-existing beat pattern.

Ezgi simply created an *ad hoc* 'usûl, to account for the unexplainably irregular rhythmical structure of the durak. This new 'usûl he conveniently named durak Evferi. The name creates a parallelism to the 'usûl Evfer, sometimes also called Mevlevî Evferi, of canonical use in some crucial parts of the Mevlevi musical ritual.[19] This new rhythmic cycle was to fit the repertoire of existing pieces, and Dr. Ezgi started to publish the notations in 1933. The few duraks published by Abdülkadir Töre, who learned them from the same teacher as Dr. Ezgi (Fehmi Efendi), were, however, notated as having no 'usûl.

Suphi Ezgi then published in 1946 a small volume containing notations of thirty-nine duraks, plus six na'ts, a *temcit* and a few other liturgical pieces.[20] This is the first and, to the present day, the only publication devoted to the duraks. There has been,

---

18 We can not totally exclude the possibility that some of the duraks composed in the seventeenth or eighteenth century might initially have had an usûl. What is to us absolutely certain, however, is that there is no way that this old usûl could have been the Durak Evferi, as it is defined by Ezgi. Dr. Ezgi himself tells us that one of the Duraks that were orally transmitted to him by Hüseyin Fahreddin Dede had an usûl ("Dilkeşhâveran makamında yegâne usullü Durak"). He does not, however, tell us what that original usûl was, and goes on by transcribing that Durak as if it had originally been composed with his newly invented Durak Evferi (Ezgi, *op. cit.*, vol.I, p. 163).

19 Kantemiroğlu tells us that the relative durations of the beats of some of the usûls were not, in his time, as strictly defined and inflexible as they are nowadays usually considered to be. Some of the usûls were, it seems, rather flexible. The three more malleable usûl were, according to him, Türkî Zarb, Evfer and Devr-i Revan. Here is what Kantemir writes : "Agâh ol ki Türkî Zarb usulün ikinci dümü... hanendelerin şartında vezne bend olmaz, öyle ki murad eylediği kadar uzatmağa ruhsatı vardır. Buna göre Evfer usulin ikinci dümü ve sonrası tek hanendelerde nâmevzun olabilir, öyle ki istendiği kadar uzun ider. Buna göre Devr-i Revan usulin dümleri hanendelerde câ-be-câ nâmevzun olabilir; lâkin sazendeye böyle olmaz zira Pişrevin şartı oldur ki name hatırı için vezn-i usûlü bozmaya." (Kantemir, *Edvâr*, pp. 85-86). These three usuls (Türkî Zarb, Evfer and Devr-i Revan) were used, according to Kantemir again, only for vocal pieces, and seem to have been, at that time, pretty changeable and open to interpretative variations. But this, of course, is rather inconclusive evidence as to the later evolution of these rhythmical patterns or as to their eventual relationship to Ezgi's Durak Evferi. What is noteworthy is that Kâzım Uz, two centuries after Cantemir, in the entry "Durak" of his *Dictionary of Musical Terms*, defines the genre as: "A hymn (ilâhi) sung by one person and composed with the usûls Evfer or Türkî Zarb". See, A. Kâzım [Uz], *Musıki Istılahatı*, (Istanbul: Matbaa-yı Ebüzziya, 1310[1893]), p. 25. (New and enlarged edition by Gültekin Oransay, Ankara, 1964, p. 20).

20 *Türk Musıkisi Klâsiklerinden Temcit-Na't-Salât-Durak*, (Istanbul: Istanbul Konservatuarı Neşriyatı, 1946). In this volume, Ezgi put five of the six Na'ts he notated to the usûl Durak Evferi, while the sixth, Itrî's Na't-ı Mevlânâ, is written in the usûl Türkî Zarb. Ezgi also adapted a few other well known liturgical pieces (salât, tekbir, mersiye) to the same usûl. Ezgi's Türkî Zarb has little connection with its eighteenth century namesake. Besides, using Ezgi's notations in order to scrutinize more closely the structure of the Durak would, for obvious reasons, be tautological. Transcriptions and notations by other musicians or scholars have to be used in a comparative perspective. Especially the Abdülkadir Töre collection of notations, now in the Süleymaniye Library in Istanbul, should be carefully scrutinized.

unfortunately, no other publication of any significance, whether analytical or simply of notations, on the topic of the durak since then.

Ezgi's 1946 volume of duraks seems to have had an electrifying effect on Hüseyin Sadettin Arel, the other "modernizer" of traditional Ottoman/Turkish music. Indeed, after the "real" *'usûl* of the durak was "rediscovered" by Ezgi and the durak and na't notations published in 1946, Arel, who had not composed a single durak until then, put himself to work and, within two years, from 1947 to 1949, produced no less than eighty duraks.[21] Needless to say, all of them had Ezgi's Durak Evferi as their rhythmic pattern.

The invention of this 'usûl met with no real resistance or opposition. With the generalization of the Arel-Ezgi pitch system and notational conventions of Turkish music, the 'usûl Durak Evferi became part of the accepted stock of rhythmical cycles. Its existence and "authenticity" were never seriously challenged, except by one musicologist, Ekrem Karadeniz.[22] Karadeniz' book, however, although written much earlier, was published only in 1983 and has not yet been successful in providing an overall and systematic alternative to the Arel-Ezgi system.

The general Arel-Ezgi setup was, from the 1970s on, adopted as the main pedagogical instrument in the Conservatories of traditional Turkish music. These Conservatories were founded thanks to the political initiatives of some of Arel's followers and students, who were also appointed as directors or members of the teaching staff of these institutions. This seems to have sealed the fate of the objections to the acceptance of Durak Evferi as the standard *'usûl* for the duraks. All subsequent Turkish publications list it as one of the well known and "age-old" 'usûls.[23]

The "Restoration" Project

How does Ezgi explain his enterprise of the "restoration" of the duraks? What justification does he have for it ? What are the arguments?

As a matter of fact, nowhere do either Arel or Ezgi provide any significant historical or musicological argument, or even any sort of supporting evidence, in favor of the treatment they chose to inflict on the durak.

As for the rediscovery of the 'usûl Durak Evferi, Ezgi and Arel obviously never had a good historical case for it. What Ezgi writes about the "restoration" of the durak is rather thin and clearly imbued with a good amount of self-righteousness. Here is what Ezgi wrote in 1935:

---

21 See Yılmaz Öztuna, *Hüseyin Sadettin Arel*, (Ankara: Kültür ve Turizm Bakanlığı Yayınları, 1986), pp. 107-114.

22 See, Ekrem Karadeniz, *Türk Musikisinin Nazariye ve Esasları*, (Istanbul: İş Bankası Yayınları, 1983), particularly pp. 44, 166, 222-223 and 710. Karadeniz adopts a middle of the road position in the matter of the rhythmic cycle of the Durak. He does not challenge the existence of Ezgi's Durak Evferi and says that new Duraks might eventually be composed using this usûl. But he strongly opposes the idea that the existing stock of Duraks were composed with the help of this usûl and heavily insists on their having no regular rhythmic pattern at all. His argumentation is, however, not well documented, as well as rather inconsistent and in general pretty unconvincing.

23 See, for instance, M. Hurşit Ungay, *Türk Musikisinde Usuller ve Kudüm*, (Istanbul: 1981); İsmail Hakkı Özkan, *Türk Musikisi Nazariyatı ve Usulleri*, (Istanbul: Ötüken Neşriyat, 1984); Vural Sözer, *Müzik ve Müzisyenler Ansiklopedisi*, (Istanbul: Remzi Kitabevi, 1986); Zekâi Kaplan, *Dinî Musıki*, (Istanbul: Milli Eğitim Bakanlığı Yayınları, 1991); M. Nazmi Özalp, *Türk Musıkisi Beste Formları*, (Ankara: TRT Basım ve Yayın Müdürlüğü Yayınları, 1992); Şeref Çakar, *Türk Musıkisinde Usul*, (Istanbul: Milli Eğitim Bakanlığı Yayınları, 1996). Some composers have continued, nevertheless, to compose Duraks which have no usûl. Çinuçen Tanrıkorur (1938-), for instance, composed in 1984 a Durak "in the old style" in the makam Bestenigâr.

Durak Evferi usulü tahminen yüz seneden beri unutulmuş... Durak ve na'tler tenbel ve cahil müezzin ve zakirler tarafından usulün zamanları birçok parçalara ayrılmak suretiyle adeta musıki hokkabazlığı yapılarak taksim gibi okunmuş idi... işte bunları usule sokmaya ve asıllarına ircaa H. Sadettin Beyle çalıştık ve muvaffak olduk... yurdumuz evlatlarına bu güzel ölçüyü kazandırdığımızdan dolayı bahtiyarız.[24]*

The usul Durak Evferi had been forgotten for about a century...the ignorant and lazy zakirs and müezzins had split the beats of the usul into many parts and, with a sort of musical sleight of hand, had performed them as if they were improvisations... H.Sadettin Bey and I tried to to put them back into an usul and to restore them to their original condition and we succeeded...we are happy to make a present of this beautiful measure to our country's children

Elsewhere, Ezgi uses almost the same expressions to justify his enterprise of restoration.

...bu eserlerin usulü unutulmuş ve cahil zakir ve müezzinler tarafından motifleri bozulmuş ve başka kötü motifler katılarak taksim gibi okunagelmişti."[25]

..the 'usûls of these works had been forgotten and the ignorant zakirs and müezzins had spoiled their melodies and added unbecoming motifs and had performed them as if they were improvisations.

Why was the "authentic" 'usûl of the durak forgotten? Why were their melodies now 'unbecoming'? Because, we are told by Ezgi, the old, primitive, pitifully traditional, backward, ignorant and, worst of all, Ottoman zakirs were unfortunately strictly instinctive and irrational transmitters of a repertoire of duraks. The rationality and the logic of this repertoire, they did not master. For Ezgi, these zakirs and müezzins were just unconscious carriers of a musical tradition with which they had no cognitive relationship of any sort. They were also faithless, because they "spoiled" the melodies during performance and transmission. These traditional musicians just memorized vast quantities of musical pieces, without ever being able to reach a solid comprehension of their significance and structure.

Ezgi stops short, but barely, of openly accusing the zakirs and müezzins of being totally unaware of the new science of Turkish music, which, in reality, he himself set out to construct. The ignorant zakirs did not know the principles of the new science of music, its taxonomy, its logic or its modes of reckoning and classifying various musical artifacts. All too clearly, an operation of "restoration" was then needed to free the durak from the grip of centuries of "ignorant and lazy" performers.

How was the durak to be restored to its original condition? What method was to be followed? What justification is given by Ezgi for the kind of restoration he precisely chose to implement?

None at all, in reality. "Restoration to its original condition" (*asıllarına irca*) is a key idea for Ezgi and Arel. Almost all the notations published by Suphi Ezgi in his five-volume work are in fact "restorations" of his own making. Rediscovering the age-old but hidden internal logic, rationality and consistency of Turkish music became sometimes an obsession for him. It is clear, however, that both Arel and Ezgi lacked historical evidence as well as analytical tools and methods. Here is how Ezgi explains and justifies the method he has followed in his enterprise of "restoration" of the duraks:

---

24 Dr. Suphi [Ezgi], *Nazarî, Amelî Türk Musıkisi*, Istanbul, Istanbul Konservatuarı Neşriyatı, vol. II, 1935), p. 63.

25 Suphi Ezgi, *Türk Musıkisi Klâsiklerinden Temcit-Na't-Salât-Durak,* (Istanbul: Istanbul Konservatuarı Neşriyatı, 1946, p. 3.

Usulleri unutulmuş veya lahinlerinin motifleri pek bozulmuş eserlerin asıllarını bulmak merakı onyedi yaşımdan beri bana hakim olduğundan o bozuk eserleri asıllarına irca etmek hususunda elli seneyi mütecaviz çalışmalarım bende o eserleri asıllarına irca edilmiş bir halde tamire ilmî ve san'atî bir kudret ve meleke hasıl etti.[26]

Ever since I was seventeen years old I have been curious about the originals of works whose usuls were forgotten and whose melodies had been spoiled. I have been working on this for more than fifty years and have developed an ability, an artistic and scientific expertise in repairing these works and restoring them to their original condition.

or,

Bu mesai sayesinde bozuk olan eserleri tanımakta benim için bir ilim ve sühulet hasıl oldu.[27]

Thanks to my hard work, I acquired the science and the ease for recognizing these spoiled works.

No other explanation or justification is ever given either by Ezgi or by Arel. Ezgi's personal musical experience, his common sense and intuition is simply raised to the status of a universal, modern, Kantian *Vernunft*. Arel and Ezgi, these two self-appointed technical modernizers of Ottoman/Turkish music, set out, first and foremost, to put order into the house, i.e. to write down, preserve and transmit traditional Ottoman/Turkish music by reformulating it as a self-contained system. This system was to be natural, logical, exhaustive and totalizing. The type of musical positivism which their views imply and the details of its implementation are, however, beyond the scope of this paper.

At all events, the canon according to which every single composition of Turkish music must have a makam and an *'usûl* could suffer no exception. Formal laxity and anarchy as well as rhythmical looseness - relics and symbols of a past age - had to be eliminated at all costs.

26-27 *Ibid*, p. 3. For a more analytical and solid attempt at reaching the "originals" of some seventeenth century instrumental compositions, see Owen Wright "Aspects of Historical Change in the Turkish Classical Repertoire", in Richard Widdess(ed.) *Musica Asiatica-5*, (Cambridge: Cambridge University Press, 1988), pp. 1-108.

An Inner History of "Turkish Music Revolution" – Demise of a Music Magazine

ORHAN TEKELİOĞLU

The founding years of the Turkish Republic were marked by a series of fundamental innovations within the sphere of culture. Referred to as "revolutions" (*devrimler*) by the state elite, these changes were designed to bring about the rapid transformation of existing society along the lines of an incipient but yet imprecise notion of "national identity". What was most characteristic of this attempt at transformation was its "state-directedness", originating from within the state apparatus and not from within the society itself. Moreover, it was iconoclastic in force since what was being attempted was the destruction of old symbols and their replacement with others carrying new meaning. One of the most striking of these cultural reforms was the replacement of the Arabic alphabet with the Latin one in the writing of the Turkish language. As a result, within a very brief period of time (no more than six months), the literate people of the new republic became illiterate. Other reforms had a deep impact on the everyday life of the masses. They included changes in attire (including the adoption of the hat), which were designed to remove public distinctions of class, profession, and religious status among the people, the adoption of a new calendar, and a new system of weights and measures, the latter two designed to conform to international standards. The reforms that perhaps had the greatest direct impact on the people were those having to do with religious law and practices: in 1926, the formal Islamic code of law was replaced by a laic Western civil code; a parallel measure against folk Islam had already been taken with the abolition in 1925 of the *tekke*s and *zaviye*s (lodges) of the dervish orders, which had had quite an influence over the masses.

The culmination of all of these reforms was in 1929 with the introduction of National Schools, the intent of which was to inculcate the new nationalistic and pro-Western socio-cultural identity. The curriculum of the new schools was designed to reinforce reforms that had already been introduced by employing the new script, emphasizing principles of secularism, and expanding upon the cultural values introduced in those reforms. It was believed that the political values of the new-born nation had to be disseminated to the fledgling generation. With this in mind, the principles underlying the newly developing national system of education, which included adult education as well, would encompass those emphazing modernization, as professed by Mustafa Kemal and his cadre. The reforms were quick to have an impact, with the literacy rate rising from about 8 per cent in 1928 to over 20 per cent in 1935. In addition to the formal education provided to school children by the National Schools, the People's Houses (*Halkevleri*) provided free education to adults - not only in the area of reading and writing, for the illiterate, but also practically-oriented programs for people having different interests and avocations.

Towards Reforms in Turkish Music

This article will focus on the politico-cultural developments (e.g., certain musical events, structural reforms, ideas) originating in the early years of the republic and continuing up to the 1940s, that paved the way for reforms in the sphere of music. The first indications of the musical reforms that were to ensue can be detected in the notion of "imposed synthesis" expounded by the leading ideologist of his day, Ziya Gökalp.[1]

Gökalp's well-known book, "Principles of Turkism" (1923), provided the ideological foundations for the Republican-imposed synthesis, and to a certain extent, constituted itself as a manual, laying out how, in his words, the fusion of its origins with those of the West was to be executed. Gökalp considered the eventual success of the new nation-state and Turkish nationalism to be inextricably linked to the development of "Turkish Civilization", which, he argued, must advance at all costs. With regard to the issue of music, he spoke of how Turkish music could become national and actually outlined a program for its future development. Gökalp maintained that the music of the elites during the pre-Republican era, while representing the pinnacle of what Ottoman culture had achieved in terms of music, was essentially Byzantine, which he called, "Eastern". To reinforce his point, he referred to ancient Greek music, which, because it is based on quarter tones and tended to repeat "the same melody over and over", he found "artificial" and "depressingly monotonous". In contrast, argued Gökalp, the musical reforms that occurred during the Middle Ages in Europe had gone far to overcome the mistakes of Greek music, with opera going even further, giving rise to the "civilized" Western music known today. On the other hand, the Eastern music that emerged from ancient Greek models, and that had been played for centuries in the Ottoman lands, continued in its "ill" state. The only "healthy" music in Anatolia was Folk music, which was enjoyed by the Turkish masses. Thus, Gökalp divided music into three classes: Eastern music, Western music, and Folk music. Only if "our national culture" welds with "our new civilization [the West]", emphasized Gökalp, can one speak of a "national music". In other words, the problem and its solution were defined as follows: Ottoman (i.e., Eastern) music was to be disregarded; Folk music was to be the primary source of the new music; and the musical reformation was to be based upon Western music and its harmonic scale - the overall goal being the creation of a new national music.

The reform-oriented attempts to reach this goal, on the other hand, reflect an astonishing lack of sophistication, possibly influenced by a naive positivism: Folk tunes were to be collected, categorized, re-worked according to methods of Western music, and finally made polyphonic. As pointed out by many scholars in the field, the model for the synthesis considered by both Gökalp and Mustafa Kemal was inspired by experiences in Russia, where a group of composers known as "The Russian Five" had followed such a path to achieve a "national synthesis" in music in the nineteenth century.[2]

The new policies directed toward establishing a new form of music based on a West-East synthesis began to bear fruit in 1924, one year after the establishment of the Turkish Republic. The Palace Symphony Orchestra (*Saray Senfoni Orkestrası*), the only institution of music where polyphonic music had been performed in the

---

1 For the notions of 'spontaneous synthesis' and 'imposed synthesis', see Orhan Tekelioğlu "The Rise of a Spontaneous Synthesis: The Historical Background of Turkish Popular Music", *Middle Eastern Studies*, 32/2, (April 1996), 194-216.

2 M. Belge, et al, *Atatürk Devrimleri İdeolojisinin Türk Müzik Kültürüne Doğrudan ve Dolaylı Etkileri* (Direct and Indirect Impact of the Ideology of Atatürk's Reforms on the Turkish Musical Culture), (Istanbul: Boğaziçi Üniversitesi Türk Müziği Klübü Yayınları, 1980), pp.34 and p.48.

Turkish Art Music Choir and Orchestra.

Ottoman era, was abolished in April. The new orchestra set up in its place was named the Presidential Orchestra (*Riyaset-i Cumhur Orkestrası*). Moreover, the training institute of the former orchestra, the Palace Military Band (*Saray Mızıkası*) [which was another vestige from the Ottoman period, comprised of musicians educated in the Palace Military Band School (*Saray Mızıka Mektebi*)], was closed down and reopened in September of the same year under the name "School for Music Teachers" (*Musiki Muallimleri Mektebi*). These changes were not simply cosmetic, but were in fact the early yet pervasive signs of the sensitivity of the political elite to the state of music existing at that time. There were other indications of this sensitivity. In 1926, the Oriental Music Section (*Şark Musikisi Şubesi*) of the *Dârü'l-Elhan*, an institution remaining from the late Ottoman days and the only public educational institution having functions similar to those of Western conservatories, was closed down.[3] The impact of this decision was reinforced by a ban imposed on monophonic music education (e.g., Turkish music having its roots in the Ottoman period) in both public and private schools in 1927.

The enactment of the law abolishing the *tekke*s and *zaviye*s in 1926 dealt a serious blow to one of the most important cultural components of the tekkes: the music used during the performance of religious rituals there. This essentially politically motivated decision paved the way for a cultural vacuum to form within the practice of what was referred to as "tekke music". More importantly, it deprived many talented *tekke* musicians of their livelihood. Especially after the 1930s, in Istanbul and other major urban centers of the young republic, some of the talented musicians from the religious tradition began to secularize their music and popularize (e.g., commercialize) their work to earn a living. In fact, they came to create a new genre, a new taste in popular music, which, in practice came to serve as a major obstacle to the Republican elite's efforts to create a West-East synthesis.[4]

Meanwhile, in the challenge of the institutions and values of the former Ottoman regime and those of its possible supporters, intense public debate ensued over the inseparable components of the politico-cultural West-East synthesis being forged:

---

3 G. Oransay, *Atatürk ile Küğ* (Atatürk and Music), (Izmir: Küğ Yayını, 1985), p.112.

4 For the conceptual difference between the 'West-East' and 'East-West' syntheses, see Orhan Tekelioğlu "The Rise of a Spontaneous Synthesis: The Historical Background of Turkish Popular Music", *Middle Eastern Studies*, 32/2, (April 1996), 194-216.

The Presidential Symphony Orchestra.

the notions of West and East. Throughout 1927 there appeared in newspapers fiery debates waged by the prominent pro-government columnists of the day who fiercely attacked the "Eastern", e.g., the "obsolete" character of the Ottoman political system.

It was in 1928 that Mustafa Kemal made his first public assessment of Turkish music. After listening to a concert where two groups - one performing Turkish music and the other "Western"- in succession, he asserted: "This music, this unsophisticated music, cannot possibly fulfill the needs of the innovative Turkish soul, the Turkish sensibility, in its yearning to explore new paths. We have just heard music of the civilized world, upon which the audience, who, in contrast to its rather anemic reaction to the whimpering known as Eastern music, immediately came to life ... Turks are, indeed, naturally vivacious and high-spirited; if these admirable traits were for a time not perceived, it was not their fault."[5] Mustafa Kemal here blamed the Ottoman intellectuals for their lack of awareness of the Turkish "character" and accused them of coercing Turks into listening to a soporific music that ran contrary to their spirit.

Throughout the period 1924-1929 there was an orchestrated ideological attempt to create a political system based on pro-Western principles. This was particularly so with respect to the so-called "music revolution", which was personally inaugurated by Mustafa Kemal. His assessment quoted above became its *Leitmotif*. From the beginning of the late 1930s, the State initiated a number of coordinated cultural policies in the field of music:

> – Formal education in Western polyphonic music began in the conservatories, which were modeled on Western schools of music. Foreign instructors were hired while some gifted students were sent abroad for training.
> – Symphony orchestras began giving free concerts in various parts of the country. Both serious and popular works of Western polyphonic music were regularly broadcast on the radio.
> – Courses in music were offered to the public free of charge in the People's Houses, where both polyphonic music and standardized monophonic folk tunes were played.

5 G. Oransay, *Atatürk ile Küğ* (Atatürk and Music), (Izmir: Küg Yayını, 1985), p. 24.

A sample of *Nota* (May 1933).

    – At "State Balls" (music and dance nights organized by the public servants of the urban centers), examples of Western dance music were selected from such forms as waltzes and tangos.

    – In the schools, although there was little in the way of teaching the actual playing of instruments, a fairly extensive coverage of Western musical history and its composers was included in the curriculum.

The Turkish audience, however, on a large scale, showed little interest either in the polyphonic music being composed by Turks or in the Western classical music that was being played. Instead, as a number of scholars have indicated,[6] the people of the big

---

6 M. Stokes, *The Arabesk Debate. Music and Musicians in Modern Turkey,* (New York: Oxford University Press, 1992), p. 93, and also see, N. Güngör, *Arabesk: Sosyokültürel Açıdan Arabesk Müzik* (Arabesque: A Sociocultural View at Arabesque Music), (Ankara: Bilgi Yayınları, 1990), p. 55.

cities began to enjoy the popular songs composed and played by the former *tekke* musicians or tuned into Arab radio stations broadcasting Arab music. This happened because of a lack of consideration on the part of the "cultural elite" toward any harmonic form of music that a broad segment of society could enjoy and identify with.

A Music Magazine Straddling Cultural Policies

This chapter aims at defining the role of a unique though short-lived magazine, *Nota*, in the 1930s - a period characterized by attempts at Westernization and consolidation of the young republic. The first issue of *Nota* was published on 5 April, 1930. According to its first editorial, it was a magazine specializing in the publication of the scores of the popular tunes of the day. The editor of the magazine, Mildan Niyazi Ayomak (1887-1947), was a music teacher and a composer of pieces in the Ottoman Classical Music genre. Mildan Niyazi had been a political activist during the Ottoman period and had, therefore, been sent into exile in Egypt, then under Ottoman control, where he was exposed to Arab and Middle Eastern flavor in music. After his many years of exile, he moved back to Izmir, the second largest urban center in the Ottoman Empire, and founded a school of music - the *İzmir Musiki Mektebi* (Music School of Izmir) in 1920. Because of the aforementioned ban placed on Turkish music education in 1927, his school had lost is *raison d'étre* and had to completely revise its curriculum and desist from teaching music. The school was reopened with a few students under the name School of Life Knowledge (*Hayat Bilgisi Mektebi*), and continued, with less success, its program in adult education up until 1932. After the closing of the school, Mildan Niyazi moved to Istanbul, where he founded an association called the *İstanbul Musiki Birliği* (Music Association of Istanbul). It was intended for professional musicians coming from the Ottoman genre of music. One of the association's projects was the publication of *Nota*. A short time after *Nota* was closed down, the association also dissolved (in 1935).

The lifespan of the magazine was a short one, ending in 1934 after the publication of its 37th issue. While it is undoubtedly possible to attribute this to poor sales figures or the personal consideration of the editor, if one examines closely the editorials, content, discussions, and score-publishing policies of the magazine, other clues emerge that do a better job at accounting for its closure. I would argue that the closing of *Nota* has less to do with economic or personal considerations than with political ones.

Nota's Idea of Synthesis

The first issue of the magazine established its position in the daily debates on musical reforms. It is clear from the motto of the magazine that *Nota* had its own notion of what synthesis meant: "While defending our personality, we should *gradually* (emphasis added) move toward the New Music." This idea of gradual development in new music was, in fact, a response to the revolutionary idea of abrupt change, which was espoused by the cultural elite in their efforts to shape a new kind of music. In the first editorial, entitled "Why We Publish", Mildan Niyazi defines the situation of music in Turkey in rather realistic terms and portrayed the economic and social conditions of musicians and composers of the Ottoman classical music tradition, most of which, as explained earlier, were from the *tekke* tradition:

> What has become the fundamental aim of contemporary music is not expertise but rather profit. Due to the shortage of trained musicians, worthless tunes are becoming

popular and are being sold throughout the country, thereby debasing the level of music appreciation to very low levels... We should thoroughly determine the route through which our music can be revived ... It must be perceived as a whole... The Alaturka [Ottoman Classical Music] cannot be transformed into Alafranga [Western music]. This is because their essentials and sounds are totally different. We cannot simply adopt Western music as it is. If we do so, then we would not be able to call it "our" music. We should preserve and accept the music that we have in our hand, as it is formed, within its own universe, and with its own instruments (*nay* and *tanbur*). To touch our own music is comparable to murder. In order to create our own international music, we should work on our own melodies, our tunes, and the way in which they are put together, and then polyphonize them [according to the rules of Western harmonic music]; this is indeed the greatest ideal of our magazine.[7]

The latter part of the quote is particularly significant. It is here that Ziya Gökalp's notion of synthesis, which takes the Anatolian folk tunes into account as the main source of that synthesis, is directly challenged. The notion of "our music" is now replaced with "Alaturka", another name for Ottoman music, and "touching" it is claimed to be comparable to "murder". After using such harsh expressions, the editorial offers a reconciliation with Western polyphony in the new Turkish music. It is suggested that the new Turkish music should be based upon the tunes of urban Ottoman music rather than on those of a fictive folk music of the countryside. Here, the term "fictive" is deliberately chosen, simply because of the fact that folk music virtually did not exist in the Ottoman urban centers. The literate musicians and composers of the day had learned, practiced, and performed music in an urban setting. This is possibly why the magazine praises Eastern music - which is considered by Gökalp as a sign of backwardness - as "our music" and has a positive view about it.

In any case, the editorial is bitter in tone and is representative of the general attitude the magazine takes toward the state of affairs confronting musicians of the Ottoman music genre. It is easy to comprehend the enormous difficulties facing them. In a similar vein, the following excerpt from the news article entitled, "We Have Also Lost Kaptanzade", about the death of a famous composer within the genre of Ottoman music, is also instructive:

In the 20 February issue of Cumhuriyet [the influential and pro-government daily newspaper of the time], on one of the back pages, it was reported under the heading "Karagöz Lovers' Society", that the chairman of the society, the composer Kaptanzade Ali Riza Bey, had passed away while on a visit to Balıkesir [a small city close to Istanbul] to perform in concerts. The report also listed the possible candidates for the post of chairman. That is to say, we would not have known about this sad event if the society had not existed or if the deceased had not been its chairman. We should never forget that we once learned from a short and awkward sentence written in one of the newspapers, about the death of Tanburi Tahsin Bey [a well-known player of the *tanbur*] as the death of the head of a cavalry regiment and painter.

Poor musicians of this country! They work, they wear themselves out because of the atrocities and miseries of this life and eventually, without disturbing anyone else's life, without hurting anyone, say farewell. Ironically, the only "reward" they receive, whether dead or alive, is a bare expression of grief from an insensitive milieu.[8]

---

7 *Nota*, 1, (5 April 1933), 2.
8 *Nota*, 22, (1 March 1934), 101.

This quote, particularly the latter part, is particularly emotive in language, portraying as it does the cessation of respect for the classical musician in the new "insensitive milieu". Beyond the emotional aspect of this assessment, it becomes apparent that the musical reforms and related efforts in this direction in the 1930s were inevitably changing the public image of the musicians coming from the Ottoman tradition. It must have been these efforts, as well as the cultural situation ("the new insensitive milieu") that made the magazine one of the targets of the pro-Western cultural elite of the day. In time, the fighting spirit of the early editorials faded away and was, especially after the 11th issue, gradually replaced with a new, notably more defensive tone. This shift in editorial tone can in part be interpreted as a response to the attention this magazine had begun to receive from the cultural elite, as well as the pressure it experienced due to its publication policy.

A defensive editorial about the reforms designed to establish a new musical genre, written personally by Mildan Niyazi in 1933, is interesting in this respect:

> [W]e cannot imagine anyone who could reject a need for clearance, reform and revolution in our music ... We think that only with these measures [reforms], can our music take off its *şalvar* [baggy trousers of the people in the countryside in the Ottoman age] and *fes* [a popular form of hat from the Ottoman era], and put on its [Western] trousers and hat.[9]

The defensive tone is quite clear here: Mildan Niyazi understood that he had no power to halt the pro-Western reforms being made in music, and thus no longer dared to speak of "touching" Ottoman music as being comparable to "murder". He was, in a way, compelled to accept half-heartedly the need for "revolution" and followed the daily jargon about the backwardness of the Ottoman age, symbolized by the *şalvar* and *fes*, and the "forwardness" of the Western culture, symbolized by the hat and trousers.

Nevertheless, the problems and criticisms of the magazine seemed to continue, with new editorials adopting an even more defensive tone. The editorial of the 25th issue nearly acknowledged the "discontent" of the pro-Western cultural elite with the publication policy of *Nota*. At the same time, however, it attempted to reach a reconciliation through the use of defensive maneuvering:

> We know very well that our magazine has been unable to satisfy readers who identify with Western music. Yet, the essence of our interest in both types of music to an equal degree is a natural outcome of our music profession. As we wrote in the editorial of our first issue, "Why Do We Publish?", we are happy to even dream of polyphonic Turkish music reaching the international arena. In our opinion, this imagined music can only be possible when talented minds know Eastern and Western music equally well. Because of this belief, we publish examples of both genres in equal size. With the same belief, we try hard to elaborate simple and discrete rules for Turkish music, especially for people involved in Western music so that they can quickly understand the rules and theories of Turkish music which otherwise would be impossible for them to comprehend in years, let alone months.[10]

This quote is definitely defensive in character and intends to redefine the main polices of the magazine. The problematic stance of *Nota* among "the readers involved in Western music" is honestly spelled out. It may be presumed from this

---

9 *Nota*, 11, (15 September 1933), p. 42.
10 *Nota*, 25, (15 April 1934), 113.

attitude that the level of criticism leveled against the magazine in the on-going music "revolution" had significantly increased, and that the editor had to justify his position. This explains the defensive words used in describing what *Nota* is for. Moreover, despite the reference to the editorial of the first issue, matters are presented somewhat deceptively. Looking back at the content of the first editorial, one can hardly get the impression that the followers of *Nota* would "feel happy even dreaming of polyphonic Turkish music reaching the international arena". On the contrary, it was boldly put forth that the music "in our hands" should be preserved as it was created, with its sounds and instruments. In the defensive editorial quoted above, it was also claimed that the magazine published examples of Eastern and Western music to an equal degree, which could not be further from the truth if one actually examines the content of the magazine. The last part of the quote, however, is a sympathetic message to the avid reader who enjoys the Ottoman genre. Here it is claimed that Turkish music (meaning, Ottoman classical music) cannot easily be comprehended in a short period of time. This is a rather indirect attack on the Western music-oriented Turkish musicians, blaming them for being slow in understanding the rules of Turkish music.

Content of the Magazine

The examination of the general content of the magazine reveals certain points of difference vis-à-vis the West-East synthesis of the pro-Western cultural elite. While *Nota* is also in favor of an West-East synthesis, it is not through serious music composed in a Western polyphonic form for the elite listener, but rather through popular monophonic tunes, mostly in song format, for the ordinary listener. One may wonder how these new monophonic compositions, many of which were published in *Nota*, differed from examples of Ottoman popular songs. The answer can be found in both the lyrics and the understanding of music composition.

The lyrics were now mostly secular, narrating a new lifestyle for a less religious listener living in an urban setting. Even though pioneer forms of such an attitude could also be sensed in some of the lyrics of late Ottoman classical music, almost all the new tunes have this orientation. Republican and secular Turkey's new urban lifestyle inevitably found its way into the whole musical scene. In some tunes, male and female choirs sang refrains comprised of flirtatious complaints about the opposite sex. Another interesting example of this mundane attitude can be found in the song entitled *Prozit Şarkısı* [Song for Cheers], which was specifically composed for drinking houses, and inspired by the German way of expressing good wishes when drinking with someone.

Traditional Turkish music is based on certain fixed modal structures (*makam*), which are written at the beginning of the score of any tune. In the new compositions that were written during the period of reform, strange and previously unheard of hybrid model structures began to appear - perhaps in the spirit of the "East-West synthesis" being forged. One of the most striking examples of these was a new *makam* called *Nihavent-Tango*, based upon the traditional structure of the *Nihavent* modality, but rhythmically fused with the Western form of Tango. Within a similar vein, another new modal structure, the *Oryantal-Fokstrot* (Oriental Foxtrot), was invented. This case was unique, however, in that traditional music lacked an "oryantal" *makam*. Strangely enough, the orientalist mind set of the Kemalist cultural elite assumed that it was a synthesis of an Eastern element[11] with a Western one (the fox-

---

11 It is interesting to note that, contrary to Ziya Gökalp's ideas, the Eastern element, namely, makam-based music of Ottoman tradition, is conceived here in a purely positive way in a possible synthesis.

trot), thus interpreting it as the kind of synthesis that they were after. Another derivative structure worth mentioning within the context of the attempts of the Kemalist regime at nationalizing Turkish music is the *Sultan-ı Yegâh*, which is, in fact, based on the traditional *yegâh makam*. Originally imperial in manner (thus the reason behind its name "Sultan's Yegâh"), upon being nationalized, it was retitled, *Milli Yegâh*, which means, "Nation's Yegâh".

In addition to the new scores of popular tunes, biographies of popular contemporary composers and singers were also presented in the magazine. What is striking about all these life stories is that most of the new popular musicians had *tekke* origins. They themselves either came directly from the *tekke*s or had been trained by teachers coming from the *tekke* tradition. For instance, one of the rising stars of the day, Münir Nurettin Selçuk (1900-1981), now considered the last great singer/performer of the Ottoman classical music genre in the Republican era, was praised. This was so even though, as it was noted, while he himself was not a direct descendent of the *tekke* tradition, his masters were ex-members of prominent *tekke*s.

Among these biographies, the most praised composer/performer was Sadettin Kaynak (1895-1961), who had been brought up in the tekke tradition and was a cantor (*hafız*) of the Koran.[12] An established star of the period, Kaynak not only collaborated with Münir Nurettin but also, in later years, was responsible for the adaptation of songs from Arab films. Through his understanding of composition, he was able to produce not simply a "synthesis" but rather a "modernization" of classical music. By creating an urban flavor to the music, a fundamental change in the musical taste of the Turkish listener was brought about. The comment on Kaynak in *Nota* was unusually engaging and gave an early and realistic evaluation of what would become the standard in Turkish popular music and "taste" in the years to come:

> Certainly, and with great success, he [Hafız Sadettin] himself has invented a "way" of
> music that portrays in song our Turkish identity having roots, perhaps, in pre-Ottoman
> times. This "way" includes the flavors found in our folk music, yet at the same time is
> definitely different from it ... These compositions offer different things to different
> people, depending on the particular blend of musical taste present in society at a par
> ticular time. It is our fervent desire that compositions of this type become the basis for
> our musical harmonics.[13]

Here again an indirect attack is launched against the cultural elite and the "folk music" notion of Ziya Gökalp. This is done within the framework of an examination of the Ottoman music - inspired compositions of Kaynak. Not only are they connected to the genuine existence of the Turk, but his composition style supports *Nota*'s idea of a popular synthesis being an alternative to an elitist one.

A Questionnaire on the Future of Turkish Music

In the first issue of its second year, *Nota* published an open letter in which the ongoing intense debate over the clash between Western and Eastern music was redescribed and a public appeal made to the musicians of both genres to present their views about the future of a possible East-West synthesis in Turkish music. In order to structure the responses expected, a very detailed questionnaire was prepared.[14]

---

12 Because of his background, he was often called simply 'Hafiz' in the musical milieu.
13 *Nota*, 19, (15 January 1934), 92.
14 *Nota*, 25, (15 April 1934), 120.

The responses, which began to be published in subsequent issues, revealed an interesting twist: there was a nearly unanimous response in support of pro-Western, pro-polyphonic music (e.g., in support of official cultural policies). Strangely enough, no replies were made by either pro-monophonic readers or directly by the editor to these letters, even though they had been written in a rather insulting tone. This strange "silence" can only be explained as a form of self-censuring mechanism exercised on the part of the majority of *Nota* readers. At the same time, the extent of the pro-Western responses demonstrate the degree to which *Nota* had keen and critical readers from among the pro-Western cultural elite.

The following response to the questionnaire can be considered typical and can serve as a basis for understanding how the "official" view on the topic was formulated. The letter is signed by a certain İlyas Bey, who was the chief representative of the Fine Arts Branch of the People's House of Trabzon. It is known that, in the founding years of the Republic, People's Houses were the main sites for disseminating the cultural policies of the State to the public. İlyas Bey, convinced by the "revolutionary" spirit, openly attacks the existing monophonic music as weak and not suitable for the masses:

> The monophonic music that has been practiced so far, including its [popular] contemporary song forms being composed, is undoubtedly very feeble compared to the music being composed for the masses. The Turkey of 1934 and its new and intellectual generations cannot be satisfied with this "tekke-sounding" music; they [the masses] demand a more expressive, lively, and energetic form of music. In order to realize this, our classical music should be reworked with the classical techniques of Western music so as to achieve a richness of expression and description that will eventually develop into concert and stage music. In addition to that, the basis of an energetic culture of music, equal to that of Western jazz music, should be constructed.[15]

The idea of how true music must be composed is clearly formulated here: First and foremost, music is for the masses, and thus must be "expressive, lively, and energetic". One may sense here traces of the mass-oriented conceptions of German and Italian cultural policies in Europe in the 1930s. Since music is for the masses, it should also have the emphasis and quality of concert or stage music. İlyas Bey continues his assessment of the structure of Turkish music, and makes a very peculiar suggestion:

> Modal structures [*makams*] that are not so different from one another and make our music vague and difficult to comprehend, should also be reworked and reduced to a single essential form. Either one of the modal structures such as *Uşak, Hüseyni, Muhayyer, Karciğer*, which are in essence not so different from one another, should be chosen or a new modal structure covering all the components of the cited modalities should be created. In regard to this, the new modalities should be based on and classified according to the Western major and minor scales and their specifications.

Therefore, according to him, all the structural developments that had taken place in Ottoman classical music should be changed immediately and be made to resemble those based on the minor and major scales of Western music. Whether such a drastic reform was actually necessary for Turkish music was not even a point of contention since he felt that the only developed and "true" music was undoubtedly Western music, with its major and minor scales.

---

15 *Nota*, 28, (1 June 1934), 134.

Two issues later, there came the elitist critique of Ercüment Behzat Lav (1903-1983), a well-known poet, theater-person, and cultural figure, who was at the same time working as a senior announcer on the radio. This critique is significant not only because Lav was a well-known public figure, but also because he held a senior post in the state-owned radio, which was to place a ban on Turkish music in November of the same year. It is also important to note that Ercüment Behzat would become the director of radio programs in 1935, just months after his assessment of the situation of Turkish music published in *Nota*. His promotion is not coincidental, if one reads closely this assessment in which Ercüment Behzat refers directly to Russian nationalism in music:

> Up until Tchaikovsky, Russian music had been an ordinary blueprint of Central European music. [Only after] Russian composers worked on the folk songs of the masses did they reach today's maturity. If Brahms had not worked on national motifs, the music of Hungary would not have appeared in the repertoire of the world orchestras ... The nucleus of tomorrow's Turkish music lies to a great extent in the Anatolian tunes ... What our millions of people require is neither mystical *tekke* music, nor *mey* [wine], nor *muğbeçe* [server in a drinking house], nor *bade* [wine-glass], nor *yar* [beloved] ... Without delay, we must give our people, now living like a spent wave, sonic food on a universal scale. The damage already done to people's minds by drinking-house songs and musically worthless jazz tunes is comparable to the use of morphine and cocaine. We should not forget that in some countries where the musical culture is not as weak as our own, jazz is forbidden in order to protect the musical taste of the people. Today, if a person were to try to organize his life along the line of Omar Hayyam or Mevlana, he would very likely be considered mad and perhaps even be locked up. Similarly, it is a social necessity in this modernizing Turkey of today to confine to the dustbin of history the opium-like music of unlearned men, which is played on the *ud* [oriental lute] and *tef* [tambourine]. As the first step in this sorting and cleansing operation for the ear, the publication and printing of records of songs should be strictly limited and controlled.[16]

This quote is very significant in that it supports the argument of this article concerning the possibility of *coercion* as a reason for the closing of *Nota*. Not only is the original formula of Ziya Gökalp repeated, but that Anatolian tunes are the source for the West-East synthesis in music is also mentioned. In addition, Lav blatantly rejects that there is any other possibility for synthesis to occur, for example, in popular music, since for him, this would be no different from "drinking-house songs" or "worthless" entertainment music, that he groups under the category, "jazz". The last sentence of the quote is particularly enlightening. It is here that Lav speaks of a "cleansing" operation and suggests a total prohibition of the printing of the scores and the publication of the records of such music. If this desire is coupled with the upcoming ban on Turkish music in November 1934, it is not difficult to imagine that his next post on the radio would be as the director of radio programs.

The ban placed on Turkish music in 1934 has an exciting history of its own. Mustafa Kemal, in his opening speech at the 1934 session of parliament, made his second public assessment of Turkish music. Stressing that advancement in the fine arts must be encouraged without delay, he asked for rapid progress to be made in music, and continued as follows:

---

16 *Nota*, 30, (1 July 1934), 143.

A measure of the change undergone by a nation is its capacity to absorb and grasp a change in music. The music that they are trying to get people to listen to today is not our music, so it can hardly fill the bill. We must not lose sight of this fact. What is required is the collection of national expression that conveys fine thoughts and feelings, and without delay, putting it to music, along the lines of the most modern of rules. Only in this way can Turkish music rise to take its place among the music of the world.[17]

One of the immediate outcomes of this speech was the broadcasting *ban* placed on Turkish music, justified as having been inspired by the speech of Mustafa Kemal.[18] This ban was announced on November 3, 1934 and lasted for twenty months. Even though this ban was later lifted, it was replaced by a much more comprehensive system of control, which was indeed a very systematic form of censorship that described the type of Turkish music that could be played on the radio and, later, on T.V. Given the fact that Lav held a senior post at the radio, the desire he expressed in his response to the questionnaire for a total prohibition of the publication of Turkish music can be traced in the later broadcasting policies of the radio. The monopoly Turkish Radio and Television held on broadcasting was not abolished until the early 1990s.

The only positive, yet oblique, answer to the questionnaire from the pro-Ottoman side came from a well-known violinist, Kemani İzzet, who used a very cautious and defensive tone. In his response, he preferred to discuss the real meaning of what is called *alaturka*, which, according to İzzet, is mostly and imprecisely mixed with what is "Eastern". For İzzet, the alaturka genre, by its very nature, is a very versatile format, and is thus suitable for Western harmony:

> Alaturka music is entirely suitable for the adoption and adaptation of motifs. If we are able to educate scholarly composers of good taste, they may help our music achieve a position praised by international music authorities. Even though the Western system of harmonics is based on major and minor scales, it is not limited to those scales. There does indeed exist full liberty. Every kind of plain music has a potential to develop into something more advanced. Therefore, the motifs found in alaturka music can easily be blended with the Western system of music.[19]

Thus in İzzet's eyes, alaturka music is full of motifs that could be combined with both the plain and advanced structure of Western music. It is interesting to note that among the many responses made to the questionnaire in *Nota*, this was the only one evaluating Turkish music in a somewhat positive way. İzzet's response was the last one to appear in *Nota*, which suspended the publication of any other responses in forthcoming issues. After its 37th issue, without prior farewell to its readers, this unique magazine was abruptly closed down.

Conclusion

The story of this unique magazine in many ways reflects the dynamics of the cultural reforms being carried out during the early years of the founding of the Turkish

---

17 G. Oransay, *Atatürk ile Küğ* (Atatürk and Music), (Izmir: Küğ Yayını, 1985), p. 26.
18 *Ibid.*, p. 49.
19 *Nota*, 32 (1 August 1934), 149.

Republic and thus provides insight as to the nature of those reforms. One of the most noteworthy of these insights is that the Republican project of Westernization was executed from above, in a rather authoritarian way, without giving consideration to any social resistance. What *Nota* represented to the cultural elite was a critical attitude directed toward the already established policies of the young state, which did not tolerate such attitudes. Another of these insights is that the ideological framework within which the new cultural policies were formulated and implemented by the cultural elite was positivistic. The intellectuals as well as the rulers of the new republic wholeheartedly believed in the existence of universal truths. As a result, they came up with an unmediated, naively positivistic solution: folk tunes were to be harmonized, using the methods of Western music, and made polyphonic.

Another consequence of this particular history of music was the disregard demonstrated by the cultural elite toward positive offers coming from *alaturka* musicians. While in the political arena, even though, at least at the level of discourse, the ruling elite totally rejected the previous Ottoman political institution, they still had to make some strange coalitions with vestiges of the Ottoman political elite. In contrast, on the musical scene, the cultural elite of the young republic not only completely rejected the musical heritage of the Ottoman period, they denied the possibility of the modernization of Ottoman music, which had, in fact, been the *de facto* "taste" of the urban listener. Instead, what they had proffered was Gökalp's notion the East-West synthesis based upon a fictive folk music, which had neither existed in urban centers nor been known thoroughly by the prominant musicians of the day. Without any intellectualization, *Nota* had come up with its own idea of synthesis - perhaps a kind of "spontaneous synthesis" - which was not a rejection but rather an alternative approach to the republican idea of synthesis. Nevertheless, this brave attempt was not only disregarded by the cultural elite but, as the story shows, was suppressed, resulting in the eventual closing down of the magazine.

The main reason that the republican cultural elite rejected the novel idea of synthesis put forth by *Nota* is more than likely related to a *lack* of interest in popular music among the cultural elite during the early years of the republic. This is particularly discernible if one considers the "from above" character of the Turkish process of political socialization that tended to cultivate political elite who were insensitive to cultural elements coming "from below". In other words, this tendency towards insensitivity is very widespread in all public discussions of cultural policies. Particularly striking in relation to the notion of an East-West synthesis in music is the absence of debate on the possibility of a synthesis in popular music. Quite to the contrary, the young republic and its limited cadre were more interested in solutions for the masses for the sake of the masses - a political reflex remaining from the state-oriented process of political socialization of the Ottoman Empire. Consequently, no thought was given to the notion that any form of popular music could be something that most of the people could enjoy or identify with.

In conclusion, it may be argued that the "from above" strategy of the 1930s had inevitably produced its "from below" counter-movements in the years to come. As observed in the editorials and the publication policies of *Nota*, musicians as well as listeners resisted through their own means and, while they lost the battle in the 1930s, they eventually developed their own synthesis in the 1950s, as well thereafter. In sum, there were, on the one hand, the cultural policies of the young republic that had been imposed by the political powers, and, on the other, a handful of skilled musicians and their listeners from a traditional background that resisted the policies imposed from above. It is within these politico-cultural dynamics that the modern popular music of Turkey has developed.

An Introduction to the History of Music Debates in Turkey

NEDİM KARAKAYALI

In this paper, I will try to give a general outline of the discursive-historical background of music debates in twentieth century Turkey. I will try to show in what basic ways twentieth century texts differ from earlier periods, what basic categorizations they utilize, what kind of discursive positions (or simply "viewpoints") exist, and what significant limitations they have in practice. I will argue that twentieth century discourses on Turkish music differ considerably from earlier periods, in that the latter tend to assume a cosmology closed upon itself, the former operates with a comparative perspective based on a grand dichotomy, Western vs. Turkish. This grand dichotomy is juxtaposed upon a series of other dichotomies: polyphonic-monophonic, artificial-natural, dynamic-static, individualistic-totalizing, local-universal, progressive-conservative, etc. I will argue that at least until the 1970s both scholarly and popular discourses on music were dominated by this grand dichotomy and that its influence is still very much alive today. Nevertheless, especially since the rise of arabesk music in the 1970s, both theoretical and empirical limitations of the grand dichotomy have begun to come into daylight. I believe that now, at the turn of a new century, as the grand dichotomy of the twentieth century is gradually weakening, we find ourselves at the threshold of a new discourse.

The Rise of the Grand Dichotomy-Turkish Music and Western Music

What significant differences can we observe between the twentieth century and earlier periods when we look at theoretical as well as other works on Turkish music? It is certainly beyond the scope of this paper to give a comprehensive history of pre-twentieth century discourses on music and the following analysis is not even remotely rigorous.[1] My aim is to highlight a few elementary differences of twentieth century discourses from earlier ones. We know that strictly theoretical works written on Ottoman/Turkish music before the twentieth century - especially in the period between sixteenth to nineteenth centuries - were few in number (Behar, 1987, pp. 26-7; Wright, 1992). Nevertheless, the works of Arabic, Persian, Turkish and Jewish theoreticians between the ninth and sixteenth centuries can be considered important sources (Farmer, 1965). This is not simply because of the multiple affiliations between these cultures, but also because contemporary theorists of Turkish music

---

1 For a clear demonstration of the complexity of this history, see, Walter Feldman, *Music of the Ottoman Court: Makam, Composition, and the Early Ottoman Instrumental Repertoire*, (Berlin: VWB, 1996).

often take these works as their starting point (e. g. Yekta, 1986 [1922], pp. 24-8). In addition to these theoretical works, there existed various other texts such as biographies, travel books and anthologies that occasionally focused on music and musical instruments. Also worth mentioning are theological, mystical or philosophical treatises about the origins and significance of musical instruments - the passages about the *ney* in *Mesnevi* being one of the most famous examples - and various parables about the powers of music.

Perhaps the most striking characteristic of these pre-twentieth century texts to a contemporary reader, the strictly technical aspects notwithstanding, is their cosmological and universalistic attitude.[2] In many of these works, mostly taking their original inspiration from Greek philosophers, one can find sophisticated mathematical models explaining the functioning of various modes, melodies, rhythms and forms.[3] Music theory, however, was seldom confined to these logical/mathematical models. More often than not, this mathematical microcosm was related to other microcosms. It is, for example, well known that Ottoman musicians classified musical works in terms of *makams* (Wright, 1992, p. 2) and that these *makams*, as parts of a cosmology, were attributed specific qualities as they relate to the times of the day, the seasons of the year, the music of the spheres, humours, primary elements, astrological signs, etc. (Wright, 1978; Shehadi, 1995).

As implied by the "doctrine of the ethos" (Farmer, 1965, p. 34; Anderson, 1968 [1966]), the influence of cultural environment and habitus on musical forms was not completely foreign to ancient theorists.[4] However, cultural origin does not seem to have ever become an autonomous and dominant theme, nor a basic means of classification of music. Rather, cultural and geographical divisions, as one "factor" among many, appear side by side with other divisions, within a general cosmology as well exemplified in the tenth century text *Ikhwan al-Safa* (Shiloah, 1978, p. 25-6). Different genres or types of music seem to matter only to the extent that they are related to different divisions of a given cosmology.[5] In this context, one of the most important distinctions appears to be the one between sacred and profane music (Shehadi, 1995; Shiloah, 1995; Uludağ, 1992).

Another closely related point which may seem rather surprising to a contemporary reader is the universalistic conception of the history of music. The "evolution" of musical instruments and forms seems to take place in a universe where geographical and cultural borders, as well as the distance between the heavens and the earth, do not constitute important obstacles. Muslim philosophers could freely quote from

---

2 Of course, this is not to say that all pre-twentieth discourses can be seen as a homogeneous whole. For a brief discussion of the changes taking place between 1250-1300, see, O. Wright, *The Modal System of Arab and Persian Music*, (Oxford: Oxford University Press, 1978), pp. 1-19. See also, Feldman, *Music of the Ottoman Court*.

3 Al-Farabi's *Kitab al-musiqi al-kabir* is perhaps the most important example. For a general introduction, see, H. George Farmer, *Al-Farabi's Arabic-Latin Writings on Music*, (London: Hinrichsen Edition Ltd., 1960 [1934]).

4 For example, Plato, an important source for Arabic philosophers, had emphasized that people enjoyed the type of music to which they were accustomed (Laws, 802c6-d6; see also, Warren D. Anderson, *Ethos and Education in Greek Music*, [Cambridge, Mass: Harvard University Press, 1968], p. 70). Note, however, that Plato was talking about different genres of music rather than different cultures. A more general comparison between old Arabic and Greek music systems can be found in the "Treatise" of the tenth century Arab historian of music, Ibn al-Munajjim (H. George Farmer, *The Sources of Arabian Music: An Annotated Bibliography of Arabic Manuscripts that Deal with the Theory, Practice and History of Arabian Music from the Eighth to the Seventeenth Century*, [Leiden: E. J. Brill 1965], p. 24).

5 Not to forget gender among such divisions. For example, ancient Greeks sometimes regarded melody as the female and the rhythm as the male component of music (L. Pearson, "The Greek Theory of Rhythm", in Aristoxenus, *Elementa Rhytmica*, [Oxford: Clarendon Press, 1990], p. xxiii).

ancient Greeks and oscillate between a divine harmony and an acoustic one. Evliya Çelebi (seventeenth century), for example, could write:

> The voice of musical instruments is drawn from the world of spirits such that when, in order to give life to the human body, God's angel gave out the "be alive" sound, the soul was taken by a dazzling fear. It took refuge in the human body and remained there. The philosopher Pythagoras who knew this effect constructed a flute from a large reed and had it played on a wedding night. Moses invented the fifer. Al-Farabi invented the lyre... (Evliya Çelebi, 1971, p. 261; freely translated)

At least in one respect, twentieth century discourses on Turkish music offer quite a different picture. Perhaps the most lucid expression of this change can be observed in an essay written at the turn of the century by the pioneer of systematic re-theoretization of Turkish music, Rauf Yekta (1986, [1922]).

At the beginning of his essay on Turkish music, written for the 1922 edition of *Encyclopédie de la Musique et Dictionnarie du Conservatoire*, Yekta notes that old theoretical works on the same subject are full of "scholastic details". He chooses to eliminate such complicated "tables and schemes" in order to achieve clarity (ibid., p. 57). At first sight, the only difference between this essay and previous ones appear to be a growing percision and rationality, and the avoidance, as much as possible, of "speculative" attributes of musical forms and scales.[6]

Underlying the explicit technical formulations of the essay, however, is an acutely visible system of classification that does not seem to exist in earlier texts: a crucial distinction between Turkish and Western music. Perhaps the most intriguing aspect of Yekta's discussion is that, although he seems to argue that Western and Turkish music should be understood from within the particular systems and not from outside, he cannot help but continue comparing and relating each system to the other. It is as if Yekta cannot talk about music without evoking this dichotomy.[7]

What makes Yekta's essay so "prototypical" is that almost all the discussions that he carries out in the course of some 100 pages recur, again and again, in the next decades of the twentieth century. Examples are the theoretical works of Suphi Ezgi, (1933), and Adnan Saygun (1976). Even in those works, somewhat reminiscent of the past, which attempt to represent Turkish music as a completely self-consistent system - mainly by demonstrating the "naturalness" of the makam system - the implicit reference to Western music persists (Arel, 1949; Öztuna, 1987; Özkan, 1990): the "naturalness" of Turkish music makes sense in comparison to the "tempered" system of Western music.

The predominance of this comparative perspective becomes all the more visible in the less technically informed debates on music that emerged in the Republican era. As is well known, from the 1920s onwards a number of new institutions mostly aiming at reforms (i. e. "Westernization") in "fine arts" and musical education were

---

6 Yekta's discussion of the origins of the mode "frenkçin" is a typical example of his cautious attitude to "speculation" (*ibid.*, p. 116).

7 Two possible objections should be answered at this point. First, it might be argued that Yekta's essay-published in French-was written primarily for European readers; therefore it is only natural that he presented Turkish music in comparison to Western music. This objection would be acceptable, if in his other works-especially his polemical writings in Turkish-this dichotomy did not also play a central role. See, for example, Yekta (Rauf Yekta, "Şark ve Garp Musikilerinde Teganni Farkı", *Tiyatro ve Musiki Mecmuası*, 6 [February1928]. Another especially interesting case is Rauf Yekta's debate with Ahmed Midhat Efendi on the issue of a "five stringed violin". Yekta spares a whole page for this debate in his essay (*ibid.*, p. 55). Secondly, one might argue that Yekta's approach stems from his lifelong familiarity with European culture and music. However, although Yekta's rather unique knowledge of European languages and literature is a necessary precondition for his theoretical works, his approach is by no means an exception.

founded. In the same period, a series of institutional restrictions were imposed on traditional Turkish music. The increasing opposition between pro-Western state policies and the excluded proponents of traditional Turkish music gradually crystallized into two discursive positions: pro-Western vs. pro-Turkish, or, alternatively, modernists vs. traditionalists (Belge, et. al., 1980; Üstel, 1994; Ayvazoğlu, et. al., 1994).

It is beyond the scope of this paper to give an exhaustive analysis of the various oppositions involved.[8] However, it is important to clarify the content of this opposition since the categories "Turkish" and "Western" are not, literally speaking, musical notions. In fact, "Turkish" and "Western" become meaningful through a series of juxtapositions that link this metadichotomy to various sub-dichotomies - hence "grand dichotomy".

Here, once again, the distinctions Rauf Yekta evokes between Western and Turkish music is rather informative. The first somewhat implicit distinction is between the "formless, soulless and monotonous intervals of the tempered scale" which is associated with Western music and the more natural and varied *makam* system of the East (Yekta, 1986, p. 56). Yekta's distinction here is a very popular one and forms the basis of the "traditionalist" view (Arel, 1949; Öztuna, 1987; Özkan, 1990).

Another important distinction in Yekta's essay is between "European polyphony" and Turkish monophony. This distinction, too, is very popular and forms the basis of the "modernist" position which interprets "polyphony" as the highest development of musical language and associates it with "universality" (Gökalp, 1968, p. 43 and 99; Üstel, 1994; Eriç, 1985; Sun, 1969; Saygun, 1984; Yener, 1985). In most non-technical discourses on music that emerge in the Republican era, we can observe further extensions of the monophony-polyphony dichotomy into other series like dynamic vs. static, individualistic vs. totalizing, local vs. universal, progressive vs. conservative, etc.

It should not be concluded here that the two discursive positions described above are absolute or mutually exclusive. Various combinations of the two (e. g. polyphonization of *makam* music), with different terminologies and intentions have existed for a long time (e. g. Ziya Gökalp's "grand synthesis," combining a Turkish "content" with a Western "form"). However, regardless of whether we find these discursive positions in "pure" forms or in combinations, they all presuppose the same discursive space, i. e. they all proceed with the same dichotomous model. In the period between 1920 to 1970, there does not seem to exist a single text on music which does not, in one way or another, herald the dichotomy of Western-Turkish and its various extensions.

As a general hypothesis, which is definitely in need of further empirical support, we can argue that, as the closed, cosmological discourse of the past dissolved, a new discourse has appeared in its place, one which consists of a range of dichotomies governed by the grand dichotomy of Western vs. Turkish. This new discourse is not necessarily less "closed" - even less cosmological - than the previous ones. Nevertheless, it presupposes a different - perhaps a more asymmetrical - "cosmos" where a "peripheral" musical system is evaluated, either positively or negatively, against a "center" (the West). The plausibility of this hypothesis becomes more apparent if we consider similar transformations in other discursive fields (e. g. on art, literature, morality, politics, etc.). As such, the hypothesis here should not necessarily be confined to music.[9]

---

8 A typical confrontation between the proponents of different positions can be observed in the proceedings of a symposium organized by the Faculty of Fine Arts at Hacettepe University in April, 1985 (Hacettepe Symposium, 1985, pp. 231-333).

9 It has often been pointed out that in the Republican era, music has been the only artistic practice that was explicitly and insistently intervened in by the state. Whether this should be attributed to

Orhan Gencebay - master of arabesk.

The Rise Of Arabesk and the Retreat of the Grand Dichotomy

It is a well known fact that some of the new art froms, new music genres and new literary forms that have emerged in Turkey since the nineteenth century had their origins in Europe. Certainly, they can be seen as various steps in a general process of Westernization and modernization of Turkish culture. The roots and the justification of the grand dichotomy, Turkish vs. Western, can, to a large extent, be traced back to such developments. The question, however, is whether these developments should be characterized as a simple form of imitation, translation or reproduction, or whether they involve much more complicated processes.

The complex nature of mimetic processes has been stressed by various authors (Rank, 1971; Borch-Jacobsen, 1988; Taussig, 1993; Lacoue-Labarthe, 1989; Deleuze, 1988). Such works voice the idea that in every case of imitation and trans-

"unique" qualities of music as an art form or to other factors is still an open question. What should be plainly rejected, however, is the notion that the discursive divisions mentioned above are peculiar to music. There does not seem to be a single cultural practice in the recent history of Turkey that escapes the grand dichotomy. Kaygı (Abdullah Kaygı, *Türk Düşüncesinde Çağdaşlaşma* [Modernization in Turkish Thought], Ankara: Gündoğan Yay. 1992), for example, provides a detailed anthology of the numerous debates among Ottoman/Turkish intellectuals since the nineteenth century. Even though the "themes" of the debates-literature, morality, art, politics, music, etc. -change, the main dichotomy, Western-Turkish, and the explanatory framework, modern-traditional, remains unchanged. For the cases of painting, plastic arts and architecture, see the contributions to: "Osman Hamdi Symposium" (1993).

lation one can also observe a transformation and trans-figuration. Similarly, reproduction is never simply the domain of preservation or conservation. Reproduction is
what makes mutations possible. For a long time now, and mostly because we were
so concerned about the overall results of these processes, we have often missed these
creative, differentiating and mutative aspects of translation and imitation.[10] Perhaps
we still tend to forget that translation and imitation do indeed have a reality of their
own, that they involve real attempts and projects, that every reproduction is an event
in itself. Seen from the perspective of the grand dichotomy, such events appear to us
as mere "accidents" or "by-products" of a generalized modernization process.

Nevertheless, the grand dichotomy has been on the decline in the last few decades
- but not so much as a result of rigorous theoretical criticism. What has been forcing
especially the scholarly discourses to reevaluate their dichotomous perspective in
recent years was an external factor, a very special *event*. This event is what has now
come to be called *arabesk*.

In the twentieth century, most debates on music in Turkey involved a clash
between two discursive positions derived from the grand dichotomy. With the emergence of arabesk, however, this discursive space went through a crucial reconfigura-
tion. In a way, arabesk appeared, quite unexpectedly, in the middle of a battlefield,
pushing the two armies farther and farther apart from each other and inserting itself
almost violently in the center of the whole debate. In arabesk traditionalists saw too
much experimentation and too many foreign elements. In contrast, modernists saw too
much tradition and too little rationality. In this strange "object" both sides saw not
only the betrayal of their own ideals but also a kind of resistance to their basic means
of categorization. It is perhaps no surprise that approximately in the same period, we
witnessed the emergence of a new social scientific literature on music, particularly on
arabesk, that breaks with these discursive positions and seeks to establish a more
detached, critical and what might be called a "sociological" approach. Murat Belge's
(1983) short, but insightful commentaries, Meral Özbek's (1991) study on Orhan
Gencebay and Martin Stokes' (1992) ethnographic work are of this kind.

Arabesk denotes, primarily, a popular music genre that emerged in Turkey in the
late 1960s. However, there is certainly more to it. Indeed, seldom can one find a
name with so many conflicting associations and plural senses. Even trying to give a
very technical definition and linking arabesk to a definite music genre would not be
easy. For we would then underestimate the fact that, originally, the term arabesk was
coined to humiliate a definite music style and its fans, and is therefore too loaded
with value judgments to be used as an objective definition. It is also difficult to relate
Arabesk exclusively to a musical style, not only because it cuts across several music
genres but also because it extends far beyond music and denotes, more often than not,
a *kitsch* culture in general

The ambiguities concerning the content of arabesk can be multiplied. For example, the word arabesk suggests a certain return to the Persian-Arabic elements of the
Ottoman culture, and yet, at same time, arabesk is often associated with rapid urban-
ization in modern Turkey. It would, however, also be somewhat misleading to associate it merely with the poor migrants of the urban centers since one of the most common settings for "arabesk culture" is expensive night-clubs, etc.

Until the 1970s, everything is different: people talk about modern/Western and
traditional/Turkish music, polyphonic and monophonic music, serious and light

---

10 There are a few important exceptions, however. See, for example, İskender Savaşır's comments on
the application of the grand dichotomy to musical practices (B. Ayvazoğlu; C. Behar; İ. Savaşır; S. Sökmen, "Müzik ve Cumhuriyet", *Defter*, 22, [1994], 10-11). See also Orhan Tekelioğlu, "Kendiliğinden Sentezin Yükselişi: Türk Pop Müziğinin Tarihsel Arka Planı", *Toplum ve Bilim*, 67 (1995).

The İSYANKÂR (rebellious) Müslüm Gürses.

music. Arabesk, however, has no specific "opposite". If anything, it refers to the very limits of these oppositions. This "out-of-place" character of arabesk often reveals itself in the difficulty of classifying it within the categories of existing discourses. Özalp (1985), for example, in his attempt to "describe" arabesk, repeats the expression "unclassifiable" [belli bir sınıfa sokulamayan] twice in a single paragraph (p. 300). Similarly, Alkan (1987) writes: "Arabesk is a river which has lost its bed. It is likely to run muddy until the heavy rain ends. It is the voice of the masses who don't know their [own] classics, who are afraid of Western music and [therefore] are "in-between" [iki arada bir derede kalmış] (p. 267).

Examples can be multiplied. But the "unclassifiable" nature of arabesk is perhaps nowhere so strongly emphasized - though within a different framework than the aforementioned passages - as in the work af an "outsider," the British ethnomusicologist Martin Stokes who studied the musical culture of Turkey in the 1980's (Karakayalı, 1995b). From the very beginning. Stokes realized that there was a very specific difficulty involved in studying arabesk: "Whilst I felt that I needed a subject, I could also see that *the search for a subject area with unambiguous boundaries was an integral aspect of what I had been observing all around me*" (Stokes, 1992, p: 18; emphasis mine). Stokes' observation here alludes to the difficulty of utilizing the grand dichotomy in analyzing arabesk. Arabesk seems to escape the clear cut distinctions between Western and Turkish music.

According to Stokes, ultimately, what arabesk texts imply is "social liminality" (*ibid.*, p. 120). Liminality is the condition of being "in-between" two things, on the borderline; being in a confused or ambivalent state: between the city and the village, east and west, modern urban life and rural traditions. Arabesk texts are *not* so much the "expression" or reflection of a *specific liminality*; rather they *generate* a kind of giant "idiom" for "expressing" *liminality in general* (*ibid.*, p. 132). Both in terms of its musical-technical inventions and in terms of its textual messages, arabesk falls beyond (or "in-between") the categories of the grand dichotomy. It implicitly denies the purity of those categories. More importantly, it highlights the possibility of a musical practice that is completely unanticipated by the grand dichotomy.

Yet, even though arabesk has succeeded in escaping the grand dichotomy, it seems to have failed in another respect. As most observers have pointed out, arabesk could not turn its escape into a new, joyful and invigorating musical culture (Belge, 1983; Karakayali, 1995a; Stokes, 1992). I tried to show elsewhere how the music of Orhan Gencebay, one of the most important contributors to arabesk, systematically avoided an active involvement in "real life", preferring an abstract, detached and self-centered attitude (Karakayali, 1995a). In Stokes' words, "arabesk does not touch the world it describes" (Stokes, 1992, p. 226). Despite its musical inventions, at the level of lyrics, arabesk almost invariably paints a resentful and passive image of life. As Stokes puts it, the liminality of arabesk is "decidedly downwardly mobile": arabesk implies "a theodicy in which natural justice is perceived to have withered, and man's lot in life is a state of powerlessness and alienation" (*ibid.*, p. 226).

Let me summarize. First, arabesk has, to a large extent, managed to escape the main categories of the grand dichotomy and occupied an "unclassifiable" status in reference to those categories. Yet, secondly, arabesk failed to create an invigorating and "upwardly mobile" sociocultural movement and is trapped in a discourse of mourning. I believe this success and failure - or, escape and entrapment - are the most significant characteristics of the history of arabesk which is likely to continue informing music debates in Turkey in the future.

Concluding Remarks

The grand dichotomy is severely limited in grasping certain musical practices in Turkish society and since the rise of arabesk this limitation has become visible. Even if we assume that at the turn of the century the grand dichotomy functioned as a means of defining and lending some kind of an identity to Turkish music, today it rather functions as an obstacle to new musical projects. In the case of arabesk, this hindrance is also observed by Stokes who documented that "no critical language exists to talk about arabesk in any positive way" (ibid., p. 129). This is not to say that arabesk involves a completely positive social movement - certainly not - but this is to say that even if arabesk had any positive potentials, there were no discursive means to identify this potential. This inability, I believe, is closely related to the fact that there has, so far, been no positive language to talk about music outside the grand dichotomy of Western vs. Turkish.

It seems that, at the turn of a new century, a new discursive opening is needed, if not already taking shape.[11] Ultimately, the aim of this paper was to highlight this

---

11 We can perhaps talk about the emergence of such an opening in practice as well. Several writers have underlined some of the current developments in Turkish pop-music and tried to point to a tendency which seems to promise a new music-a music which is no longer a theoretically strived-for objective but one that is already in the process of actualization (O. Tekelioğlu, "Kendiliğinden...", Orhan Kahyaoğlu, "Türkiye'de Pop Müziğin Oluşumu ve Tüketim İdeolojisi (1960-1970)", *Defter*, 22 [1994]; see also the comments by Cem Behar and İskender Savaşır, Ayvazoğlu et. al., *Defter*, 22 [1994]).

opening rather than offering a closure. At a practical level this opening suggests that we avoid sweeping generalizations and grand categorizations. Unlike the perspective of the grand dichotomy that ceaselessly reduces all cultural practices to their "Eastern" and "Western" components, this perspective is likely to focus on elements that escape this dichotomy.

The concept of liminality may, to a certain extent, prove to be useful in this endeavor but it is certainly not devoid of problems. The most salient problem of the concept of liminality is its extremely general nature. Indeed, this problem is clearly recognized both by the originator of the concept (Turner, 1967) and his critics (Geertz, 1980). Stokes, who applies the concept to arabesk, is also aware of this problem. In the concluding remarks of his book he notes that liminality can take many different forms and that its outcome may be positive ("upwardly mobile") as well as negative ("downwardly mobile"). In the case of arabesk, this outcome, he suggests, is largely negative but he ends his book on the note that some sort of positive potential might exist in arabesk as well. Stokes, however, does not discuss what this positive potential is and under what conditions it can be actualized.

It is quite likely that this question that Stokes apparently left open for future research will continue to animate discourses on music. The example of arabesk suggests that escaping the grand dichotomy in no way guarantees a positive outcome. If a new discourse on music is to build on the experience of arabesk, the reasons behind both the "success" and the "failure" of arabesk are likely to be the main problems of this discourse. More generally, it is quite possible that as the focus shifts from grand categories to "liminal" practices, the question of the outcome or the *value* of such practices will come to the foreground.

Perhaps the most important point to note here is that this "value" can no longer be determined on the basis of a preestablished dichotomy such as Turkish vs. Western. Once these grand categories are dissolved, the criteria for evaluating musical practices turn into an open question - and this open question may prove to be the most important topic of new debates on music. A new discourse on music in Turkey, then, is likely to *begin* with the observation of liminal musical practices that escape the grand dichotomy, but it certainly does not end there. Rather, its most essential problem is likely to be the *consequences* of such "escapes".

References

Alkan, A. Turan (1987), "Musikimiz Üzerine Derbeder Notlar", *Türkiye Kültür ve Sanat Yıllığı.*

Anderson, Warren D. (1968), *Ethos and Education in Greek Music*, Cambridge, Mass: Harvard University Press.

Arel, Sadettin (1949), "Türk Musikisi Sistemi: 1", *Musiki Mecmuası*, n. 17

Ayvazoğlu, B.; Behar, C.; Savaşır, İ; Sökmen, S. (1994), "Müzik ve Cumhuriyet", *Defter*, n. 22.

Behar, Cem (1987), "Sunuş" [Introduction], in Charles Fonton, *18. Yüzyılda Türk Müziği* [Turkish Music in the eighteenth Century], İstanbul: Pan Yay.

Belge, Murat, et. al. (1980), *Atatürk Devrimleri İdeolojisinin Türk Müzik Kültürüne Doğrudan ve Dolaylı Etkileri*, İstanbul: Boğaziçi Üniversitesi Türk Müziği Kulübü Yay.

Belge, Murat (1983), *Tarihten Güncelliğe*, İstanbul: Alan Yayıncılık.

Broch-Jacobsen, Mikkel (1988), *The Freudian Subject*, Translated by Catherine Porter, Stanford, Calif.: Stanford University Press.

Eriç, Daniyal (1985), "Çok Sesli Türk Müziğinin Gelişimi ve Geleceği", in *Hacettepe Symposium.*

Evliya Çelebi (1971), *Evliya Çelebi Seyahatnamesi*, Book II, tr. Zuhuri Danışman, İstanbul: Zuhuri Danışman Yayınevi.

Ezgi, Suphi (1933), *Nazari ve Ameli Türk Musikisi* [Theory and Practice of Turkish Music], v. 1, İstanbul: Milli Eğitim Basımevi

Feldman, Walter (1996), *Music of the Ottoman Court: Makam, composition, and the early Ottoman instrumental repertoire*, Berlin: VWB

Farmer, H. George (1960, [1934]), *Al-Farabi's Arabic-Latin Writings on Music*, London: Hinrichsen Edition Ltd.

Farmer, H. George (1965), *The Sources of Arabian Music: An annotated bibliography of Arabic manuscripts that deal with the theory, practice and history of Arabian music from the eighth to the seventeenth century*, Leiden: E. J. Brill

Geertz, Clifford (1980), "Blurred Genres: The Refiguration of Social Thought," *American Scholar*, Spring, pp. 165-79

Girard, Rene (1986), *The Scapegoat*, Baltimore: Johns Hopkins University Press

Gökalp, Ziya (1968), *The Principles of Turkism*, Leiden: E. J. Brill

"Hacettepe Symposium" (1985), *Türkiye'de Sanatın Bugünü ve Yarını*, Ankara: Hacettepe Üniversitesi Güzel Sanatlar Fakültesi Yayınları

Kahyaoğlu, Orhan (1994), "Türkiye'de Pop Müziğin Oluşumu ve Tüketim İdeolojisi (1960-70)", *Defter*, n. 22

Karakayalı, Nedim (1995a), "Doğarken Ölen: Hafif Müzik Ortamında Ciddi Bir Proje Olarak Orhan Gencebay", *Toplum ve Bilim*, n. 67

Karakayalı, Nedim (1995b), "*The Arabesk Debate* by Martin Stokes" [book review], *Toplum ve Bilim*, n. 67

Kaygi, Abdullah (1992), *Türk Düşüncesinde Çağdaşlaşma* [Modernization in Turkish Thought], Ankara: Gündoğan Yay.

Lacoue-Labarthe, Philippe (1989), *Typography: Mimesis, philosophy, politics*, Cambridge, MA: Harvard University Press

"Osman Hamdi Symposium" (1993), *Osman Hamdi Bey ve Dönemi*, [Proceedings of a symposium/workshop held in İstanbul December, 1992], İstanbul: Tarih Vakfı Yurt Yayınları

Özalp, M. Nazmi (1985), "Türk Musikisinde Yabancı Musikilerin Etkisi ve Sonrası", in *Hacettepe Symposium*, pp 291-302

Özbek, Meral (1991), *Popüler Kültür ve Orhan Gencebay Arabeski*, İstanbul: İletişim

Özkan , I. H. (1990), *Türk Musikisi Nazariyati ve Usulleri*, İstanbul: Ötüken

Öztuna, Y. (1987), *Türk Musikisi*, İstanbul: Türkpetrol Vakfı

Pearson, L. (1990), "The Greek Theory of Rhythm" in Aristoxenus, *Elementa Rhytmica*, Oxford: Clarendon Press

Rank, Otto (1971), *The Double: a Psychoanalytic Study*, translated and edited with an introd. by Harry Tucker, Jr., Chapel Hill: University of North Carolina Press

Saygun, A. Adnan (1976), *Bela Bartok's Folk Music Research in Turkey*, ed. Laszlo Vikar, Budapeşt: Akademiai Kiado

Saygun, A. Adnan (1984), *Atatürk ve Musiki*, Ankara: Sevda Cenap And Müzik Vakfı

Shehadi, Fadlou (1995), *Philosophies of Music in Medieval Islam*, New York: E. J. Brill

Shiloah, Amnon (ed) (1978), *The Epistle on Music of the Ikhwan al-Safa*, Tel-Aviv: Tel-Aviv Univeristy

Shiloah, Amnon (1995), *Music in the World of Islam: a socio-cultural study*, Aldershot: Scolar Press

Stokes, Martin (1992), *The Arabesk Debate: Music and Musicians in Turkey*, Oxford: Clarendon Press

Sun, Muammer (1969), *Türkiye'nin Kültür, Müzik, Tiyatro Sorunları*, Ajans Türk Kültür Yayınları

Tekelioğlu, Orhan (1995), "Kendiliğinden Sentezin Yükselişi: Türk Pop Müziğinin Tarihsel Arka Planı", *Toplum ve Bilim*, n. 67

Turner, Victor (1967), *The Forest of Symbols: Aspects of Ndembu Ritual*, Ithaca: Cornell University Press

Uludağ, Süleyman (1992), *İslam Açısından Musiki ve Sema*, Bursa: Uludağ Yayınları

Üstel, Füsun (1994), "1920'li ve 30'lu Yıllarda 'Milli Musiki' ve 'Musiki Inkılabı', *Defter*, n. 22

Wright, O. (1978), *The Modal System of Arab and Persian Music*, Oxford: Oxford University Press

Wright, O. (1992), *Words without Songs: A Musicological Study of an Early Ottoman Anthology and its Precursors*, London: SOAS, University of London

Yekta, Rauf (1928), "Şark ve Garp Musikilerinde Teganni Farkı", *Tiyatro ve Musiki Mecmuası*, n. 6 (February)

Yekta, Rauf (1986, [1922]), *Türk Musikisi* [Turkish Music], İstanbul: Pan Yay. (Orginal: "La Musique Turque," in Encyclopédie de la Musique et Dictionnaire du Conservatoire, v. 1, Paris: Lavignac)

Yener, Faruk (1985), "Müziğe Yaklaşım", in *Hacettepe Symposium*, pp. 247-54

Tasavvuf, Music and Social Change in the Balkans since the Beginning of the Twentieth Century with Special Consideration of Albania

NATHALIE CLAYER

The following pages is the fruit of the work of an historian, and not that of a musicologist or ethno-musicologist; an historian, who until now, most certainly wrongly, did not attach enough importance to music when working on *tarikat* in the Balkans, Moreover, the writer had no possibility to fill this gap by doing field research in Albania before writing this paper because of the events that occurred in that country in 1997. Nevertheless, I shall try to give first a brief picture of the context in which Sufism survived in the Balkans after the end of the Ottoman domination. Then I shall present some features concerning Sufi music in these regions in the twentieth century, before considering in more detail the Albanian case by studying two periods of transformation: after the end of the Ottoman domination, and the other after the breakdown of the communist regime.

Social Changes Endured by the Balkan Muslims and the Survival of the Mystical Brotherhoods in the Twentieth Century

If we compare the situation of Balkan Muslims since the collapse of the Ottoman Empire with that of their co-religionists within Turkey, it is obvious that it is not at all the same. Even within the Balkans, we have discrepancies from one country to another, and from one period to another. The Balkans consist of five countries: Albania, Yugoslavia, Greece, Bulgaria, and Romania; and they have lived through three different periods during the twentieth century: the period between the two world wars; the period during the communist regimes; and the period since 1990.

Except in Albania, and in certain regions of the former-Yugoslavia, the end of the Ottoman domination was followed by a numerical weakening of the Balkan Muslim communities (following, in the early periods, massacres, conversions, and, later, above all, migration during or after the wars, and emigration resulting from the lower status of Muslim minorities in the newly created countries (on this subject, see Toumarkine, 1997). The phenomenon was more accentuated in the Eastern part of the Peninsula where the Muslim population was predominantly Turcophone. As well as the small group of Muslims in Romania, there remained, in these regions, the two substantial groups of the Muslims of Bulgaria and those of Western Thrace in Greece. However, the biggest Muslim communities remained in the Western part of the

Balkans, in Albania (where the majority of the population was Muslim) and in the for-mer-Yugoslavia (i.e. Bosnia-Herzegovina, Kosovo-Metohija and Macedonia).

In addition to the weakening of and change in social status, two other factors were fraught with consequences for the Balkan Muslims: the fact that emigration had been particularly important among the elite, be they religious or non-religious; and, later on, the establishment of communist regimes in all the countries being considered except Greece (about these phenomena, see Popovic, 1986).

In this context, the Sufi networks were also weakened, because of the emigration of numerous sheikhs and dervishes to Turkey. In Romania, Bulgaria and Greece, they disappeared almost completely, except in the case of the *Kızılbash* community of Eastern Bulgaria.[1] In Bosnia-Herzegovina, they had already been weakened dur-ing the Austro-Hungarian occupation, from 1878 onwards, but survived till the inter-diction of 1952. In Macedonia and Kosovo-Metohija, where stronger groups of Muslims (Albanians, Turks and Slavs) remained, the networks were affected above all in the towns, and later on also in the Turkish villages of Macedonia during the great wave of departures which took place in the fifties (see particularly Clayer-Popovic, 1992). When the Yugoslav regime relaxed its position towards Islam from the seventies on, the Sufi activity had a new start in Bosnia-Herzegovina, as well as in Kosovo-Metohija and in Macedonia. In the latter regions, this revival was rein-forced by the creation of gypsy networks.[2]

Some Features of Sufi Music in the Balkans and its Development in the Twentieth Century

Being a non specialist, and also because, as far as I know, the subject has not been really studied until now, I can give here only a few rather disparate elements con-cerning the development of Sufi music in the Balkans in general during the twenti-eth century. In view of what I said about the survival of Sufi networks, one can imag-ine that Sufi music could survive and develop itself above all in the Western part of the Peninsula.[3]

Some information was provided about Macedonia around the year 1925 by Gliša Elezovic. According to him, *ilahis* were sung in *tekkes* at this time in Turkish and Arabic.[4] These *ilahis* had a lyrical or philosophical character, and were composed according to a special rule and sung monophonically on the metric cycle called *dü yek* (4/4), or, for some, on the pattern 2/4 or *marš usuli*. Among the Bektashis, the *nefes* were sung on metric pattern called *aksak* (9/8).[5] The Mevlevis used the *ney*, *tümbelek* and *kudum*, and also the *ud*, the violin and the *kanun*. The Rifa'is and the

---

1 On this *kızılbash* community, whose members do not belong to a *tarikat*, but to an alevi-like reli-gious group, cf. Irène Mélikoff, "La communauté kızılbaş du Deliorman en Bulgarie", in I. Mélikoff, *Sur les traces du soufisme turc. Recherches sur l'islam populaire en Anatolie*, (Istanbul: Isis, 1992), pp. 105-113. About the survival of some *tarikat*s in Bulgaria, see F. de Jong, "Notes on Islamic Brotherhoods in Northeast Bulgaria", *Der Islam*, 63/2 303-308.

2 See A. Popovic, *Les derviches balkaniques hier et aujourd'hui*, (Istanbul: Isis, 1994); and N. Clayer, *Mystiques, Etat et société, Les Halvetis dans l'aire balkanique de la fin du XVe siècle à nos jours*, (Leiden: E. J. Brill, 1994), pp. 275 ff.

3 The case of the *kızılbash* of Bulgaria constitutes certainly an exception in the eastern part of the Balkan Peninsula.

4 Here I suppose that G. Elezovic refers to the use of Arabic words, or to Arabic prayers includ-ed in some ilahis.

5 The patterns *düyek* and *aksak* can be found in the treasure of metric cycles of Ottoman and modern Turkish art music (I thank Dr. Anders Hammarlund for this remark and for a set of other suggestions).

Chorus of Bektashi *muhib*s during the ceremony of *ashura* in the central Bektashi *tekke* of Tirana (*kryegiyshat*a), in 1995.
Photo: Nathalie Clayer

Sa'dis used *def*s (tambourines with cymbals, or *daire*), *kudum*s and cymbals (*zil*s). In the other brotherhoods only *kudum*s were used (Elezovic, 1925, 16-19).

In fact, even in the Western part of the Balkans, some traditions like the Mevlevi one vanished with the closing between the 1930s and the 1950s of all the Mevlevi establishments.[6] Regarding the Bektashi tradition, we shall see hereafter what occurred in Albania, the stronghold of the brotherhood. For the other *tarikat*s, one can imagine for the period up to the outbreak of the Second World War, a kind of stagnation, or a phenomenon of "nationalization" for non-Turkish groups, comparable to the process that I shall describe for Albania.[7] In fact, with the communist takeover in Bosnia-Herzegovina, Sufi music was forbidden in 1952, when the *tekke*s were closed down in this Yugoslav republic. When the *tarikat*s re-emerged in the 1970s, the Sufis were allowed to recover places and objects which had belonged to them, except for the musical instruments. In Kosovo and Macedonia, where the activity of the *tekke*s was not prohibited, but where the Sufi networks were weakened by the political pressure and by migration, in the mid seventies the tradition re-emerged and the ceremonies of *zikr* were multiplied through the opening of new *tekke*s, notably by the sheikh rifa'i of Prizren, and the creation of gypsy networks (Sufi networks developing and recruiting members among Gypsies).

For the last few years, one question could form the basis of future research: to what extent were (and are) the dervishes from Bosnia-Herzegovina on one hand, and those from Kosovo and Macedonia on the other, influenced by the production in Turkey (or elsewhere), of audio-cassettes diffused through the Turkish television, or contacts with friends or relatives who have emigrated to Turkey? Besides modernization, this could be a main factor in the evolution of local Sufi music, since there

---

6 In fact, the Mevlevi tradition survives in Bosnia-Herzegovina, through the existence of annual meetings, called "Academies of Şebi Arus", but without any music.

7 Let us point out the fact that, in spite of the political change, a strong *mevlud* tradition remained all over the Balkan, among the Muslim communities.

is no longer pressure from the political side, and no real interest coming from the surrounding non-Muslim society.[8]

The Albanian Case

As already mentioned, Albania was the only Balkan country born after the collapse of the Ottoman Empire that had a majority of Muslims. But approximately one-fifth of the Albanian Muslims belonged to the Bektashi order of dervishes, which, in the new state, became a semi-official (and thereafter, official) religious community. Among the non-Bektashis, a lot of Muslims were members of other *tarikat*s, especially of the Halvetiyye, but also the Kadiriyye, the Rifa'iyye, the Sa'diyye, the Gülsheniyye or the Tidjaniyye. Except for the Tidjaniyye, and probably also the Bektashiyye,[9] all the *tarikat*s that were active in Albania until 1967, the date of the absolute prohibition of religion in the country, used musical instruments: the Sa'dis (standing), the Rifa'is, the Kadiris (on their knees, using *kudum*s, *zil*s and *mazhar*s) and even the Halvetis (sitting and standing). It is said in a document preserved in the Archives in Tirana, that Halvetis had "strong" *nefe*s, which were not to be divulged or to be sold - which is an allusion, I supposed, to a « business » regarding the nefes of other *tarikat*s.[10] The Mevlevi tradition, which was present during the Ottoman period only in central Albania in the town of Elbasan, survived in the twenties through the unique existence of a *türbedar* (keeper of a mausoleum).[11] Thus it is doubtful whether the rich Mevlevi music could have continued under these conditions.

But can we detect an evolution in the Albanian Sufi music between the end of the Ottoman period and 1967, in view of the social and political changes? Before 1944, in Albania - as in Turkey - the question of modernity versus tradition arose. The politics of the President (and thereafter King) Zog was a kind of mixture of both. Besides the two trends - let's say "orientalist" for that of the Ancients (*Të vjetër*), and "occidentalist", for that of "The young" (*Të rinjtë*) - a movement of "neo-Albanianism" developed which insisted on the individual soul and essence of the Albanian people, and which was sympathetic to Bektashism and Sufism in general.[12] In the field of music, the political authorities made some efforts to develop occidental music (Selenica, 1928: CLXVI). On the other hand, the ties with Turkey were weakened after 1925, the date of the ban on the *tarikat*s in this country, while the Albanian *tarikat*s, like all the religious communities in Albania, were restructured on a national level. In this context, an important factor in the evolution in *tekke* music before World War II, which I want to stress now, is a kind of "Albanization" and "nationalization" of Sufi music, especially among the Bektashis.

Through "Albanization" and "nationalization" I want to talk about two phenomena which certainly had already begun during the last century of the Ottoman peri-

---

8 Maybe an interest will be aroused as in Greece, where there is a movement very sympathetic to ancient Turkish music and Sufi music and where big concerts are organised, or as in Hungary, to a lesser degree, where in 1984 an audio-cassette was taped of "Ancient Turkish Music in Europe" (Kecskés Ensemble, 1984).

9 Until now, I have found no evidence concerning the use of musical instruments among the Albanian Bektashi dervishes, but I have never assisted at a ritual ceremony.

10 Cf. Arkivi i Qendror i Shtetit (Tiranë), F. 882, d. 15, pa vit, fl. 2, 6, 11; and d. 16, viti 1953, fl. 1.

11 Cf. Arkivi i Qendror i Shtetit (Tiranë), F. 882, d. 5, Viti 1922, fl. 122-124.

12 Cf. Bernhard Tönnes, *Sonderfall Albanien, Enver "eigener Weg" und die historischen Ursprünge seiner Ideologie*, (München: R. Oldenbourg, 1980), 80 sqq.; Michael Schmidt-Neke, *Entstehung und Ausbau der Königsdiktatur in Albanien (1912-1939)*, (München: R. Oldenbourg, 1987), 250 sqq.; and the newspaper *Illyria*, I-28, 26 *Tetuer* 1935, p. 5; *Illyria*, I-37, 4 *Kallnuer* 1936, p. 3.

od, but which were considerably amplified and increased in the framework of the Albanian state: on the one hand, the creation of an Albanian repertoire through the translation - or rather the "adaptation" - of the Turco-Arabic one, or through the composition of new pieces; and on the other, the introduction of national and nationalist motifs. Already in the nineteenth century, there were translation-adaptations of religious works recited or chanted in *tekkes*: the most famous example is that of the *Hadikat üs-suada* which is recited and partly chanted during the *matem* (beginning of *Muharrem*) in remembrance of the martyrdom of Imam Hüseyin. In 1258/1842, it was adapted from the version of Fuzuli, and translated from Turkish into Albanian by Dalip Frashëri.[13] *Nefes* and *ilahi*s were also translated into or composed in Albanian, always in order to make their content understandable to people who did not know Turkish.[14] Furthermore, some Bektashi "clerics" began to compose *nefes* having a patriotic or nationalist spirit (Clayer, 1995, 292-296) - indeed the Bektashi element was very active in the awakening of Albanian nationalism.

From the 1920s onward, the activities of Baba Ali Tomori, one of the most modern educated Albanian Bektashi *Baba*s, (he studied in the gymnasium of Yannina) tended more and more in this direction.[15] Like his predecessors of the second half of the nineteenth century, he composed *nefes* and *gazel*s, but tried progressively to purify the language.

In a small collection published in 1934 by one of his *muhib*, we can read in the introduction:

> The Bektashi *nefes* and *gazel* are not only hymns. They possess a high degree of philosophy or theology, through which the sick heart of the human being is cured.
>
> Bektashi poets in the Albanian language existed already before this language had its own script. They wrote in Arabic script, and, because this language remained undeveloped, they of necessity used Arabic [in fact Arabic, Turkish or Persian] terms, which, because of their individual taste, they need to use as they are, without any changes (Lumani, 1934, 6).

I shall give three examples of this kind of *nefes* composed by Albanian Bektashis. One composed by Baba Abidin of Leskovik (South-East Albania) at the end of the Ottoman domination, begins as follows:

> *Një dylber [dilber] kur e vështrova / me sy të hakut [Hak]/ në gjonul ç'u përvëlova / për ashkut, Shahut...*
>
> When I looked at a beloved / with the eyes of God / how my heart was broken / for desire of the Shah [Ali]

The *nefes* written by Baba Ali Tomori, when purely religious, are on the same model, using Arabic and Turkish words, considered "to have a special taste" (in fact,

---

13 See Osman Myderrizi, "Letërsia fetare e Bektashive", *Bulletin për Skhencat shoqerore*, Tiranë, 1955/3, pp. 131-142. According to Faik Konica, at the end of the Ottoman period, the Hadikat was recited in Toskeria (i.e. South Albania), in Albanian or in Greek, and, among the Bektashis of the region of Tetovo/Kalkandelen, in Turkish (cf. Kalendari i Malévé mé zbukurimé per 1900, Bruxelles, Perlindja é Shqiptarevé, p. 25-26. Today, the Bektashis of Tetovo are chanting nefes in Albanian and Turkish (cf. Murat Küçük, "Makedonya'da Hacı Bektaş Velî Mührü, Harâbâtî Baba Tekkesi", *Cem*, 6/61 (Aralık 1996), 35.

14 See Baba Rexhebi, *Misticizma islame dhe Bektashizme*, (New York: Waldon Press, 1970), pp. 166 sqq.

15 About Baba Ali Tomori (d. 1947), cf. N. Clayer, "Tomori, Ali, Baba", in *Dictionnaire biographique des savants et grandes figures du monde musulman périphérique, du XIXe siècle à nos jours* (sous la direction de Marc Gaborieau, Nicole Grandin, Pierre Labrousse et Alexandre Popovic), Fascicule no 2, janvier 1998, (Paris: Ehess, 1998), p. 72.

often "technical" terms of the mystical doctrine), even if, on the other hand, he tried in general to use a clear form of Albanian, without foreign words, as in the second part of the following verses:

> *Të zgjuar vakt' i sabahut / më zu në Bahçen e shahut / të mërguar prej gjunahut / se ishte vakt i sualit / Pranë luleve qëndruar / prej të qarit i pushuar / nga të pamët i hutuar / se më zû koh e zevvalit...*
>
> Awake the time of the morning / caught me in the garden of the Shah / exiled from the sin / Because it was the time of the judgement / standing near the flowers /stopped by the tears/ disconcerted by the appearances / because the time of the sinking of the sun after noon caught me..."

But Baba Ali Tomori composed others *nefes* on a totally new model, without any oriental words and, thus, without their flavour. For example:

> *Çilni sytë e shikoni / jetën si u bë / fletë-fletë tá lëxoni / botën gjer më një...*
>
> Open the eyes and look /at life how it / blooms; read / the word...

The above-mentioned collection, published in 1934, contains also four other pieces which belong to quite another genre. There are two hymns composed by Baba Ali Tomori - one in honour of the king, the other in honour of the Albanian flag - taken from an unpublished book of his of "hymns for solemn Bektashi ceremonies". The second one, for example, begins with the following verses:

> *Ky flamur ësht i bekuar / se çudira ka dëftyer, / Zoti udh' i ka rrëfyer, / gjith' armiqtë i ka thyer / dhe atdhen e ka shpëtuar. / Shum i shënjt' është ky flamur / shum i shtrënjt' është ky flamur*
>
> This flag is blessed / Because it has shown wonders / God has indicated the way / All the enemies he routed / And the fatherland he has saved / Very holy is this flag / Very dear is this flag).

The two other poems are entitled "Kombësija" (Nationality) and "feja" (Religion). They are, like the two hymns, testimonies of what I called the "national-ization" of the Albanian Bektashi works, i.e. of the integration of nationalistic motifs.

> *Zoti math në këtë baltë / më ka bërë Shqiptëtar, / gjuhën shqip t' ëmbël s' i mjaltë / ma ka fal për kombëtar / ...*
>
> Dieu le Haut de cette boue / m'a fait albanais / la langue albanaise douce comme le miel / il me l'a offerte pour [que je sois] national[iste]...

Here I want to stress the parallel which can be made between the position of Bektashism in Turkey vis-à-vis Turkish nationalism and the position of Bektashism in Albania vis-à-vis Albanian nationalism. Bedri Noyan writes:

> *Görülüyor ki Türk millet ve milliyeti Bektâşiliğe çok borçludur. Çünkü Bektâşilik dünyadan geçmiş, ukbadan geçmiş, mal, mülk para, şöhre ve şandan geçmiş, sadece vatandan geçmemiştir. Türk milletinden ve Türklükten geçmemiştir." (Noyan, 1985, 174).*
>
> We see that the Turkish nation and nationality is very indebted to Bektashism because Bektashism renounces the world, renounces eternity, renounces goods, possessions, money, renounces fame and glory - only the fatherland it does not renounce. It does not renounce the Turkish nation or the Turkish soul."

Interior of the Rifaʻi *zaviye* in Tirana; on the walls, instruments for the piercing (*şiş* and *darb*), calligraphies, musical instruments (*zils* and *kudums*), and two pictures, that of the Rifaʻi sheikh of Prizren and that of the former Rifaʻi sheikh of Tirana before the interdiction of religion.
Photo: Nathalie Clayer

After the works of Baba Ali Tomori, I shall take the example studied by Frances Trix of the Mersiye sung on the occasion of the day of the *ashura*, as a remembrance of Imam Hüseyin's martyrdom. According to her, between the First World War and the Second World War the Mersiye was still sung in Turkish, in one of the Bektashi *tekke*s of Gjirokastër - and probably elsewhere in South Albania.[16] When a new *tekke* was founded in 1954 near Detroit (USA) by one of the dervishes coming from this establishment, this dervish - Baba Rexhebi - "translated" the lament into Albanian. Frances Trix compared the two versions and analysed the process of "adaptation". She wrote as follows:

> A striking similarity of the Ottoman[17] and Albanian laments is in the melodic contour. This is, of course, not apparent from written texts, and metric analyses only distract. The Albanian is in trochaic octosyllables, an accentual meter; where the Ottoman is analyzed as a quantative sort of remel. But when Baba chants the Ottoman *mersiye*, and when he, or the people he trained chant the Albanian one, the melodic contours are very similar. This is not particularly unusual as melodic structures are some of the most persistant of cultural structures, preserved beneath the conscious level of words.
>
> Another similarity between the Ottoman and Albanian laments, and one apparent to both ears and eyes, is the refrain. Both have unvarying refrains that invoke Husein: "Ya Huseyin" in the Turkish, and "O Imam Hysejn" in the Albanian. [...] These invariant refrains also allow for participation of many people or people new to the ceremony. [...]

16 Nevertheless, Baba Ali Tomori published in 1928 an Albanian version of the *Mersiye* ("Mersija" apo ceremonija e shenjte e Bektashivet kur shenjtërohet ashyreja [Mersija ou la sainte cérémonie des Bektachis lorsqu'on bénit l'ashure], translated and completed by Atë Ali Turabiu, Tiranë, 1928, p. 9). So it seems that the process of "Albanization", which arose also through the efforts made to "Albanize" the terms used to describe the religious hierarchy: dede/gjysh, baba/at, etc, was not completed at this time.

17 The Ottoman reference is that of Şeyh Safi, "Mersiye", in Ahmed Rifat Efendi, *Mi'ratü'l-Mekasid fi def i'l-Mefasid*, (Istanbul: İbrahim Efendi Matbaası, 1293[1876]), pp. 202-204.

After the first couplets, however, the Ottoman and Albanian laments part. The Ottoman proceeds to laud the beauty of Husein in multiple couplets, whereas the Albanian strikes a more narrative note. This is a pervasive difference in the two laments. Where the Ottoman extolls, the Albanian recounts and instructs. [...]

The metric structure of Baba's lament places it squarely in this Balkan tradition [of lamenting the dead]. The line in epic verse and dirges in Albanian folk poetry is an eight-syllable trochaic line with special emphasis on the penultimate syllable. The lines in Baba's lament have this same structure.

[...]

Besides line structure, the imaginery in Baba's lament is typical of Balkan laments. This is not to say that the Ottoman lament does not contain some of the same images. [...] the images in Baba's lament are restricted to those of light and water, and build in more narrative fashion with standard Balkan terms. [...]

Besides the use of the images of light and water in Balkan fashion, Baba's lament contains an ethical dimension related to codes of honour and bravery in combat. These elements are especially characteristic not of Balkan laments in general, but of Albanian dirges and Albanian epics and songs" (Trix, 1995/b, 415-420).

To summarize, whereas the "melodic contours" seem similar to the listener , the metric structure has been changed for a local one, and the content has been adapted to local folkloric imagery and epic tradition. In spite of the transformation, however, the model remains. Nevertheless, sometimes this could have curious consequences. Here I am thinking in particular about the creation of *ilahi*s in Albanian, composed on the following model: a succession of verses, beginning by the successive letters of the Arabo-Turkish alphabet (Elif, Ba, Ta, Tha, Jim, and so on). I found two examples of this: the first dates from the mid-nineteenth century, and was consequently written down in Albanian in Arabic script (Myderrizi, 1957, 183-186); the second one, more surprisingly, is a composition of a certain Sheh Ramazan Picari, a rifa'i sheikh from the environs of Tirana, but published in 1933, several years after the adoption of the Latin alphabet for the Albanian language. The words placed at the beginning of each verse were both Arabo-Turkish (Allah, Xhevap, Hin, Selamet, Shehid, Zullum, ...) or purely Albanian (Besa, Ti, Thirrje, Dishrojnë, Rruga, Zemra, etc.).[18]

Let us take now the problem of the revival of Sufism and Sufi music after the break during the communist period of 1967-1990. Since the "rehabilitation" of religious beliefs and practices at the end of November of 1990, a few *tekke*s have reopened, especially Bektashi and Rifa'i ones (the Halvetis, Kadiris and Sa'dis reopened as well but in most of them there is no real Sufi life).

As far as the Bektashis are concerned, we have a testimony from Frances Trix who attended a ceremony of the blessing of a *türbe* rebuilt in 1991, during which traditional laments for religious *baba*s were chanted by young women. In the villages, unlike the situation in towns and cities, the tradition was transmitted during the communist period, publicly before 1967, and then privately. A tape was made of the chanting during the ceremony, and thereafter copies have been circulated, playing an important role in the revival of the community. In the same way, official ceremonies in the central *tekke* of Tirana (*kryegjyshata*) have been filmed and videos circulated, which have contributed to the rebirth of the Bektashi community (Trix, 1995: 540-544). When I was in Tirana for the Bektashi Congress, in July 1993, I realized for myself how important the chanting of *ilahi*s was during the meals which took place in the great dining room of the *tekke* with participants coming from all over the Bektashi regions. These *ilahi*s were sung in unison by the entire congregation

---

18 See Sheh Ramazan Picari, *Vjersha fetare. Ilahi*, Vorë-Tiranë, Maj 1933, 9-11.

with a leading chanter, or by a single person in the case of *gazel*s. The rhythm used was 4/4, in a non-pentatonic scale (unlike the popular music of South Albania), and the melodies showed diverse influences, coming from different types of Balkan music (from the Aegean coasts, from the Pindus, from Macedonia, from *Rumeli Türküsü*, etc.).[19]

As for the Rifa'is, a *zaviye* was opened in Tirana, as well as three or four other centres of this order elsewhere in the country. In a former Kadiri *tekke* of the capital, a Rifa'i sheikh is accustomed to leading the *zikr* also. I was able to attend the ceremony of *zikr* several times in 1993, 1995 and 1996, in both of these establishments. The quite young sheikh of the first one (quickly promoted to this rank by the sheikh of Prizren, in Kosovo) is a professional flautist at the Albanian National Opera, who is much helped by an older *zakir* who was certainly affiliated to the *tarikat* before 1967. In the first years, the assembly performed a "minimal" *zikr*, not very elaborated, if we compare it, for example, with the *zikr* of the Rifa'is dervishes of Prizren (sometimes there were some problems in the recitation of *ilahi*s, when the participants did not know the words well). But in time, the sheikh took more and more care over the musical aesthetic, preferring some more complex formulae in the *zikr* to show his expertise. Contrary to the Bektashi *ilahi*s and *nefes*, the *ilahi*s chanted in the two afore-mentioned establishments are, it seems, on oriental modes (*aksak*, etc.), sometimes executed to the accompaniment of a *kudum* beaten with a strap. Here we can see, probably, the difference in nature of these *tarikat*s, the Rifa'iyye being of Arabic origin.

To conclude, in the Albanian case, which differs from the other ones in the Balkans by the fact that the country had a majority of Muslim citizens, one of the main factors of the evolution in Sufi music seems to have been the process of "Albanization" and "nationalization", at least in the Bektashi works. By "Albanization" and "nationalization", I mean a process of adaptation from a Turkish model, regarding the metric structure of compositions (as in the case of the Mersiye), but above all regarding the language, and, beyond the language, sometimes the image and the spirit-epic as in the case of the Mersiye, or "nationalistic" in the case of some *nefes* or hymns composed by Baba Ali Tomori for Bektashi ceremonies.

And, last but not least, I want to stress the fact that the principal aim of this contribution was to draw attention to a quite virgin field of research, and to inspire some musicologists, or ethno-musicologists, to study the numerous aspects of Sufi music in the Balkans, and especially in Albania.

Bibliography

Clayer (Nathalie), 1994: *Mystiques, Etat et société, Les Halvetis dans l'aire balkanique de la fin du XVe siècle à nos jours*, Leiden, E.J. Brill.

Clayer (Nathalie), 1995: "Bektachisme et nationalisme albanais", in A. Popovic et G. Veinstein, *Bektachiyya. Études sur l'ordre des Bektachis et les groupes relevant de Hadji Bektach*, Istanbul, Isis, 1995, pp. 277-308.

Clayer (Nathalie) - Popovic (Alexandre), 1992: "Sur les traces des derviches de Macédoine yougoslave", *Anatolia Moderna/Yeni Anadolu, IV. Derviches des Balkans, disparitions et renaissances*, Paris-Istanbul, Librairie d'Amérique et d'Orient/Institut Français d'Etudes Anatoliennes, pp. 13-63.

---

19 I am very much indebted to my friend Leonidas Embiricos for giving me indications concerning the types of registered melodies which seem to be common to the Christians of the regions mentioned. Of course, these are only indications, and real research is to be carried out in this field by ethno-musicologists in the future.

Elezovic (G.), 1925: *Derviski redovi muslimanski tekije u Skoplju*, Skoplje, "Stara Srbija".

Lumani (Asqeri F.) (éd.), 1934: *Nefeze dhe Gazele bektashiane të marruna nga libri i posaçmë i Baba Ali Tomorit*, Tiranë, Shtyp. K. Luarasi.

Myderrizi (Osman), 1955: "Letërsia fetare e Bektashive", *Bulletin për Skhencat shoqerore*, Tiranë, 1955/3, pp. 131-142.

Myderrizi (Osman), 1957: «Një dorëshkrim shqip i panjohur i Gjirokastrës», *Bulletin për Shkencat shoqerore*, XI, 1957/1, pp. 177-200.

Noyan (Bedri), 1985: *Bektaşîlik Alevîlik nedir*, Ankara.

Popovic (Alexandre), 1986: *L'islam balkanique. Les musulmans du sud est européen dans la période post-ottomane*, Berlin-Wiesbaden, Otto Harrassowitz.

Baba Rexhebi, 1970: Misticizma islame dhe Bektashizma, New York, Waldon Press.

Schmidt-Neke (Michael), 1987: *Entstehung und Ausbau der Königsdiktatur in Albanien (1912-1939)*, München, R. Oldenbourg.

Selenica (Teki), 1928: *Shqipria më 1927*, Tiranë, Shtyp. Tirana.

Sheh Ramazan Picari, 1933: *Vjersha fetare. Ilahi*, Vorë-Tiranë, Maj 1933.

Tönnes (Bernhard), 1980: *Sonderfall Albanien. Enver Hoxhas «eigener Weg» und die historischen Ursprünge seiner Ideologie*, München, R. Oldenbourg.

Toumarkine (Alexandre), 1997: *Les migrations des populations musulmanes balkaniques en Anatolie (1876-1913)*, Istanbul, Isis.

Trix (Frances), 1995: "The resurfacing of Islam in Albania", *East European Quarterly*, XXVIII, 4, January 1995, pp. 533-549.

Trix (Frances), 1995/b: "The Ashura lament of Baba Rexheb and the Albanian Bektashi community in America", in A. Popovic et G. Veinstein, *Bektachiyya. Études sur l'ordre des Bektachis et les groupes relevant de Hadji Bektach*, Istanbul, Isis, 1995, pp. 413-425.

PART V

SUFI MUSIC AND THE MEDIA

Sufi Music and Rites in the Era of Mass Reproduction Techniques and Culture

JEAN DURING

In the past Oriental music could only be transmitted orally: from master to disciple. Without this personal transmission, it risked being lost forever. All this changed with the advent of modern technology. Today modern recording devices make possible the collection of Oriental music. The development of various media allow for its dissemination on a wide scale. Thus it has become possible to learn Oriental music without having to rely on the personal relationship that is at the heart of the traditional process of transmission.

Considering the fact that music and mysticism share many of the same structures of transmission, it would be interesting to examine how modern means of diffusion have influenced Sufi music. It is significant to note not only the reaction of the dervishes to these new factors, but also the influence the media have had on the public. In this vein, it is interesting to investigate how public demands have changed the orientation of the musical practices of the dervishes themselves.

The contemporary attitude of dervishes toward the transmission of their music ranges from a very strict conservatism, having as its goal the preservation of secrets, or at least the sense of the secret, to a kind of liberalism that condones the use of the means of transmission and distribution of their music in order to create a new attractive image of themselves. This is not a new phenomenon. In fact, in the past, some Sufi lodges owed a part of their success to the quality of their *samâ'*, which was attended by music lovers; however, with the diffusion of music through concerts, records and cassettes, the narrow field of Sufi music has become considerably enlarged. On the one hand, forms of music that are strictly Sufi have become popularized due to the impact of the media; on the other hand, the dervishes are in a position of having to adapt their practices to the new means offered by modernity, the "mediatic brewing," and the circulation of cultural goods and information.

The phenomena considered here provide a cultural framework within which the traditions existing in Iran and especially in Kurdistan can be examined. However, this framework can be used to examine other traditions as well. In order to better understand contemporary dynamics, an attempt is made to contextualize forms of music called "Sufi", in other words, to consider them in relation to their public as well as other genres. It is necessary, in effect, to limit the cultural terrain in which the "mediatic factor" has contributed to transformations, the ruptures and the levelling, which have defined the actual musical landscape. It is sometimes possible to discover the origins of changes that ultimately occur. Through an examination of the context in which change has occurred, it becomes possible to locate its source. In certain cases, the vulgarization of traditional musical style is the natural consequence of the interaction of Sufi music, and different forms of art music. Before laborating on the central issue of this article, I want to give a few examples. What needs to be addressed is how the sense of the secret, or of the obligation of preserving it, has become transformed by the diffusion of Sufi music through the media. How has this diffusion encouraged the development of new forms of unveiling of the deeper secrets that are brought about both through the performance of the music and through the rites associated with it. This process is not unlike that brought into the foreground by the concepts of *aura* and of *cultural value,* found for example in the philosophy of Walter Benjamin who has argued that the quality of being a work of art is lost under the effect of mass reproduction.

Sufi Music and Persian Art Music

Sufi music, as its culture in general, is not homogeneous. Thus, musical forms and repertories vary from one Sufi group to another. In the past, it was common practice for Sufis to invite (and pay) professional musicians to play in their *samâ'* rites. These musicians would interpret classical melodies and solemn songs having literary content in ways compatible with their *ahvâl*.[1] Exchanges between art music and Sufi, or spiritual, music occurred from the very beginning, because boundaries between them were porous or fluid.[2]

The Sufis or dervishes of Iran have therefore not generated music unique to themselves. The melodies and styles of their songs are in line with classical Persian music, generally without instrumental accompaniment. In the Shiite brotherhood of Ne'matollâhi Gonâbâdi, one of the most important in Iran, musical practices reflect the strict conformance to Islamic Law (*shar'iat*, which was in some periods a vital necessity). Accordingly, for example, women remain in an adjacent room, and the only form of music allowed is the song performed *a cappella*. If a dervish with a beautiful voice is found among the performers, he is asked to sing something to close the meeting. He usually choses a poem by Hâfez or Sa'di or a passage from *Masnavi* by Mawlânâ Rumi, which he cantillates using classical modes and melodies (*gushe*). Even within a repertoire of simple tunes having secular lyrics (*majâzi*), the dervishes may interpret them in a spiritual sense. In other settings, the chanting may be accompanied by an instrument considered less mystical than others, such as by the *ney* or

---

1 The Sufis undoubtedly began by summoning professional singers who would interpret the songs in a symbolic manner. After the hagiographs, it appears that the musicians of Rumi or Abu Sa'id Abi'l-kheyr were such professionals. An old Tadjik bard tells of how in the past he would sometimes be invited by dervishes to play and sing at the mosque. It is likely that some brotherhoods avoided the development of specific repertoires in order to conform to the *shar'*.

2 It is the same for such genres as the Shiite Persian song (*nowhe, marsie,* etc.), the classical song (*radif*) and the dervish song, not only because the modes and rhythms were the same, but also because certain religious songs were at the same time also performed by dervishes. Classical musicians were often affiliated with a Shiite lodge, where a place was reserved in seances for the mystical song. These songs did not make up an organized repertoire, a style or a specialization of their own. Nevertheless, they were not expressed in the same way in a *xânegâh*, or in a private gathering as in a concert. In the former it was not expected that dervishes exhibit vocal prowess or subtle modulations, but warm expression and feeling. Such interpretations appear alongside demonstrations of virtuosity or performances of extremely gay or exuberant melodies. Pieces having a particular emotive or meditative character are chosen from the learned repertoire. By using nostalgic modes, they include many soft and emotive melodies (for a discussion of this, see the rather lengthy article by M. Frishkopf on the Egyptian *inshad*). In Iran, the Shur, Homâyun, Esfahân, Dashti, and Afshâri are often played. Of the classical repertoires most suited to the Sufi mood, the most current are the Sufinâme (and Sâqinâme), Gereyli, which have a slow and sober melody, and the *gushes*, Gham Angiz, Leyli and Majnun, Râz o Niâz, *Jâme darân*, as well as others that are more gay in spirit such as the Tusi and the Chahârpâre, and, of course, nearly all of the Masnavi (primarily that of Afshâri) since this genre is by definition a mystical one by virtue of its literary component.

A group of dervishes posing in front of the photographer (İstanbul: end of nineteenth century).

setâr.[3] Generally, when, under these conditions, they listen to music *a fortiori* dervishes practice their interior *zekr*. Notably, in the meetings of this brotherhood, the Koran is only chanted during Ramadan, where custom requires one *joz'* to be recited each day at sunset.

The frontiers between art music and Sufi music are difficult to trace since the public as well as artists and producers continually mix up the classifications. This partially stems from the fact that the distinction between the sacred and the profane is not very clear in Muslim cultures. Moreover, if a classical singer is himself dervish, one can assume that all the music he performs, at least at the *xânegâh*, is spiritual in nature. The question can be raised as to whether otherwise religious music reproduced by someone else, but in another, non-religious, context can still be considered Sufi music. Examples of the circulation of repertoires include that of the *ta'zie*, the Shiite religious opera. A great number of its tunes have been incorporated into the body of classical music. Since the singers of *ta'zie* were often classical masters, it is possible to argue that the tunes constituting the repertoire of religious opera were in fact originally borrowed by these musicians. Even in the highly specific case of the sacred Kurdish music of the Ahl-e Haqq, an essential piece such as *Jelô Shâhi*, "before the King," would be considered *majâzi* (profane) by some, and mystical by others, who would argue that the "King" being referred to is the "spiritual King". One interpretation of this phenomenon is that the melodies of this genre were originally sacred, then have become profane, and then have eventually been restored to their mystical dimension. In other cases, it is recognized that the music in question actually has its origins in festive music, although it is argued that the *jam* (the spiritual meeting) is also a festival. Moreover, few people concern themselves with the real origin of the melodies; what matters is that someone with authority decrees that they are of a particular origin. Differences of opinion appear not as a result of any real difference in origins of the melodies but rather as conflicts of authority and legit-

3 Cf. J. During, *Musique et Mystique dans les Traditions de l'Iran*, (Paris: IFRI-Peeters, 1989). At wedding celebrations a much smaller tambourine, called a *dâyre*, is used.

imacy. Two examples of the circulation and interaction between the artistic and spiritual domains can be given.

In general, Persian art music tends to look for the subject matter of its renewal in rural or provincial popular melodies. The songs of Kurdistan, Gilan or Persia have enriched the repertory, and have even given birth to such new modes as *Shushtar*, *Bayât-e Shiraz*, *Kord*, *Gilaki*, or *Amiri*. Historically, it was not uncommon for musicians to become interested in ritual music as well. Moreover, the fact that many were of Kurdish origin contributed to the integration of Kurdish elements. Another factor which favored these borrowings was that there has always existed in Persian music (at least for the last two centuries) a tendency towards spiritualization - a tendency which has been favored by the cultural climate of the Islamic regime.

With "mediatic brewing," classical musicians, who for the most part live in Teheran, have become acquainted with the music of the Qâderi Kurds and, to a lesser extent, of Ahl-e Haqq, which differs from the Persian tradition of Sufi music. Since about 1977, these musicians, in particular those of the Qâderi, have exercised an influence on Persian music, or at least on those arrangements designed for concert or for cassette recordings.

An example of Kurdish influence in Persian music is the introduction of the grand Qâderi *daf* into classical ensembles. The *daf* is a sacred instrument charged with symbolism. In principle, it can only be played at *zekr* ceremonies; it would be considered a sacrilege to play it at a wedding party. Despite these restrictions, the *daf* has experienced a growing success among secular musicians for the last 10 to 15 years. The first time that it was used in a classical concert (at the Shiraz festival in 1976), it was with special permission from the sheikh of the brotherhood. Actually, the dervishes permit its use for serious music, such as art music, or to accompany Kurdish songs having a moral and spiritual content (close to the *xânegâh* repertory). It was first played by Kurdish dervishes, then by secular musicians, and finally by non-Kurds. Certain "uninitiated" *daf* players have reached a high technical level, but dervishes say that it is necessary to be initiated and affiliated in order to play correctly.

The powerful resonance of the *daf* justifies its use in the center of large ensembles, but it has subsequently carved out an increasingly important place for itself within smaller ensembles. Acoustic considerations are not the only priority,[4] however, and even in large ensembles the *daf* is requisitioned not only for its power, but for its scenic image and the symbolism attached to it. In addition to the dervish touch, the *daf* puts into effect a rich and powerful gesture, which is very effective on stage. Furthermore, considering the ease with which they have integrated Kurdish pieces into their Persian concerts, it is not unusual for the classical Persian groups having Kurdish origin, such as the eight-member Kâmkâr family or the Andalibi, to have adopted the *daf* as a distinctive element in their music. These groups sometimes play *xânegâh* tunes, which lend themselves to instrumental interpretation, and some (such as the "classical Persian" singer of Kurdish origin from Ta'rif) go as far as composing half of their program with Sanandaj Qâderi *xânegâh* songs, despite the fact that they themselves are not dervishes. For connoisseurs, these interpretations are noth-

---

4 The use of the *daf* within the classical context is rather different: The main difference is the sound quality. This is because of several factors, one of which being the choice of finer skin (from sheep rather than from goat). Another has to do with the quality of the stroke. Most importantly is the fact that the percussionists are asked to play rather softly so as not to drown out the melody being played by the other instruments. Thus on commercial recordings, the sound of the *daf* is loosing ground in comparison to even the delicate lute, the *setâr*. On account of technical ingenuities, it has become possible to replace the traditional cup drum (*zarb*) with the *daf*, even in very light ensembles.

ing bat fairly flat imitations compared to the performances of the adepts. The fact that the former make use of an instrumental accompaniment of the utmost finesse does not make them any more captivating.

Another mystical instrument that has recently appeared on the scene of art music is the *tanbur* of the Ahl-e Haqq of Kurdistan.[5] It is a kind of two-string lute (one string generally being doubled), a very close variation of which played equally with the fingers of the right hand, is found among the Alevis of Eastern Anatolia. For the adept, the *tanbur* is sacred: it is embraced when it is picked up; it is never placed on the floor, and must be arranged in its cover in a high place in the room, from where it spreads its *barakat* throughout the house. Reserved for ritual or mystical use, its repertoire has only recently begun to be divulged. Nevertheless, despite its sacrosanct character and the mysterious aura that the Ahl-e Haqq maintain around this music, and although the instrument is poorly adapted to any other repertoire than its own, it has progressively come out from behind its veil and has become integrated into classical ensembles, notably by Shahrâm Nâzeri, a celebrated Persian singer of Kurdish Ahl-e Haqq origin. While he may use it for playing one or two sacred melodies in concert, he generally uses it for profane Kurdish melodies. He plays it in a systematic manner in order to accompany himself in certain melodies and to give himself countenance. Recently he released a cassette (entitled *Motreb-e mâhtâb ru*) where the main accompaniment is carried out by a group of *tanbur* players. It goes without saying that the constitution of such a group is a recent innovation in Iran.

The Kurdish mystical mode does not permit further use of the *tanbur*, because this instrument is traditionally fretted to give a chromatic scale, which limits its use to a few Persian modes only. Curiously, no one has ever dared to add more frets, arguing that one would then detract from the specific character of the *tanbur*. The intention was indeed to introduce a "mystical citation" and a Kurdish element in Persian performances, and not simply to recruit a new instrument as had been done with the *rabâb* and the *qichak* of the Sistan. Moreover, they could have used the *dotâr* of Khorassan, a variant of the *tanbur*, but with a more "Iranian" scale, but they did not do so, since this instrument does not have the mystical aura of the *tanbur*. In contrast, it is the players of the *dotâr* who have borrowed it from art music. The improvisations on the *tanbur* have also inspired such musicians of classic tradition as Jalâl Zolfonun in recordings made on the *setâr*, accompanied by the *daf*. We will further see that he has developed a sacred repertoire himself.

Preservation of the Secret and Diffusion of Patrimony

The position of the dervishes varies considerably with respect to the divulging of their music and of their rites, and above all, the modern means of diffusion and reproduction. Even when it is only a question of preserving their tradition, they can be reticent. For example, a Tunisian doctoral student at the Institute for Turkish Studies in Strasbourg working in Tunis has not been able to obtain authorization to take video films of dervish seances, despite his family's support. A well-known Arab ethnomusicologist no longer had the right to film or record the Qâderi or Rifâ'i dervishes of Aleppo, even though she was very well-received by the sheikhs. The argument, she says, was only that it was necessary "to preserve the secret," or probably more accurately, the sense of the secret, or, the sense of the sacred, an essential point we will return to.

---

5 Cf. During, *Musique et Mystique*, Livre III, 2nd part.

In contrast, in Bagdad and in Iranian Kurdistan, the Qâderi dervishes open their doors to all and gladly allow themselves to be filmed. Contrary to the Ahl-e Haqq, who, in certain periods had to carry out their *jam* and their *zekr* ceremonies in secret, for example in underground sheepfolds, the Sanandaj Qâderis have a home of their own and hook up loud speakers to diffuse their songs outside to the entire neighborhood, as is sometimes done in the mosques.

Although the dervishes are not particularly given to showing off their prowess on the stage, they are prepared to make use of video films to make themselves known. Cassettes recorded in the grand Kasnazani *xânegâh* in Bagdad and distributed in Iranian Kurdistan demonstrate the most extraordinary of exploits performed in front of foreign witnesses who verify absence of deceit. If one were to visit one of the well-known Sanandaj *xalifes*, it is likely that the visitor would be invited to watch such cassettes. In contrast, to my knowledge, one has never filmed a Ahl-e Haqq *âtesh xâri* seance, where burning coals are placed in the mouth.

I will here give a few examples of this sense of mystery, as it is expressed in musical traditions, as well as the subtlety with which the secrets are unveiled. Hâtam Asgari Farahâni (born 1932)[6] considers the old masters of song, several of which he has visited, as spiritual authorities or Sufis who knew certain secrets, such as the therapeutic power of modes, and who did not transmit their music to anyone. He says that his master, Aqâ Ziâ, did not want to teach even his most beautiful melodies to his own son, since he was convinced that he would immediately pass them on to another singer, who would then record them and have them broadcast over the radio. Aqâ Ziâ himself was "tested" for eight years by his own master before the latter decided to show him all he knew, without concealing anything. The secret was preserved for a long time by Asgari; it is only recently, as he approaches sixty, that he has begun to transmit his repertoire.

However, even in this context of initiation and esotericism, the technical means and processes of divulsion and diffusion have influenced the transmission of this jealously kept music in different ways. The repertoire of Asgari is three or four times larger than those of other masters of song; even his better students have had the chance to go on tour. In order to transmit his repertoire, he has begun to resort to cassettes and has published a *dastgâh* (*Navâ*), as long as eight hours - it would fill eight cassettes. His memory is not infallible, especially when it comes to the melodies that he has created or that he receives as inspiration through a dream. Therefore, when something is revealed to him, he immediately records what he has heard, and wherever he goes, he carries a small portable recorder.

Furthermore, commercial recordings have the advantage of designating certain people as the veritable keepers of repertoire. This phenomenon of appropriation has appeared with recordings which, from this point of view, have had the same effects as writing had in the Western world. The public attributes authorship of a melody to its interpreter (one says, for example, "Sharjarian's Bidâs," as one would say, "Pavarotti's Aria of Figaro"). Aqâ Ziâ refrained from singing in front of the famous master, Abolhasah Sabâ (d. 1957), whom he reproached for claiming authorship of the melodies that he interpreted. Asgari bore a large grudge against the author of these lines, after an incident in which a piece from his repertoire, the *gushe* Bidâd, which he had recorded for himself, was copied by others and ended up falling into

---

6 For a discussion of this master and his very original approach to the history of Persian music, as well as its symbolic significance, cf. J. During, "La voix des esprits et la face cachée de la musique? Le parcours de maître Hâtam 'Asgari'", in M.A. Amir Moezzi (ed.), *Le Voyage initiatique dans l'islam, Mi'raj et ascension céleste*, Paris: E.P.H.E., 1997.

the hands of a celebrated artist who sang it in concert. This kind of incident, made him decide to publish his own repertoire. These examples show that at one important level, the sense of the secret has been principally linked to an object whose exclusivity one wants to maintain; however, on another level, it is also a question of preserving the sense of its value, without which the object would lose its aura. These two levels do not exhaust the sense of the secret, as will be seen.

The idea that elements having inestimable value exist in the preserved musical repertoire has its origins in the evolution of Arab-Persian music itself. It is said that the famous Abbasid singer, Ishaq al-Mawsili, heard a woman in the street sing a melody so captivating that he offered a large sum of money in order to find her again, so that he would be able to learn it. Asgari tells how his master thanked him one day for a particularly chivalrous gesture, by singing a rare tune to him on a street corner. His master found the tune so precious that he has not yet been able to find anyone worthy enough to receive it. The following testimony by Asgari demonstrates the value that the dervishes attach to certain melodies as well as the place that the classical song occupies in the Ne'matollâhi assemblies.

> One evening I had a dream in which three dogs were attacking me in the middle of some ruins. They were at the point of devouring me when the sheikh Hâjji Mohammad Râstin arrived: he beat the dogs and chased them away. The next morning, a soldier appeared at my house to inform me that Mr. Râstin wanted to see me. I went to his house, and after the greetings he said to me: "Good! I saved you from these dogs but there is a stipulation: you must give me an interpretation of Leyli and Majnun. It is I who will tell you when and where" ... Hâjji Mohammad Xân loved dawn and his dervishes would come to find him during these hours. One morning while I was with him with his dervishes, he asked me to sing the *gushe* Leyli and Majnun. I was intimidated in front of all these Sufis and attempted to get undressed, but he said: "you owe me this song". Then I sang. It was always the same thing; each time I had a meeting with him, he asked me to sing and I would interpret an entire *dastgâh*. He knew the music and he would play the *târ*.

It is quite clear that profane and sacred music do not constitute distinct categories. What equally concerns the sense of the secret is that art music obeys Sufi structures of initiation. In the ensemble, the entire canonical repertoire of Iranian *radif* was, up to a certain point, considered a precious treasure that one transmitted only to those who had been judged dignified. Abdollâh Davâmi (a master of the same tradition as Asgari, d. 1980) said to his close relatives that he would prefer to leave this world taking with him his repertoire, rather than to leave his songs to the disposition of the first comer who would want to sing them.[7] In the past, said Asgari, there were three levels of instruction and one only attained the third level after many years of proving oneself on the moral plane. According to him, even the most well-known singers have not gone beyond the second level, perhaps not even the first. The repertoire is fundamentally the same, but it develops and becomes more complicated at the second and third levels. These degrees reproduce the Sufi stages of *shari'at*, *tariqat*, *mar'refat* or those of disciple, *sheykh*, and *qotb*.

---

7 In the musical tradition of Lucknow, the percussion repertories (*tabla*) of certain great family lines (*gharana*) have totally disappeared. This is because their trustees did not consider their sons worthy enough to receive this musical tradition, which, especially within Shii circles, was considered to be a sacred deposit. Similarly, Ravi Shankar dispenses a special recording (*xas talim*) to a few advanced students who are responsible for keeping secret certain principles of *alap* composition (S. M. Slawick, "Ravi Shankar as Mediator Between Traditional Music and Modernity", in S. Blum, P. Bohlen, and D. Neuman (eds.), *Ethnomusicology and Modern History*, (Urbana-Chicago: University of Illinois Press, 1990).

Under these conditions, it seems rather paradoxical to divulge this third stage so widely, as has been the case through recordings, and this after thirty years of silence. Consequently, a general question can be posed: why (and how) are the secrets revealed? Asgari is content to say that he received the permission to divulge his repertory through a kind of inspiration from the souls of the old masters with whom he is in contact - a frequent case in the traditional music of Asia. We will, nevertheless, propose alternative responses to this question.

Even as Asgari has been practicing the maintenance of the mystery while revealing a part of it, other masters have certainly been more discrete. That is the case of Ostâd D., a learned person, dervish, or 'âref with Zoroastrian tendencies, versed in the esoteric sciences and in chanting. He does not claim kinship with a prestigious line like Asgari, but presents himself as the semi-exclusive trustee of an ancient body of songs that have disappeared, or of semi-secrets that he has collected on campaigns in Kurdistan, Persia and Lorestan. He recalls the repertoires of caravanners, shepherds, xânegâh, masnavi xân, etc. but discloses very little of these melodies. During a discussion, a well-known classical musician, fascinated by these songs and with the personage who concealed them, proposed to record them, accompanying himself with his own instrument. Ostâd D. responded: "it is impossible for you since I must sing these songs at dawn, towards 4 o'clock in the morning, and you would not be able to maintain the rhythm." His esoteric vision of Persian music, classical as well as popular, has made an impression on certain reputable musicians of whom he has become adviser or master; however, contrary to Asgari, he has never lifted the seal of the secret on his art or on his powers. Apparently, musicians are content with his rather poetic-like aura, through which he breathes life into these secrets. In his company, they maintain the highest idea of the value of their patrimony and their mission as trustees and transmitters.

Even in a more banal recording, such as the one made by the National Television of the music of N. A. Borumand, one of the important transmitters of instrumental repertoire, the recordings remained inaccessible for many years.[8] When someone was finally allowed to listen to them, it was under the condition that he would speak about it to no one. Gradually, there were leaks, and copies began to circulate to a point where all musicians were able to have access to them. Fifteen years later, two transcriptions and five complete recordings could be found on the market. The sense of this attitude was the maintenance of the myth of the value of the repertoire and of the restraint maintained by the circle of the initiated. For pedagogical reasons, N.A. Borumand taught orally while forbidding all recordings. Nevertheless, another reason may have been of the potential impact they might have: perhaps, if he had permitted recording, he would have lost the exclusivity of his repertoire. Suddenly rendering it accessible to all through cassettes, an important part of the process of transmission, which is the basis of tradition, would be erased. Moreover, the repertoire would be reduced to the level of simple merchandise that anyone could buy and keep in his home. This is contrary to the conceptualization of the repertoire as a *word* that one could receive only after many years in the apprenticeship of a master with whom one is intimately connected, and gathers the spirit of tradition.

The group that has best protected its music from propagation by the media has been the Ahl-e Haqq (apart from the fact that their *tanbur* has been used in classical ensembles). Their music was kept secret, only performed in rituals, where nobody but the adepts partcipated. Among Iranian musicians no one knew about this tradition.

---

8 In this connection, it is necessary to know that for the last 2000 years in China, musical repertoires have been under the control of the army. Some of them, such as the Uygur Onikki Muqam, are as inaccessible as military secrets.

The sacred and secret character of this music stems from its thematic contents that are drawn from the revealed books of this tradition (*Kalâm, Daftar*) and to the fact that it has been jealously preserved by the *kalâm xân* (reciters) and *seyyeds* (the equivalent of the Alevi *dede*). The veneration for the sacred texts can be illustrated by this anecdote: a dervish who was reciting the *Kalâm* while working in his field has a loss of memory and is unable to remember a verse. He immediately puts aside his plow and takes to the road in order to consult a *kalâm xân*, an connoisseur of *Kalâm* in a distant village. Thus the sense of secret and of the *takie*, which is still very strong in the Ahl-e Haqq, has contributed to raising the value of religious and musical patrimony.

In the 1970s, Darvish Hayâti, a somewhat impassioned Ahl-e Haqq dervish obtained mediatic success by singing with his *tanbur* a song dedicated to Ali, which was based on a classical Persian poem by Sâber Kermâni. The fact that he played the *tanbur* in public and that he was paid, earned him the reprobation of many adepts. Recently, a few Ahl-e Haqq soloists have appeared who sing *kalâm* while accompanying themselves on the *tanbur*. It becomes a matter of forging a compromise between original performance (the *jam*, which requires the presence of a group) and the concert, where without being an accomplished master (or an "enthusiast" as the dervish mentioned above), no Ahl-e Haqq *kalâm xân* would be able to hold his audience with only his song and accompanying himself on his instrument.

Towards 1977, a concert recording that included a traditional *zekr* was even diffused (in small quantities) by the cultural center of Niâvarân. This was the first public dissemination of Ahl-e Haqq music. However, it was a very tentative appearance at best, probably due to the reticence of the adepts. The true *zekr*s, which include ecstasy and invoke non-typically Islamic personalities such as Dâwud or Soltân, cannot easily be disclosed to the profane public, even if many Ahl-e Haqq own *zekr* cassettes and listen to them at home or in their car.

The obstacle has been surmounted in two ways: by creating new hymns, often in Persian, and by using the *tanbur* to accompany profane Kurdish or Persian melodies, as Nâzeri has done. A third way consists of having the hymns played by five or six, or even more, *tanbur*s at a time. Here, too, something of the repertoire is presented but without revealing the essential, which is the character of the *zekr* and of spiritual states. In effect, the melodies stand out from these ensembles as laminated, cut up and stripped of their flavor. It is necessary to note that one of these distortions imposed by state representation in general is the search for the mass effect: one cannot just present a single musician lost on the stage; a large number has to be assembled.

In the face of all these manifestations, which give only an incomplete and imperfect idea of the sacred repertoire and of the performance of the *tanbur*, certain guardians of the grand tradition succumbed. Breaking the seal of the secret, they permitted a young *tanbur* player, Shahâb Elâhi, youngest son of the great master Nur Ali Elâhi, to play in public the transcendental pieces of the repertoire, which had previously been transmitted exclusively within the family. Nevertheless, it was done with parsimony, interposed between two spiritual songs in Persian composed for the occasion and interpreted by a mixed choir, as is often the case among the Ahl-e Haqq Kurds. It seems that the concern was not simply to perform to an Iranian public (by introducing the *târ* and the *ney*, by singing in Persian).[9] The idea was to *show*

---

9 The integration of Iranian or "foreign" elements is not, moreover, new in the Ahl-e Haqq musical tradition. There is reason to believe that the use of the *daf* is not traditional but rather inspired by Qâderi *zekr*s or borrowed from folklore (for the *daf* in question is different from those of the Qâdaris.) Through their contacts with the other brotherhoods, certain Ahl-e Haqq groups have also learned to sing in Persian, particularly the hymns dedicated to 'Ali. They have also adopted Iranian styles. It was said that a singer and player of the *tanbur* who was also a very respected spiritual personality composed many songs within this genre in order not to "use" the ancient *kalâm*s through repetition.

something (the competence of the performer, the authenticity of the repertory, etc.), while at the same time *hiding* the essential, namely the emotional or mystical dimension of the sacred music.

This music, which had so many times to emerge from the shadows, received recognition in the media with the publication of the album "Le chant du Monde" ("Songs of the World"). It consisted of six compact disks of the repertoire of Ostâd Elâhi, the unequalled and charismatic master of the sacred Kurdish *tanbur*, taken from archives dating back to the 1960s. These exceptional documents, recorded in private seances, were guarded as relics by his family for thirty years. Their being brought to light is also indirectly due to the power of the media, in response to either the opportunism or laxity of certain Ahl-e Haqq dervishes, who broke the rule by playing for the profane, and above all by usually playing in a mediocre fashion. The publishing of this music determined who the heirs to the music would be. At the same time, it demonstrated at a single blow the nature of this music and who its true trustees were. However, even though the recordings of this master have been made public, nearly nothing has been revealed of the conditions under which he played his music or of the incredible effects that it had on the audiences, effects attested to by many written testimonials in the family archives. In the unveiling by recordings, the magical aspect of the musical performance and of the devotional context (of the interior *zekr*, or *samâ'* type) have been disregarded. Perhaps the reason is that explications of this type of phenomenon were not permitted and a recording could restore only the artistic or purely acoustic aspect of the performance. We note as well that the publication of these archives was made possible due to highly sophisticated restoration techniques (such as the program, "No Noise").[10]

Sufi Music on the Oriental Scene

As all these examples demonstrate, to a certain extent at least, that the sense of secret is compatible with the unveiling or popularization of musical practices and mystical rituals. A remarkable example of the popularization of the Sufi chant is that of the Pakistani *qawwâli*, a professional genre intended for the public of Sufis, *qalandars*, *malangs*, dervishes, or simply for pilgrims visiting the tombs of saints. With radio, record, and then the recovery by World Music, the *qawwâli* has become an international commercial product. Many of these hymns can be heard in every disco club in India and Pakistan, arranged in diverse ways. These include the pop style of the famous *Jule La'l*, whose adaptations are innumerable, as well as variations of *Dama dam mast qalandar*. This rather banal phenomenon is occurring everywhere, under less commercial forms as well. One can think of, for example, the Alevi bards, whose audience has gone beyond the circle of initiated.

But above all, the emergence of Sufi music in the field of the profane is not a new phenomenon. The most ancient case of mediatic success is perhaps that of the great mystic and poet, Erâqi. While on a forty-day retreat ordered by his sheikh, he continually hummed mystical chants he had composed. The dervishes who heard him from behind the door were seduced by these chants and began to repeat them - so well that in a few days they were known throughout the whole town and sung in the taverns. Learning this, the sheikh ended up releasing Erâqi from his retreat early.

---

10 Moreover, there is reason to believe that the transmission of this music will not remain in the cloud of *jamxâne* but rather will use official channels and modern techniques. It is even possible to learn the rudiments of *tanbur* in Paris or in Köln in some cultural associations in the presence of representatives of the Guran tradition, just as one can learn the Mevlevi *ney* or the Qâderi *daf*.

The texts of classical Sufism furnish a number of allusions to what can be called the *samâ'* of the vulgar (*avvâm*). In light of current phenomena, it can be deduced that it was a question of mystico-religious festivals organized by some non-affiliated, but in which specialized musicians produced themselves in a mystical repertoire (cf. especially, Frishkopf).

Even certain spectacular structures have deep traditional roots. If, for example, the *qawwâli* can be commercially recovered, it is because it had certain predispositions. In fact, the classical *qawwâli* unite on the same stage a well-knit group constituting a hierarchy of singers, choristers and percussionists. In this setting, the dervishes assume the role of passive listeners: they can only express themselves by getting up to dance and by bringing their offering of wads of small bank notes that they drop on the heads of the performers. If the *qawwâli* has become a mediatic commodity, it is because it was already a religious commercial product. In short, it was a spectacle, a dramaturgy of ecstasy confined to professionals. This is completely the opposite of Kurdish traditions, where the roles are distributed between one or two soloists and a participant assembly, intensely and in a less formal manner.

A broad spectrum of practices exists since the ceremonies emerge from "popular Sufism" or "informal Sufism," and range from dates on the religious calendar to those which serve to mark a social event such as a marriage. In certain cases, the Sufi component is completely lost but a certain sense of the sacred subsists nevertheless in the performance. The following is an example of this.

With the disappearance of lodges in Tajikistan, certain particularly striking practices, such as those of *zekr*, have subsisted in the collective memory as vestiges. In Panjkent, for example, within the context of a wedding party, a senior member of the party designates a few young people and directs a *zekr* with them, beyond all explicit reference, but executed with concentration and seriousness, after which the festival continues.[11] As for the southern Tajiks, they have conserved some songs and a sketch called *qalandar bâzi*, in which a person puts on a patched gown, hold a staff and declaims a *qalandar* chant. The Turkmen, too, practice a *zekr* completely cut off from its roots and context, during private festivals. They do not hesitate to present this *zekr* during their folkloric spectacles or their concerts.[12]

These manifestations form part of a trend toward "folklorization." They border on parody when they are staged by the cultural authorities. This was formerly the case in Teheran in the seventies, where official spectacles were given in large halls. In the middle of these spectacles, Darvish Hayâti would be placed on stage as if he were already in ecstasy and performing his *zekr* while chanting all alone with his *tanbur* and waving his dishevelled hair. The discomfort was accentuated by the fact that in the same spectacle, the ballet troupe of Rudaki Hall would dress up as dervishes and interpret a choreography inspired by a Mevlevi, crying *hu* and *haqq!*

---

11 This custom is not unrelated to the survival of the *zekr* tire (called *zarb*) beyond the brotherhood in the Yaghâb valley, an extremely remote region in Panjkent, where many traditions have been preserved (cf. Th. Levin, *The Hundred Thousands Fools of God: Musical Travels in Central Asia* Bloomington: Indiana University Press, 1996, p. 235).

12 We saw a much more interesting spectacle put on by the Turkmen (of Iran). They staged two healing rites in a folkloric and theatrical fashion. They first presented an "insane person," a *djinni*, or lunatic. A player of the *dotâr* would then play an appropriate melody in the effort to cure him. Next, a *porkhân* healer armed with a horsewhip (like the *qamchin bakhshi* of Central Asia) who would attempt to frighten the *djinn* by whipping and threatening him. Finally, a group of "dervishes" would arrive singing hymns and performing *zekr*, standing in a circle in the manner of the Yasavi or Qâderi of Central Asia. Then the patient would become calm and enter their circle, soon followed by the *porkhân*. Thus, without even directly intervening, the dervishes would succeed where the power of the shamans had remained impotent. This fifteen-minute spectacle was performed as part of the Hôze Honari festival (cf. infra).

Is it necessary to deplore such representations, and if so, according to what principles? Understandably, one could invoke the obligation of discretion (*takie*), which binds the adepts to one another, or the taboo of spiritual commercialization. However, in the eyes of the public, the dervish passed for a *majzub*, an enthusiast avoiding his obligations, as is often found among the *malang* or *pakir* of the Sind, for example. On the other hand, what can be said about the *mevlevi* spectacles organized by the Ministry of Culture for years in Konya, in which the dancers, originally at least, were not even dervishes? And what can be thought of the latest initiatives, apparently spontaneous, consisting of having women dressed in colored gowns dance, within the context of Turkish *mevlevi* dervishes? Is it a question of opportunism, of the argument of marketing, of adaptation, of innovation, or of the liberation of women? In order to settle the debate, it would be necessary to know if the impulse for change comes from within or from an external force, such as a political will or commercial demagogic stakes. However, these changes are not as abrupt as they appear since they occur on a well-prepared terrain: as artificial as the official *mevlevi* ceremony in Konya may seem, it is only the end of a process of ritualization that has been transforming the *samâ'* for a long time as a representation of the *samâ'*. Furthermore, in an important sense, it is a representation of the *samâ'* of Mevlânâ Rumi, a highly codified commemorative rite, a dramatization with a well-measured dose of ecstasy, not so much true-to-life as signified by symbolic gestures. The example of the *mevlevi ayin*, liturgy of the well-established and completely anticipated repertoire, prefigures what generally becomes the transpositions of the Sufi rites used on the public stage.

As it is not possible to reconstitute the stages of this process of dramatization, one will try discerning the underlying motivations and the implications of these different types of adaptation. It is equally essential to understand why and how different groups get involved in the processes of diffusion. It could be interesting to follow the transformations of the rituals in spectacles through their presentation on the Western stage. There has been an increase in the number of Western concert programs including what is called "Sufi" groups, whose performances contain as often as not as much art music as music truly coming from the Sufi tradition. Raising this issue, however, is a digression. We must, rather, restrict ourselves to the manifestations situated on the margins of the concert circuits, stemming directly from the activities of lodges and organized by them.

Between Concert and Ritual

The diverse Ne'matollâhi Gonâbâdi Safi' Ali Shâhi branches do not possess a particular repertoire. Some of their adepts have been fine musicians or even great masters. Yet, while they sometimes made a contribution, they didn't have a regular function in the meetings.

In the branch whose *qotb* is the psychiatrist J. Nurbaxsh, ritual music holds a less important place. Nevertheless, during festivals held by this brotherhood in the 1970s, classical musicians (*ney* players and singers), as well as Kurdish Qâderi groups, who perform their *zekr* completely, and sometimes even Ahl-e Haqq[13] were invited. This

---

13 It may seem curious for a relatively orthodox Shii brotherhood to invite pure Sunni Qâderis as well as such heterodox Imamites as the Ahl-e Haqq. It is more surprising yet to see some Qâderis to invite some Ahl-e Haqq to perform their *zekr* under the guise of an introduction to the Qâderi ceremony that they held for us near Tehran in 1989. In this case it was Kurdish solidarity that was the driving force, rather than mystical ecumenical sentiments.

lodge was very powerful and had sympathisers among the ruling class. When it established itself in England after the revolution and opened its *xânegâh* in Europe and the United States, it became necessary to respond to the new public demand composed of Iranians in exile and a minority of Europeans. The lodge developed two aspects: publications, which were still very embryonic in Iran, and, music thanks to the formation of groups of "Sufi music." In their concerts, the stage is generally decorated with the paraphernalia of the lodges: *kashqul*, *tasbih*, hatchets, etc. as well as large *daf*s, tambourines, borrowed from the Qâderis. A dervish dressed in old-fashioned attire with all his accessories walks into the room. The participants are dressed in long white shirts (as the Qâderis and some Ahl-e Haqq) and felt headdresses, which was not their custom in Iran. One notices among the men the presence of one or two women, dressed the same way, who sing and play the *daf*. It is noteworthy that the entrance of women in the ritual circle may constitute the decisive innovation at the end of this millennium.

The music is composed of measured or free improvisations by the *ney* - thought to be the universal symbol of the Sufi soul - which is played by a good professional, of non-measured *âvâz* songs, or a singer accompanying himself on the *tanbur*, equally improvisational, a practice that is borrowed from the Ahl-e Haqq *kalâmxân*. A choir resumes with refrains and *zekr*s, but pronounced in Persian. The styles and rhythms are of the Persian genre and are reminiscent of the religious songs, the *rowze xâni*, and the songs of *xânegâh*. In themselves, these songs and melodies are not any less authentic than what one hears for the most part in the *xanegâh*, but it is the ensemble, the composition of the group, the chain of sequences and above all the organization "in concert" or spectacle (with Sufi decor) which seems in contrast to tradition. In general, this music is not sufficiently artistic to be presented as "concert." Nor is it sufficiently strong or authentic to pass as a simple Sufi manifestation. To what end, then, are they organized? It could be argued that their objective is to reinforce the adepts and sympathisers in their affiliation while presenting their ritual within a public and official framework. However, it is necessary to note once more that this concern is not new: Mawlânâ Rumi gave *samâ'* with his dervishes in the palace of the Emin Parvâne, within a framework which is perhaps not far from the one of our concert halls and other cultural centers.

The question of the authenticity of Sufi representations is open to a number of interpretations. Without making a value judgement, one can distinguish levels of authenticity, such as *fidelity* to an original model, *sincerity* of the implication, or *intensity* of experience. For the majority of dervishes, an authentic *jam* is one where there is some *hâl*, emotion and a just intention. After that, the forms can adapt themselves. The following example is evidence of the problems that present themselves when one goes from the restrained sphere of ritual and its music to the public sphere.

Recently, a group of Ahl-e Haqq formed in Germany took a decisive step in presenting to the public (in a concert hall) the *jam* ceremony, as it is practiced among the Kurds. I had the occasion to closely follow their preparation. The purpose of these representations was to appear in public as a spiritual and cultural group in the heart of their adopted country. This emigré position favored their awakening and also made possible the elaboration of such a program, which would be difficult to conceive of in Iran. There was also the concern to preserve or restore a tradition which was in the process of being lost in exile, notably in the transmission to their children. The group worked a lot in order to rediscover the old melodies or their non-altered versions and to enhance the artistic level about which the adepts no longer seemed to care to much.

The strongest motivation, however, was highly symbolic and mystical: the group wanted to create an atmosphere of spiritual dynamism. The event had to evoke spiritual reflection in their adopted country and to bring *barakat*. This is all well and good, but in this case, why must there be a public? First of all, for any event there must be witnesses, with whom their fervor can be shared. In this way, people were not considered as simple spectators since blessed offerings, *niaz* (under the form of sweets), were distributed to them. This type of consideration runs through all mystical religions, but the degree of conviction these adepts had, concretized by the force of their ecstasy, was particularly prominent. These different interpretations are not contradictory, because they are situated on different levels; nevertheless, "the divulsion of the secret," if it can be called that, has certain paradoxes.

In the passage to stage representation, the group has been surrounded by multiple precautions in order to simultaneously respond to the requirements of authenticity and sincerity. Nevertheless, the requirement of being understood by the public obliges it to sometimes act contrary to the principle of authenticity. Moreover, while the innovations have not failed, when looked at more closely, or while discussing the subject with dervishes, it becomes clear that there are actually precedences to these innovations or adaptations such that nothing can really be considered artificial. The most striking innovation is the presence of women around the circle of men during the free *zekr*, something that was an exceptional occurrence in Kurdish villages. However, it is known that women have an elevated status in Kurdish homes, particularly those of the Ahl-e Haqq, who in this sense, too, are close to the Alevis. This tendency can only be highlighted while bearing in mind the Western context. With respect to the costumes, there is some uncertainty as to what should be worn. "Natural," e.g. everyday clothes, would be detrimental to group harmony. On the other hand, Kurdish clothes are elegant but artificial (because this group only wears the Kurdish pants). One ends up opting for long white robes, which, while being conscious to accentuate the element of liturgy in the *jam*, is "in reality" more relaxed, event though there is some risk of presenting the image of a Sufi lodge, which the Ahl-e Haqq defends itself as being.

The problems associated with scenic representation are derived from the inexorable misalignment between the existence of transparency and the need to be understood correctly. In other words, what is demonstrated needs to be shown well, and in a manner that avoids misunderstanding. What this concern reflects is the underlying tension inherent in attempts at revealing rituals without disclosing fundamental "secrets" contained within them. All representation is still an anamorphosis. It is a kind of "translation" that carries with it the danger of excess and deficiencies as it is transformed into different idioms.

Several paradoxes emerge. The fundamental one is that the essence of the ritual is a type of secret. It is through the performance of the ritual (which was formerly accomplished in secret) that its substance is revealed. In order to get around this, the assumption is made that the spectators are fully capable of participating to a certain degree in the fervor of the adepts; this is why they were integrated symbolically in receiving the *niaz*. However, for the spectators to become part of the process, the dervishes had to curb the free course of their emotion and of their *hâl*, so as not to frighten the public or be seen as savages. Nevertheless, the force of the *zekr* and the ecstasy that it provokes (and which was supposed to touch little of the public) were actually the *raison d'être* for the representation. The need to simultaneously show and retain produced a paradoxical situation that was difficult to manage. The question arises as to whether it wouldn't be better if all the dervishes were to refrain from all manifestations of enthusiasm, with perhaps only one or two of them being caught up in an expression of ecstasy.

The idea of ecstasy upon demand constitutes yet another paradox. Under such conditions, the process of reaching and demonstrating a state of ecstasy is questionable. The authenticity of ecstasy comes into question when it can be programmed in advance to reach varying degrees of intensity or to assume different theatrical forms. A similar concern over authenticity appears in the classical question of the authenticity of the Sufi concept of *tavajud* (translated as "excitation" or "conditioning"). Originally, the Sufis would assimilate it into the simulation and later on, to a stimulation, freeing a real ecstasy (*vajd*). Carried out in this manner, it was considered praiseworthy. From this perspective, this group of Ahl-e Haqq can be seen as practicing a sincere, albeit controlled, *tavajud*: only one member of the group was permitted to transform it into *vajd*, with the rest of the group prohibited from doing so. Even though this *vajd* is not "real" in some sense, it can still be considered valid and not simply a simulation since those experiencing it considered it to be an intense form of *tavajud*.

A distinction also has to be made between the existence of quality music and the principle according to which the song served to connect the function of the melody and its inspiration: the preference was to repeat a well-established program in order to palliate all musical slippage. However, while acting there was the risk of dulling the sensibility of the participants and ending up with a *jam* without *hâl*. It is probable that this same aesthetic greatly affected the rituals, which passed from the stage of participation to that of representation.

The program should culminate, as is the custom, with very rapid refrains on two or three notes. For the Kurds, it is these melodies that are the most stimulating since it is through them that the final state of ecstasy (called *hâl*), is reached - passing through the body with the speeding up of the tempo. This is far from being the rule among spiritual music, however. Accordingly, in order to signify the *hâl* to the emigré Iranian public or to Westerners, whose customs are different, it was decided to put aside these rapid and agitated refrains and to limit themselves to melodies that were more moderate, less primitive and more pleasant to Westerners and Iranians. But in doing so they also conformed to tradition since according to the Ancients, the rapid and agitated refrains and simplified melodies did not have a place in the *jam*.

The final paradox is that if this group is in the process of becoming the guardian of Ahl-e Haqq musical tradition, it has only been possible by breaking out of the narrow circle in which it is confined, in order to set itself up as an object of representation, under the gaze of the Others. However, during the evening of the concert they fargot all these problems and performed a wonderful *zekr*, with a very deep, even though slightly controlled, *hâl*.

The reason I have paid special attention to the problems encountered by this particular group in the process of transforming a ritual into a public performance, is because these problems might as well have been the same for many other Sufi groups opening their rituals to the public.

Of a completely different nature is the crude Sufi and para-Sufi representation of musical rituals that we are going to describe now. In 1994, a festival of popular Iranian music was organized in Teheran. It brought together for many weeks the best non-classical musicians from the four corners of the country. While its aim had not been to reach a very large public, this event attained unprecedented dimensions. The initiative came through the *Howze honari* (the Arts Foundation), a powerful semi-private institution, run by the *hojat ol-eslâm* Zamm.

Many points in this enterprise merit discussion. The most striking aspect was the way in which the Iranian culture presented itself on stage, contemplated itself as in a mirror, apperently without the slightest shade of ideology. The musicians of the mountains and deserts were simply invited to present their songs and their melodies as they had customarily done in their own context, without artificiality, and without particular *mise-en-scène* decorations or costumes.

This type of concert is not new. Since the festival of Shiraz and Tus, in the 1970s, Iranian intellectuals and artists have learned to appreciate their popular bards, their religious opera and their story-tellers. The first of these manifestations always addressed themselves to a cultivated and Westernized elite. In the case of the festival of the *Howze honari*, the 'distanciation' implicated by the detour of Westernization was much less clear after 14 years of Islamic regime. A desire to bring the whole world together on friendly terms was demonstrated in the generous hospitality offered to the musicians. The participants, which numbered about a hundred, were invited to remain during the festival to listen to their colleagues who had come from other provinces. Thus, seated in the first rows were not the notables, but Kurdish or Baluchi musicians listening for example to the *ashiq* of Tabriz.[14] Let us, however, return to the question of Sufi music.

The pinnacle of this festival, at least from the point of view of drama and paradoxal representation, was reached with the Sufi seances and the rites of trance. First to perform were the Qâderi of Sanandaj, directed by Mirzâ Ghowsi, who gave a complete seance, with 12 dervishes and 4 cantors. During the 1970s, this *xalife*, also cantor, was sometimes invited to participate in religious festivals in the grand Ne'matollâhi *xanegâh* and was even invited to sing with his group in front of the Empress during a religious concert given in Teheran (Niâvarân).[15] In these concerts, the few dervishes who accompanied him would be limited to the initial part of the ritual, the *zekr tahlil:* a few adepts would listen to the cantor (*xalife*) and a chorus of two or three subordinates would accompany him on the *daf* tambourin (a *samâ'* would be performed on the basis of antiphonic chants.) The part of the *zekr* proper (*zekr-e here or qiyam*) was always slurred. But why, in effect, were the chants authorized but not the *zekr*? Perhaps it is because the chants appear to induce emotion and tears, which are admitted by religion, whereas the *zekr* brings ecstasy and agitation, which are more problematic for the common people. Furthermore, the organizers did not want to portray this violent aspect of the ritual. Whatever the reasons were, it remains that (in contrast to the Ahl-e Haqq) the Qâderi always opened their doors to the local public, who evidently respected their practice. Moreover, they sometimes practiced *zekr* in a public place, in their own milieu.

It can be assumed that the conditions were different in Teheran in 1994 because there Mirzâ Ghowsi's group performed an integral *zekr*, with the one exception that the adepts did not practice their well-known fakir prowess (*tiq bâzi*). While several reasons can be proffered for this change of attitude, the main one is probably the fact that one was now in an Islamic Republic and that, *a priori*, the spectators were taken up by the cause and that they could be considered as a public of sympathizers.

If this *qâderi zekr* unfolded as a normal seance, another *zekr* brought together other Sunni dervishes from Khorasan (*Torbat-e Jâm*) in a seance completely astonishing by its total absence of stage quality and by the anarchy that reined. The dervishes belonged to the Naqshbandi Mojadadi order. Some were completely absorbed in themselves, while others performed their individual *zekr*, each according to his own technique. Among them there were two who played the *dotâr* and sang or sighed exclamations, each for himself, without listening to the other. The cameramen

---

14 At other Ne'matollâhi concerts, the unifying effect of large numbers used to bring together a group of some thirty dervishes with many instruments, under the direction of a well-known musician, himself a dervish.

15 The best Sufi singer of Sanandaj, Xalife Karim, has never accepted any invitation, whether it be from the Empress or the Islamic Republic.

had to slip in among the participants to capture these extraordinary images, unperturbed by the many incidents that occurred, such as, for example, microphones falling from their tripod. This seance remains in itself an enigma. It may seem astonishing that it was given in front of an assembly comprising religious shiites and intellectuals of the capital. Nevertheless, the global religious context may help explain how dervishes were able to continue performing their usual *zekr*, without the public being fully aware of all its connotations.

This festival also devoted an evening to a seance of Baluchi *mâled*, a semi-Sufi rite with seated dances culminating in trance. In addition, eight evenings of trances from Baluchistan (three *guâti* seances and one from *zâr*) and from the Persian Gulf (three seances being directed and sung by a woman and one by a man) were held. It is no longer a question here of Sufi or para-Sufi rite, but of a cult of devotion to the spirits (*zâr, nobân, mashâyex*). The trance is the result of making contact with spirits, which from the Islamic point of view, is even more suspect (without speaking of the fact that four of these rites were reserved to give priority to women). None of this seemed to be problematic to the organizers, even though the *xalife* are considered pagans by the local authorities in the Persian Gulf, where they are from, and have difficulty performing their rites there.

There remains the question as to how these rites, which are by nature secret and at times have been suspected of being heretic or paganistic, were able to be carried to the stage without their actors being the least embarrassed, and without the trustees of Islam declaring them an anathema. Even if the young and dynamic *hojat ol-islam* Zamm has grand ideas, and represents the liberal avant-garde, he is obliged to maintain a certain theological coherence. It is perhaps for this reason that before the seances, a general presentation is given that explains how seances function as curative rites. The chants, melodies, and rhythms are said to generate a therapeutic power, well known by doctors of the past. Moreover, the many religious invocations expressed by these chants made it easier to admit the legitimacy of the rituals.

But perhaps the fundamental reason for the tolerance manifested towards the rituals can be found in the fact that these rites were isolated from the social and cultural system in which they exist. Presented on stage, the rites are seen less as a spectacle than as simply an object of observation. As is often the case in Iran, beauty was the main objective, camouflaging the rest. The impeccably dressed participants were seated on an enormous and magnificent carpet surrounded by vases and bouquets of flowers. The staging of the spectacle, although very sober, constituted an essential *alibi* which enabled it to be brought into the domain of the arts, as one could expect in this "Art Institute." The idea of representation or *mise en scène* was so strong that all these events were recorded in three simultaneous ways: through audio, video, and film. In order to put together a "complete file," the plan was to film the best traditional masters in their own environment, and devote an entire film to each of them. All this undertaking is evidence of an intention to enhance the value of a cultural heritage through staging of a spectacle, where the actors are invited to look at one another mutually. This method was much more sophisticated than ordinary fieldwork, collection of films or recordings, or gathering "folkloric" groups for the sake of entertainment.

In addition to the aesthetic touch, there was in this method a scientific concern, which is one of the conditions for justifying musical exercising. It is in regard to this criterion that western or eastern art music or even jazz are authorised, where as other varieties of music are banned. But if so, how can folk music be justified? Through its moral authenticity, its purity, its conformity to tradition, and/or its functionality. The way chosen to avoid this difficulty was to present it an "objective" framework of culture and erudition, to wrap it in a discourse, and to consider the traditional musicians as holders of a knowledge and treat them as high artistic personalities.

Conclusion: The Sense of Secret and the Time of Transparency

The last examples mentioned are rare cases where the rituals are delivered as spectacle. No recourse is made to accommodation such as "reframing" since the public is considered as initiated. In all the other cases, there are distortions, displacements, paradoxes, ambiguities, understatements, and intentions. The most important of these follow.

First, it is necessary to remark that for a secret to function, or for one to consider it as such, it must be expressed in a particular manner. It is at least necessary that one knows that something exists as a secret, to which some have access or keep. It is for this reason that the mystics play with the unveiling in all the required nuances. As it has been seen, they only give signs of it and are far from delivering it.

There are reasons to believe that this has always been the case; however, it is necessary to consider a new factor: the propensity to display everything into the open, which is so characteristic of our period. One of the effects of the flow of diverse information is the evoking of a form of indifference or, at best, tolerance. With the broadening of perspective of Muslim society, a phenomenon such as Sufism risks becoming unnoticed. Under these conditions, the Sufis, instead of hiding (as the Ahl-e Haqq did, for example) are, on the contrary, obliged to signal their presence. The music is an excellent means, as understood from such groups as the Alevis or the Ne'matollahis of the diaspora, who literally have elaborated new forms of Sufi concerts.

Finally, with the "cultural brewing," the sense of the secret and of the mystery looses ground. Faced with the invasion of music of all sorts, the value of ritual music becomes relativized when it simply becomes part of a mass consumption of goods, as is the case of *qawwâli*. The veneration for secret or rare repertoires, transmitted or performed within a framework of initiation, is dulled with their divulsion. It is the same for sacred and secret texts, such as the ones of the Ahl-e Haqq: no longer known by heart by the pious adepts, nearly all of them have been published. No one can withdraw from this current, and when an individual or a group takes the first step towards divulsion, the others are annoyed and often end up by giving up in turn in order to advance their personal idea of the veracity or out of a spirit of rivalry. To the phenomena of mediation can be added the explosion of "societies of proximity" (and from them, "secret communities") under the effect of rural exodus and demographic pressure.[16]

In order to counterbalance this process, a new sense of the past is developing, which expresses itself through the official preservation of traditions. However, it is difficult to escape the perversity of taking recourse in the media to rescue patrimony. It has the contradictory effect of both fixing it and reproducing it through such means as recordings and/or films. In other words, it is kept alive by the media by finding for it a public. All of this amounts to demystifying the traditions and to transforming spiritual as well as cultural values.

Certain aspects of these processes were described more than sixty years ago by Walter Benjamin[17] in terms applicable to the object of our discourse. According to

---

16 This phenomenon is particularly striking for the Alevis and other related groups.

17 Benjamin, W. 1971: "L'oeuvre d'art à l'ère de sa reproductibilité technique," in *L'homme, le langage et la culture*, Paris, Denoël-Gontheir.

him, there is in the history of the work of art, a movement of "cultural value" towards "exposition value." Originally, the preponderance of cultural value made the work of art a "magical instrument" and prevented it from being recognized as art: "it is the cultural value that acts to keep the works of art secret".[18] When this value is lost, one begins to expose them and reciprocally, "in times of the techniques of reproduction, what is attained in the work of art is its aura".[19] Thus with their reproduction (e.g., writing, recording), the aura of the melodies and of the sacred texts of oral tradition fades, and one of the consequences is that the faithful do not want to make the effort to learn them since they have them at their disposal as object. To ensure the continuity of tradition, it would have been more profitable sometimes to preserve the mystery and not to unveil it all.

But this is exactly the point: if the Sufis have so easily conformed to this mode of transparency, it is perhaps because they have learned that these means do not bring about a true divulsion of secrets, given that they only deliver the appearance in the form of the musical object. All the rest, which makes tradition not preservation of an object but a process of transmission, does not become evident in the recording, the spectacles, or the video, so that when all is said and done, the true secrets are themselves preserved.

One of the lessons to be drawn from these examples is that even if the media make accessible all sorts of music, including ritual music, it is not sufficient to ensure a correct transmission of patrimony. For example, the *daf* is propagated by recordings and videos, whereas classical singers have believed that they have the power to appropriate the repertoire of Qâderi song simply because they were Kurds. Therefore, the dervishes have always affirmed that it is necessary to be a dervish in order to play the *daf* appropriately, and one can conclude that it is the same for the song. Some Ahl-e Haqq say the same thing with respect to the *tanbur*.

What the imitators do not know, and what the reproductions do not transmit, is the nature and quality of the existential experience lying behind this form of music. They constitute its "aura", "the authority of the thing", intimately tied to its "here and now".[20] Thus, when a Qâderi *xalife* sings for the Prophet, for 'Ali or for the *Ghaws*, he creates a fervor and a communicative conviction which upsets the dervishes, and even the laity. He is himself familiar with "states of altered consciousness" and subtle energies activated notably by the *zekr* and asceticism. It is the same with the listeners. There is some reason to think that when he plays the *daf* and when he sings (done only within the framework of a ritual), his music disengages something else, especially when clever imitation is provided by a good percussionist. In the case of the Qâderi, it is the impression of force which dominates. In other traditions, on the other hand, there are other qualities that are not taught any more in conservatories. These include such qualities as emotion, sincerity, purity, liberty or gracefulness.

At a most elementary level, the same phenomenon is seen in the transmission of the patrimonies of art music: one can have at his disposal all existing sources and even have them memorized; it is only in the relation of master to student or in a "milieu of proximity," among the "people of the secret," that the art of performance can be learned. The same can be said for mysticism: it does not matter that the rites, texts, secret *zekrs* reserved for the initiated, and those familiar with the hermeneutic and the esoteric sciences are revealed, because it is only through personal contact with a sheikh that one can actually become a dervish.

18 Ibid. p. 151.
19 Ibid. p. 143.
20 Ibid.

The real secret is not what is hidden; it is not circumscribed in a closed space upon itself, as an "interiority." As Deleuze and Guattari explain,[21] the secret, on the contrary, is a pure form of externality - the absolute outside, something which always extends beyond us, which is stronger than we are and something that no one can "hold" or enclose. The fact is that it is not simply a matter of contents; neither is it something that can be transmitted or reproduced. Rather, it is through a moment of grace that the process of transmission is achieved.

Thus, through the confrontation of the ritual with the means of mediatic reproduction and diffusion it becomes understood that the secret, the mystery, and the sacred are not enclosed in relics, objects, words, sounds, or books. Furthermore, it becomes clear that by rendering these forms or symbols accessible, one does not release much of the spiritual essence - essence that, as soon as one believes that it has been unveiled, has already been invested with other symbols and has found other forms of effectuation.

Accordingly, a historical approach to the Tradition should not limit itself to the description of this process by pointing out with nostalgia how the "inner" is submerged by the "outer", how the aura and the cultual values are swept away by the stream of mass reproduction and diffusion. Instead, it should localise the space where the 'secret game' takes place, the way in which it is represented and exposed. It should follow the shifts of meaning through the bias of the "communities of the secret", the outline of which are shaped and reshaped according to the exposition of the secret. Degrees of unveiling of the secret exist between different groups: lines of division are continually being redefined between initiated and affiliated, people of the community and sympathisers, spectators, critiques and observers. Hierarchical degrees of genre, such as avvâm, xâs and xâs al-xâs are constantly being created. Concomitantly, a group can unveil secrets or, on the contrary, create others in order to redefine its range of extension, playing alternately with mystification and demystification. This is also what the examples demonstrate to us: the position of the spectator is not the same in a Sufi concert, in a ritual-spectacle, or in a classical concert. A deep analysis of the "strategies of unveiling" must also bear in mind the ways through which reception occur by the public, an aspect that has only been touched upon in this chapter.

Translated from the French by Sylvia Zeybekoğlu

---

21 Deleuze, G. and Guattari, F. 1980: *Mille plateaux*, Paris, Editions de minuit, p. 440.

List of Participants

Professor Cem Behar, Department of Economics, Boğaziçi University, İstanbul.

Mr. İlker Evrim Binbaş, Department of History, Middle East Technical University, Ankara.

Dr. Natalie Clayer, CNRS, Paris.

Professor Jean During, Institute de Turc, Strasbourg, France.

Anne Ellingsen, Institute for Music and Theater, Oslo University, Norway.

Professor Walter Feldman, New York, USA.

Dr. Anders Hammarlund, Department of East European Studies, Uppsala University, Sweden.

Nedim Karakayalı, Department of Sociology, University of Toronto, Canada.

Professor Irene Markoff, York University, Canada.

Professor Tord Olsson, Department of History of Religions, Lund University, Sweden.

Professor Annemarie Schimmel, Bonn, Germany.

Professor Edwin Seroussi, Department of Musicology, Ball-Ilan University, Ramat-Gan, Israel.

Professor Amnon Shiloah, The Hebrew University, Jerusalem.

Dr. Razia Soultanova, Goldsmiths College, London.

Dr. Orhan Tekelioğlu, Department of Political Sciences, Bilkent University, Ankara.

Professor Dag Osterberg, Institute for Music and Theater, University of Oslo, Norway.

Professor Elisabeth Özdalga, Department of Sociology, Middle East Technical University, Ankara.